Gardening Southern Style

University Press of Mississippi
Jackson and London

GARDENING
Southern Style

Felder Rushing

This book is a companion volume to the public
television series *Gardening Southern Style*,
produced by the Mississippi Authority for
Educational Television.

Copyright © 1987 by the
University Press of Mississippi
Manufactured in the United States of America
91 90 89 88 87 5 4 3 2 1

Designed by John Langston

The paper in this book meets the guidelines
for permanence and durability of the Committee on
Production Guidelines for Book Longevity of the
Council of Library Resources.

Library of Congress Cataloging-in-Publication Data

Rushing, Felder, 1952–
Gardening southern style.

Bibliography: p.
Includes index.
1. Gardening—Southern States.   I. Title.
SB453.2.S66R87   1987   635.9′51′75   86-33997

ISBN 0-87805-390-5

British Library Cataloguing in Publication data
is available.

Front cover photo by David King Gleason

Back cover photo courtesy of Mississippi Authority
for Educational Television

Contents

Preface

Things grow bigger in the South. Our climate is one of roller-coaster extremes, one warm day slipping into sudden frost, then turning warm again for the rest of the winter, with—oops!—one more light freeze slipped in on Good Friday just in time to nip the tomatoes and impatiens we had set out in the sweltering heat only the week before. Our weather, our soils, and even our altitudes make for some interesting but often frustrating experiences. We use crops not often planted in other areas (sweet potatoes, okra, peanuts, and southern peas). Our flowers and ornamentals have gaudy, outsized blooms. Our gardens sport native muscadines, paw-paw, gourds, and dozens of African and South American imports. Even our insects differ from those seen farther north and west.

According to surveys, people who live in the South enjoy gardening, whether for food or for pleasure, more than people who live in the North or the West. We southerners believe, as Thomas Church observed, that "it is worth any amount of effort to be able to see your house through the arch of a tree," partly for the beauty and partly for the shade—and partly for the challenge.

While our weather changes madly from extreme to extreme, becoming tropical one week and arctic the next, our never-ending struggle with the earth becomes a matter of pride. No organic gardener farther north has ever encountered stinkbugs with the size and ferocity of ours. And only south of the Mason-Dixon Line do the natural enemies include the soilborne fungus called simply southern blight. Despite such adversity, we persevere. We stubbornly lime the naturally acidic soil. We cover tender azalea buds in the frosty nick of time. We lift our beds above the floods and mulch away the torrid summer. We swat bugs as big as dragons and suffer the onslaught of their seemingly endless reinforcements. We joke about tying our tomatoes to giant nut grass while weeping over the fire ant. Collectively we brave the elements and use our fruits and flowers to raise our spirits. If the truth be told, our southern gardens are reflections of ourselves.

This book in no way represents official sponsorship or dogma on gardening. It is hardly definitive or authoritative. It is merely a collection of my own thoughts and experiences, based upon years of professional and personal contacts with southern gardeners. My horticultural skills are those of a gardener born and bred in the South. In addition to my work with the Cooperative Extension Service, I have spent hundreds of hours as the host of a weekend talk show on live radio. For years I have written garden columns for a newspaper. I have spoken to garden clubs almost more times than I can remember.

Having lived in Texas, Virginia, and Mississippi, I am accustomed to plants and practices that succeed in an area shaped somewhat like a sweet potato, with Austin on the western border and running across Shreveport, Jackson, Montgomery, and ending up with Richmond on the east. Gardens just a few miles north of the coast of the Gulf of Mexico, from Houston to Pensacola, fall within the zone I have defined; the lower reaches of Texas and Florida become nearly subtropical, however, and lie beyond it. The stretch across Florida's panhandle to Jacksonville, then up the Atlantic coast through Charleston to Norfolk, completes the territory that is usually called zone 8. The climate of the coastline itself is moderated by breezes from the ocean and the Gulf and by rainfall, so that it differs somewhat from that of places even a few miles inland.

The northern boundaries of my South are generally wherever the normal winter temperature rarely drops below 5 or 10 degrees. Another way of describing the region is in terms of the limits of St. Augustinegrass, a southern turf that is killed by freezing weather. Elevated areas, especially in the foothills of the Ozarks and the Smokies, are generally colder in the winter than the flatlands, and some of my favorite plants may suffer there.

Each chapter in this book deals with one aspect of southern gardening. Some information appears more than once so that you can dip in at random without necessarily reading from cover to cover. The monthly guide at the end is just a calendar of activities; you should turn to the text for greater detail. The additional resources at the back suggest some other books and magazines for further reading and provide addresses of Cooperative Extension Service horticulture departments, plant societies, mail order firms, and gardens that are well worth visiting.

Apart from the specific suggestions that the book offers, it reflects my belief in the value of local resources (nurserymen, neighbors, and the local Cooperative Extension Service) in providing solutions to local problems. Reputable nurseries can inspire new gardeners and old as well as offering the first line of defense against pests and disease. Your neighbors' tried and true planting practices and experience with different varieties will give you fresh local knowledge of unparalleled specificity. Then, too, the publications on home gardening available at no charge from county or parish agricultural services can't be beat for up-to-date information. I recommend them wholeheartedly to any reader with questions that I could not or did not answer in this book.

As Allen Lacy wrote in *Home Ground,* "To garden is inescapably to be involved with other people, to be indebted." In my work I have benefited from countless helpers, especially the callers and visitors and other folks who asked me questions I could not answer, making me ask others in turn. These people taught me to be honest, and the many fine men and women in the nursery industry (as well as a few incompetent ones) made me stand up for what I believe is right. They also made me check and triplecheck information until I was satisfied.

I am indebted to a number of specific individuals. For their great influence on my approach to horticulture I thank Milo Burnham, Jim Perry, and Richard Mullenax, who have generously shared with me their senses of humor and attitudes toward life. I am also grateful to Kent Schwartz, who knew I would never be satisfied unless I could ask questions; to Gail Barton, who never gave me a break; to Wilma Gene and Karl, who showed me their gardens after I began to learn that they were gardeners; to Melodie Avery, who put up with me for all those years in the office; and even to Betty and Arch, who never knew me but who showed me the way off the farm. Finally, I owe a great debt to Terryl, an unsung hero.

Felder Rushing

Gardening Southern Style

The garden should fit its master or his tastes, just as his clothes do; it should be neither too large nor too small, but just comfortable.

Gertrude Jekyll

1

Planning the Successful Landscape

A well-designed landscape enhances the surrounding community, adds to a property's resale value, and gives pleasure to the people who use it. Landscapes supposedly also perform other functions, for example hiding people from prying eyes and ugly views (a two-way proposition) or helping conserve energy. Some landscapes happen just because some folks like to plant things. Unfortunately, most people waste money on too many plants and end up with hidden homes and higher maintenance costs than they expected. The visible results may include unkempt, weather-beaten plants and confused, overworked homeowners.

It is vitally important for you to know what purpose you want to achieve *before you choose the plant or material*—even before you choose books on landscaping or approach your local extension agent or nurseryman with questions. Do you want shade for a patio? Then you want something that grows fast and won't be affected by insects—perhaps willow and water oaks, river birch, ash, honey locust, red or silver maple, or tulip poplar. Are you trying to screen out your neighbors? If so, choose a plant that will grow into an easily maintained hedge without dying of leafspots and without getting leggy. Are you looking for color? Then you

3

must know whether the plants will get hot sun, dense shade, or a combination of the two, for the survival of your plants will depend largely on light.

Whether you are building a brand-new landscape or adjusting a mature one, you need to start with a bird's-eye view of the property. How long and wide is the lot, and which direction does the house face? Where are the power lines, water faucets, slopes, good views, bad views, patios, and other *physical* components of the existing landscape, including plants in good health and in bad? Without an overall view and plan, your plants will succeed only through sheer luck. Your plot plan (or site analysis) will also help you decide *how many* plants you may need for a hedge and where to put trees for shade and for wind or sound screens.

As you plan, don't forget the opportunity to save on fuel bills. Landscaping to conserve energy is no idle concept; it works. But there is much more to it than summer shade. You can protect yourself from winter winds with evergreen hedges placed near the house's northwest corners. You can also channel summer breezes by remembering that most of them come from a southerly direction. Small trees on the south side of a house will lift the breezes to the roof line, where they will carry heat off the top of your house. (Southerly spring breezes are generally of warm air rising, which lifts upward, while autumnal breezes come from the north-northwest and are of cooler, descending air, which presses downward.) By choosing plants that are deciduous, you can keep them from blocking the warming sun in the winter.

Throughout the South, the winter sun remains low in the sky, while in the summer it rises north of due east, passes almost directly overhead, and sets nearly 30 degrees north of due west. We should plant accordingly. It does little good to set shade trees on the south side, given the sun's path in summer, since trees rarely have branches that hang over the roof. In fact, shade trees on the south will actually *decrease* energy savings by blocking the rare summer breezes!

In planning your landscape you will need to know your land, its soil types, and its faults and good points. Where are there overhead obstacles to trees? Know how much sun or shade your landscape will have, in all areas of the yard and in all seasons. Know where water flows during heavy rains—and know where it might come from, too.

Use Areas

"It may be argued that real beauty is neither in garden nor landscape, but in the relation of both to the individual, that what we are seeing is not only a scenic setting . . . but a background for life," remarked Sir George Sitwell. Landscapes are more than looks. They reflect on the places where we live and tell us who we are and how we like to spend our lives. The most important part of a landscape is a point of view.

Some folks just want to relax in the yard after work; others expect a landscape to make a statement. The front yard (also the side yard if you live on a corner) is the most visible to neighbors and passersby. Most people want it to be at least neatly kept. The fellow who was taken to court for having a weedy lawn insisted that it was a wildflower garden, but even wildflowers can be in tidy borders.

While you are at the planning stage, divide the landscape into different use areas, considering the view from inside and from outside. You will probably want the front to be for public view, the back for private use, and the work area to stay out of sight from all angles. The public area should be made to fit somewhat into the scheme of the neighborhood, with the architecture of the house dominant and everything else visually secondary. Drives and park-

---

I hate for visitors to come in through my kitchen, but that's the door they usually come to. How can I get people to use the front door?

Ask Felder

I have seen beautifully landscaped homes with attractive front entrances—with no sidewalk leading to the steps! You may have unwittingly made it so convenient for you and your family to use the closest door from the car, and forgotten to make it clear how to even get to the front. Drive slowly by your house, and look at it objectively (if you can). Is the front door clearly visible, or is it hidden by shrubs? Is the sidewalk leading to the front easy to get to from wherever people park, or is it simpler to wander up the driveway to the side? Also, is there anything accenting the front door, perhaps a lighted doorbell or a "welcome" sign of any sort?

To use a door, visitors should be able to see it clearly and be able to easily get to it from their car. That may mean that you should slightly "conceal" the door you normally use, perhaps with a lattice screen or a large potted plant.

ing ought to be directly accessible from walkways, which in turn should lead to a door—something people often forget, leaving visitors to guess how they should approach the house. (If visitors to your house often pick the wrong door, try concealing it slightly, perhaps with a lattice or large potted plant, so that the main door is the more visible one.)

The plants around the front should need little maintenance. Basic landscapes usually have entirely too many shrubs, most of which need pruning. At the corners place some shrubs that upon maturity will reach only about a third, no more than half, the height of the house, then accent the entrance with an unusual plant or unique accessory (an American flag alone can dramatically draw attention to the doorway). A few low-maintenance borders here and there will go a long way toward filling gaps. Add a group of trees (not less than ten feet from the house) to help frame it, and all the basics are in place. Avoid the common mistake of cluttering the front of your home with too many plants. The problem will only worsen with time, as the plants grow.

Hedges and fences both will often help hide the garbage cans, the old car, the tool shed, the woodpile, and the dog's yard. People frequently fail to consider such camouflage, but a simple wood lattice on posts with a vine or two can go a long way toward concealing the work area and anything else that lacks aesthetic appeal.

The last big use area of the landscape is the private area, the patio or deck with its bird feeder, swing, grill, pool, sandbox, vegetable garden, and everything else you enjoy with your old shirt on. You probably have these things near a window (so that you can keep an eye on the kids and the flowers) and a door, through which guests and food may flow freely. You should be able to breathe easily, or even to rant and rave, in the privacy of your own backyard without wondering who is peeking in.

The private area should visually pull you outdoors when you view it through a door or window. As you gaze across the backyard in the wintertime, the birds should seem as nearby as if they were in the kitchen or den. A small salad garden or bed for herbs or cut flowers should be handy and visible. The private area should be inviting and fun.

Do you *really* enjoy gardening enough to drag a garden hose around the yard in July, to pull weeds in August, to mulch in December, and to prune in January? Do you want a few beds full of

> Only man deliberately rearranges the setting he lives in simply because he prefers the look of it.
>
> *Nan Fairbrother*

perennials to be tended every now and then, or would you rather have lots of annuals, which will need replanting, deadheading, watering, and mulching on a regular basis?

Does your family share your gardening enthusiasm, and will you be able to count on help with the planting, pruning, and harvest? Also, if you like to entertain, have you left enough room per guest on the deck? How many people are likely to be relaxing, socializing, or working in the landscape? Do they have any allergies or other special needs? It makes little sense to grow an abelia, which strongly attracts bees as well as butterflies, if someone is allergic to bee stings. Then, too, some plants are absolutely dangerous—oleander, poison ivy, and the seeds of wisteria and lantana are examples—and should be avoided or planted in full awareness of their hazards. Do you plan to install a pool or some other structure in the future for which you should allow space now? Is there room for a pickup truck to drive through to deliver sand for the raised beds?

When my wife and I moved into our present house, the trees were there, the shrubs were large and healthy, and even the ground covers were in pretty good shape. The drive needed resurfacing, and some poison ivy had invaded the back. All in all the landscape was acceptable—but it did not reflect my own needs as a gardener, and the backyard was too open for private entertainment, so some changes had to be made.

The first thing I did was to walk around a couple dozen times and discuss things with my wife, who also likes to garden. I knew I wanted flower beds and borders, lots of them, and I hate mowing the lawn (I hope I never own a lawn mower). With plenty of sunshine and some weed killers, I figured I could start by killing the grass and planting some flower borders at the same time. Next I went about building raised beds for herbs and perennials and began the compost bin. The big, overgrown magnolia had to be removed, since it shaded the winter sun, blocked the summer breeze, buried my perennials in leaves, and clogged my sewer line with roots. That's as far as I got the first year. While I waited for spring to come around again, I noted drainage patterns in case I had to dig water canals in the winter (when the ground is softer). I also set about preparing for shrubbery and ground covers.

Americans, including southerners, want landscapes to look finished right away. Immediate perfection is impossible, and besides, no yard or garden looks the same any two months in a given year, much less three years down the road. Most of us cannot afford to have a landscape company come to our homes and install turf and shrubbery. Hoping for the best instantly, people all too often set out the biggest plants they can afford and can load into their cars. Not surprisingly, the trees and shrubs eventually dominate the house, the yard, and the owner's weekends.

Keep in mind a few general principles. Accent the entrance with something attractive or unusual, so folks know which door to come to. Use medium-sized bushes at the corners, so that the house doesn't appear awkward. Avoid scattering single shrubs up and down the front; use ground covers or borders to tie them together if necessary. Try not to use more than one accent, or the view may become cluttered. Aim for low maintenance by selecting plants that will eventually reach the desired size rather than setting out big expensive ones that will have to be controlled by constant pruning. Most important, choose plants that will perform their jobs well with as little trouble as possible. Also bear in mind that you can always move bushes later if their location doesn't suit you.

How should you decide what goes where? Look at your site plan. Do you need a hedge or screen somewhere, but a fence or wall is out of the question? Then you have a place for some tall shrubs. You need some color by the door but don't want to paint? An attractive container full of plain flowers (or a plain container with gaudy flowers) would perhaps do, but let's assume that you want to plant something and are willing to do a good job of soil preparation and to provide the regular attention and care that a living, breathing plant will require.

Functional Planting

There are only four possible ways to use plants in the landscape— as specimens, in borders, in groups, and massed.

Specimen plants grab attention, functioning as accents or show-offs. Small trees with pretty flowers or bark or shape, odd plants like mahonia or cactus or palm, container plants, espalier, or topiary—these plants are used one at a time, like giant rocks, to catch the eye and to lead it toward or away from an area. They usually stand near the entrance to a home or garden to show the way to

Ask Felder

What are good border plants to plant along my driveway? It is partly in the sun.

For one thing, most driveways and walks do not need additional high-lighting with border plants—they only emphasize the obvious. It is better design to use groups or masses of plants here and there to soften the artificial line created by the pavement. Leave the lawn as a border to keep from promoting the difference. Besides, your sun/shade situation would only cause part of the border to do better or worse than the other.

But if you must, it would be hard to beat any cultivar of *Liriope muscari,* daylilies and daffodils mixed (for year 'round color and foliage), cotoneaster, groundcover junipers for the sun, and the truly ubiquitous southern border plants of creeping phlox (thrift) and pink oxalis.

---

the welcome mat or gate. They may add interest to a little-used corner or light up a dull spot. Such accents are most effective alone or at least where only one can be seen at a time. Avoid placing more than one in the public area of the landscape.

A second very common way of using plants is to create a line to emphasize or to deemphasize an area in the landscape. Borders along scattered shrubs can create continuity; along a walk or drive they will only draw undesirable attention to an existing pavement. (Along a drive it is better design to use groups or masses of plants to soften the artificial line created by the pavement. Leave the lawn as a border.) Rows of tall plants can create living walls, or hedges, as we call them. Snaking lines can break up monotonous areas, for example under shade trees, where no grass will grow, to make the area seem smaller and to add interest. Wavy lines can also lead the eye more slowly from one point to another. Perennials as well as annuals can be used to create seasonal lines or borders, but the soil and amount of light must remain the same all the way along the line, or the results will be uneven.

A third and very effective way to use plants in the landscape, and one of the least exploited except by knowledgeable professionals, is in groups of three or more of the same kind. Even container plants can be grouped together for emphasis. In groups, azaleas, forsythia, or trees stand out much better than single specimens spread out around the lawn and in some cases are aesthetically more appealing than long lines. Perennials and flowering shrubs work together much better when they are grouped than when they are separated. Groups of plants repeated two or three times around the landscape can enliven an otherwise dull expanse.

Mass plantings, a fourth major category, create strong horizontal effects that tie the landscape together. A lawn is a mass of grass plants, and other ground covers can be equally effective in unifying large areas or dividing them into component spaces. Shrubs and trees en masse are powerful statements.

Accent, line, group, and mass: these techniques can help you plan and implement an effective design.

Gardening shouldn't be a grim business. If you've forgotten that, it's time you learned a lesson from your children.

Richard Nicholls

Choosing Wisely

Plants used to arrive at the nursery when it was time for them to be dug, and that was when they were to be set out. Some had bare roots, some were balled and burlapped, and some were just on a wheelbarrow, with a clump of dirt around the roots. Nowadays, with the development of new fertilizer types, soilless media for growing, tough containers, fancy irrigation systems, and mist propagation, anyone can buy almost any plant at just about any time of the year and find it in good enough condition to set out immediately or next week.

Although any potted plant may be set out at any time of the year (with allowance for watering, freeze protection, and so on), my personal rule of thumb is not to plant anything in July, August, January, or February. The reason is simple. In order for a plant to have a good chance of surviving, it must be set into a well-prepared soil. Even if pieris, forsythia, or elephant ear can tolerate the weather, there is the chance that I as a gardener may not be able to. If it is too hot, or if the soil is hard, I am not about to get out the pickax, hose, and straw hat to plant a bush—and I hope I never plant bushes for a living in the dreary winter, either, when the soil is cold and mud-cloddy and influenza hangs heavy in the air.

Once you know for sure how you want to use plants in a given area, it is important that you choose the best varieties for the situation. Bear in mind two simple rules of thumb. What should the plants look like upon maturity? Will they survive where you want them to grow?

First consider the questions of color, height, spread (or canopy), and the season or duration of foliage and fruit. Will the plant you have in mind need a lot of pruning to stay the shape you want?

Many people make the mistake of setting plants too close to each other, prune them too often, and ultimately kill them by overcrowding. If you want a big plant, choose a big plant. If you want a hedge only five or six feet high, remember that many fast-growing hedge plants would rather be ten or twelve feet tall and will need constant pruning if they are to stay at medium height.

Choose plants after considering their size potential at maturity. To determine chances of survival, you must know whether the area gets lots of shade, lots of sun, only early morning sun, or periods of hot afternoon sun. Sun-loving plants will grow poorly or will become weak and die in the shade. Shade-loving plants will burn in the sun or will become more susceptible to other problems. Some plants like sun if it's not hot (some of my best roses withered when they were set against a brick wall facing west, with heat reflected off a sidewalk).

Cold exposure is another consideration. Many beautiful plants would rather not be grown in the South for one reason or another, and while you may succeed in getting them to survive, don't expect them to perform well (lilacs are prime examples). Heavy or soggy soil, or dogs chewing on the bark, or insects and diseases may cause otherwise fine choices to do poorly.

Having decided what you want, what you need, and what conditions it will be subjected to, you are ready for the advice of experienced landscapers and nurserymen and for generous amounts of experimentation with your garden.

Distinctive Design

The overall design of any landscape has less to do with plants than many people realize. Most of the successful designs have broad, sweeping plantings, it's true, and lots of borders and ground covers. But what makes a landscape stand out is the walks, patios, borders, edging material, statuary and other accessories, containers, fences and walls, and arbors and trellises. These objects, and anything else that is more or less permanent in the landscape, add visual appeal if they are used carefully.

Outdoor lighting can contribute interest and utility to the landscape, whether it is a hidden spotlight used to highlight certain features or a floodlight installed for safety purposes along walks and near steps. Dimmers, low-voltage units, and other special accoutrements make outdoor lighting much simpler and more versatile today than it has ever been before. Outdoor lighting can obviously be used to excess, however, and "bug zappers" or strings of multicolored plastic owl lights can make a landscape the object of neighborhood ridicule. Used with discretion and properly installed, outdoor lighting can nevertheless multiply the number of enjoyable hours you spend in the garden.

Paving materials, such as washed aggregate cement, bricks, and flagstone, are best selected to blend in with existing construction material or to complement it, but contrasting textures may help you break up wide expanses into more appealing components. Weathered or stained wood, rocks, and mulches can all lend charm to the landscape if they are combined to create specific effects or moods. The natural wood shavings on my wide paths are soft under foot and have a golden glow when they are moist. They also help provide a transition between the pressure-treated pine of the deck and the flagstone beneath my arbor.

The tasteful use of different materials in the landscape not only simplifies edging and makes walking easier but also helps screen sights and sounds, reduce maintenance, promote the flow of foot traffic, and generally complement the architecture, giving the garden a more spacious and finished appearance.

Paths should be at least four feet wide and more if possible, so that people can comfortably walk side by side to or from an area. Then, too, by widening paths you can reduce the planted area that will require tending. Steps should be carefully laid out, being seven inches or less in rise (rule of thumb: riser plus tread should equal twenty-one inches). And if you have only one step some-

---

Ask Felder   *What is the best type of wood to use for a deck?*

Southern woods are subject to humidity, heavy rains, drying winds, water leaking from potted plants, and hot sun. It is fine to use cedar, cypress, and redwood (although redwood may not be worth the price morally, considering its limited source), but the best wood by far for decking and posts is pressure-treated pine. While it may cost half again as much as untreated, it will last fifteen, twenty years or more. Avoid pentatreated material (penta is now a restricted material and may pose health hazards). Word to the wise: pressure-treated wood is hard as the dickens to cut, so be prepared to sweat a lot if you don't have a power saw!

where, somebody is going to trip sooner or later. Use no fewer than two steps anywhere, and keep the dimensions of the steps consistent up the entire stairway.

Furniture should be useful, attractive, in good repair, comfortable, and weatherproof. Built-in furniture can enhance the overall garden design, and so can the surface of a raised bed or retaining wall. As Henry Mitchell observed in *The Essential Earthman,* "A good place to sit in the garden is worth having, and will count strongly in the design—far more than other ornaments."

Landscape accessories (plastic flamingos, statues, wagon wheels, or wind chimes) are fairly nonfunctional additions, mere ornaments, yet they dramatically affect people's opinion of a landscape. While they should express the gardener's personal tastes, some are best left in the backyard. My bottle tree, for example—a naked cedar tree covered with cobalt blue milk of magnesia bottles, old brown snuff jars, and green wine jugs—is a sight to behold when the sunshine hits it in the morning, but my wife thinks it is best unseen by neighbors and all but my closest, most understanding friends. The same goes for the massive birdbath I fashioned from my greatgrandmother's freestanding porcelain sink and for the cast iron bathtub I call a lily pond. I like these things but not in the front yard.

Accessories should not be overdone—they can quickly produce visual tension and confusion—nor should they be afterthoughts. Plan them so that they add a dimension to the garden, fitting into the overall design in a beautiful or inspiring manner. Avoid overusing driftwood, rocks from vacations, hanging baskets, statues, "antiques," and even birdbaths and feeders.

> Making a garden, no matter how simple, is a creative endeavor and it should relate to the person who owns it and be in some way a conscious expression of himself.
>
> *Nancy Gransby*

Soil and Culture

Most of the ornamental plants we set about the yard are foreign—imported from Asia and Europe and Africa—and often fare none the better for having been subjected to the vagaries of our soils and predictably fickle weather. Although nurseries may assure us that the plants they offer us are perfectly hardy in our climate, the fact remains that often they are not unless we give them a little "culture." As Goethe once noted, a plant "is like a self-willed man, out of whom we can obtain all which we desire, if we will only treat him his own way." We must therefore expect to give our landscape shrubs and trees occasional help in coping with un-natural stresses.

Even the most carefully chosen plant, carefully placed, has no choice but to deal with the soil in which it finds itself. My yard is clay, the sort that shrinks and cracks in the summer (or during dry spells in the winter) and swells to half again its volume during Mississippi monsoons. It is called "Yazoo clay," and it is responsible for the roller-coaster highways in my part of the South. When I was a kid, we called it "gumbo" clay. My trees and shrubs struggle mightily to keep from succumbing to its death grip on their roots.

Rather than dig out all the clay and haul in "good" soil, which would be expensive and which would eventually turn into clay anyway, I have been using raised beds for delicately rooted plants that cannot stand wet feet (roses, peonies, lilies, hosta, and azaleas). Raised beds are simple to construct and solve several problems at once.

To begin with, I arranged for delivery of several yards of clean, coarse builder's sand and piles of organic amendments. Clay or sand, whichever you have, may be improved dramatically by the addition of generous amounts of humus and organic matter. Indeed, soil preparation is critical to plant performance. Without good soil, a plant may survive, but it will not thrive.

The preparation of good soil is like making a pot of chili. You start with either tomatoes or meat, whichever you have on hand, and add the other. Then you chop in a few peppers, throw in some

---

Ask Felder

The fill dirt around my house is mostly red sand. What will grow there? Should I add any peat moss or something else?

By all means, add some organic material to that soil! Even cactus would have trouble there, since red sand usually also has a high clay content. Refer to the section on soil preparation, and be sure to do a thorough job of working any amendments in with the existing material. Raised beds and other planters may be easy to work with there, also. Don't feel as though you need to plant all the way around the house, either—it is much better to do a good job in a small area than to spread yourself too thin. As for what will grow there, first decide how big a plant you want in the long run, what color flowers you want (if any), and whether you'll be setting them in sun or shade. Your nurseryman can help you from there.

onions, perhaps add beans, and spice the pot with garlic and cumin and whatever else your secret recipe calls for. The point is, you start with one of two major ingredients and add the second. The rest is extra.

Soil is the same. Sand or clay? Start by adding the other. Then blend in peat, compost, old manure, finely ground bark, or other type of organic material. These ingredients will help the soil drain and will enable it at the same time to hold fertilizer and moisture between waterings. Add lime if the soil is acidic and the plants are not acid lovers. Fertilizer, like salt and pepper, will enhance the pot, but a little goes a long way. Proper soil preparation is the key to getting the most out of your investment in plants, whether you consider the expense of buying them alone or add in the time spent making your choice and setting it in the ground.

If your soil is so loose and well drained that water will not stand in a hole for more than a few minutes, you will have no problems preparing a nice bed or deep hole for new plants. If you have nothing but sand, no amount of organic material will last more than a season or two in the Deep South, so a deep hole won't be permanent enough to warrant the effort. If you have clay, as my neighbors and I do, a deep hole is still an extravagance.

Except for the very first root, or radicle, roots do not grow down, up, sideways, or in any particular direction. They respond to water and air: the deeper your soil is loose and friable, the more deeply air can penetrate, and the farther down your plants' roots can breathe. If moisture is there also, roots will go many yards.

An excess or dearth of air or water will limit the territory available to roots. If your soil is sandy and deep, then you must water deeply to provide roots with moisture, or they will dry and die. Likewise, if your soil is heavy, and water stands in the bottom of a freshly dug hole, then a nine-inch rainfall one week would probably drown any deep roots, starving them for air.

Dig down a foot or two, or as deep as practical, and turn over the soil thoroughly, adding organic matter and sand. Most roots will be less than a foot deep in the long run anyway. It is far better to prepare entire beds than to dig individual holes. Thoroughly break up the native soil (getting rid of noxious weeds and smashing clods), add sand and till it, and then add organic matter (plus any lime that is needed) and till once more. This is the method I use, and it is easier in the short run (tilling three times seems like

The home gardener is part scientist, part artist, part philosopher, part plowman. He modifies the climate around his home.

John Whiting

extra work, but the amendments are so much easier to blend in one at a time); the third time is the charm. If soil is correctly prepared from the beginning, the process will not need to be repeated.

Trees and shrubs often die from cold and drought and other forms of adverse weather that they would have been able to withstand had they been properly fed. The most important of these nutrients—carbon, hydrogen, and oxygen—come from air and water. Plants usually have no problems getting these chemicals except when they are grown in pots or under eaves of houses and someone forgets them (too much water, by the way, starves roots for oxygen and sometimes causes shrubs to drown).

The most important fertilizers that plants need from us include nitrogen, phosphorous, and potassium supplied in fairly large amounts but not all at once. Calcium, sulfur, iron, and magnesium—the other chemicals that plants need in relatively small amounts—are called trace minerals, or micronutrients.

Fertilizers are not as complex as they appear. All plant food bags and boxes, by law, bear three numbers printed under the words "guaranteed analysis." These numbers indicate how strong the material in the container is. Even bags of manure carry these numbers, as do bone meal and rose food. The first number indicates how much nitrogen is in the bag. Nitrogen, probably the most important nutrient for plants, is used largely for vigorous green growth. A fertilizer with a high first number will make plants grow lush and green if it is used according to the directions on the label. Lawns, ferns, trees, vines, and other foliage plants like nitrogen. Lack of nitrogen slows plant growth and causes leaves to be off color. Too much nitrogen will make plants grow more than they should and may burn their roots in short order. It can prevent flowering plants from flowering, since vegetative growth assumes priority when excess nitrogen is present.

Nitrogen does not last very long in the soil. There are slow-release nitrogens, such as cottonseed meal and urea, but generally the nitrogen is depleted or washes down to the river within a short time. It should be replaced occasionally but should never be applied in heavy concentrations. Ammonium nitrate, contained in most generic garden fertilizers, is very potent and must be used with discretion.

The second number on the label indicates the amount of phosphorous in the fertilizer. Phosphorous promotes early root formation and flower and fruit production and also gives plants energy and other vital benefits. Too much phosphorous prevents plants from being able to use nitrogen and other minerals, so it is important not to overfertilize with phosphorous. Unfortunately phosphorous lasts a long time in most soils and is heavily concentrated in most generic garden fertilizers. Excessive amounts of phosphorous are hard to avoid.

One glaringly bad practice that is widely promoted is the use of bone meal under bulbs and other flowering plants. Bone meal is all phosphorous (the analysis on the bag is 0-11-0, or 11 percent phosphorous and the rest inert ingredients). Phosphorous only *helps* flowers; it doesn't *make* flowers. Bone meal alone is not adequate for total plant growth, and it overdoes the phosphorous.

The third and last number on the bag indicates potassium, or potash, content. Plants need nearly as much potassium as nitrogen, although its function is not well understood. We know that potassium promotes winter hardiness (it is the main ingredient in so-called winterizers) and improves resistance to disease; it also improves the quality of fruits and vegetables and helps develop full, plump seeds. Lack of potash causes stunted growth, weak stems, increased susceptibility to disease, and loss of dark green color. Potash dissolves and leaches out of soils somewhat, so that it must be reapplied every year or so (more often on sandy soils, which do not hold nutrients very well).

Nitrogen, phosphorous, and potash, in other words, are the essential ingredients supplied by fertilizer. Micronutrients should be provided in only very sparing amounts. A soil test will of course identify deficiencies and is especially useful for sandy soils and potted plants.

West of the Mississippi River, out toward Dallas and past Houston, soils begin to become alkaline. Where an area of the country gets more rainfall, however, especially from eastern Louisiana on up beyond Virginia, the soils tend to be acidic. Acid soil is a natural result of excess hydrogen in the soil. We know that water is made up of hydrogen and oxygen, and so we can infer that, once the oxygen has evaporated from rainfall, the hydrogen that remains may be a problem.

On a scale of 1 to 14 (the pH scale), anything above the midpoint (7) is said to be alkaline, and anything less is acidic, or sour. Soil pH may vary from very acidic to slightly alkaline, even in the same yard or from town to town or from the top of a hillside to the bottom. The pH value depends largely upon the type and texture of the soil. To determine your soil pH, have your soil tested at a commercial soil-testing laboratory or through your county agent or local university.

Some fertilizers simply do not work in acid soils. The nutrients become bound up chemically so that they don't dissolve, and roots cannot absorb them. The best plant in the best spot in the best soil with the best water and fertilizer will languish, in other words, if the soil is too sweet or sour.

At this point lime enters the picture. If soil is too alkaline, for example out west or in gardens on limestone outcroppings, sulfur can be added to adjust the soil pH downward to the desired level. Most southern soils are acidic, however, so we must generally neutralize the acids with ground limestone.

Wood ashes, being highly alkaline, will do the job if they are not piled on too heavily in any one spot. Ashes from the fireplace have many valuable micronutrients and generous amounts of potash as well. Unfortunately, they are strong and must be used sparingly. They are also highly water soluble, so that they wash away quickly. Slag, a by-product of the steel industry, will also raise the pH of an acidic soil. Like ashes, slag is short-lived; it lasts only a year or so. Ground limestone, then, is best for long-lasting benefits. Lime will take a few weeks to begin dissolving (more or less, depending upon rainfall or irrigation), but it will generally last for three or four years, maybe five. It is worthwhile if your soil is known to be acidic (too much lime will of course make soil too alkaline). Lime is most effective when it is worked into the soil rather than left on the surface. Mix it into soil that is being prepared, or work it into the top of the ground beneath existing plants if it is practical to do so and if plant roots won't be damaged by tools.

By neutralizing acids in soils, lime helps roots and earthworms grow better, helps make fertilizers available to plants, and in general promotes plant growth over a period of several years. Lime is one of the best investments you can make if your soil is acidic.

Please note that, while most of the plants we enjoy prefer to be grown in a soil that ranges from only slightly acid to barely alkaline, they will often tolerate minor deviations from the level they prefer. Azaleas, camellias, blueberries, centipedegrass, and blue hydrangea, however, grow poorly except in acid soils. Do not add lime around these plants unless a soil test indicates that the pH is below 4.5.

Special fertilizers sold for acid-loving plants provide nutrients that become available slowly and sulfur, which lowers the pH. The types of nitrogen found in most such fertilizers also gradually make the soil more acidic. You will want to remember that these special fertilizers, like other specialty plant foods, are often extra strong and may burn exposed roots or stems. Apply them sparingly, and water them into the ground after each application.

In addition to scads of brand-name and generic granulated (dry) fertilizers, there are many liquid formulas. These are great for quick pick-me-ups for actively growing plants, but they are generally too short-lived to be practical for shrubs, trees, and ground covers. They are readily soluble in water, are quickly absorbed into the soil and plant roots, and may even be applied to foliage as a fertilizer—a shot in the arm, if you will. Be very sure, when using liquid or water-soluble plant foods, to follow the mixing directions and recommendations for application. These materials may be excellent (although temporary) sources of nutrients, but you don't want them to burn foliage or roots.

Rarely will more than two feedings a year help a mature tree or shrub. In fact, forced extra growth caused by feedings three times a year or more often, though occasionally helpful in forcing blooms for flower shows, penalizes the plants sooner or later. Perpetually forced plants may become unwilling candidates for health problems. On the average, plants can best use fertilizers at about the time they begin active growth—late winter or early spring for most shrubs and trees, late summer or fall for bulbs which grow during the winter. Avoid feeding plants as they try to go dormant. Late summer feeding of shrubs and lawns may tempt them to stay succulent and tender, which would be devastating come frost. Likewise, bulbs trying to go into rest in the spring may be exposed to undue pressure from diseases if they are fed at that time.

Put fertilizer under the branches if there is soil there. Roots, especially the feeder roots that carry the brunt of the workload, are not right up against trees or shrubs. They are spread out under the outer parts of the canopy and beyond. That's where the fertil-

The best fertilizer for a piece of land is the footprints of its owner.

Lyndon B. Johnson

izer should be watered in. Fertilizer will burn if it is put onto trunks and stems and also if it is applied too heavily over shallow roots.

Broadcast the fertilizer lightly over the general area around and beneath the plants. Right on top of old mulch is as good as beneath, maybe better if roots would be damaged or exposed when mulch was pulled back. Broadcasting fertilizer under the outer spread of tree branches and watering it in is as effective as the time-honored method of punching holes and filling them with concentrated plant food.

The Importance of Watering

The Deep South is notorious for prolonged drought during the heat of the summer and fall. Even during the winter there are weeks on end with no relief from desiccating winds. Plants, especially the popular broad-leaved evergreens (cleyera, aspidistra, pyracantha, sweet shrub, live oak, and so on), simply dry out and freeze in the winter without water. In August, road tar melts, vinca wilts, and mature oaks literally shrink in girth.

Still, some folks are surprised when plants suddenly brown out because of drought and never recover. Whereas some plants wilt, shed leaves, or otherwise plead for attention when they need water, others can't give warning signs and abruptly turn completely brown from damage which has been accumulating over several months. Such plants rarely recover. Most people don't understand why only a couple of shrubs in an entire hedge die. It's important to realize that all of the plants are very badly off, and the weakest or most damaged are only the first to go.

Water plants once every week or so, depending on the weather. If it is really hot, and there is an incessant, drying wind, water more often. If the weather is overcast and cool, plants may not need water for two or three weeks or more. Plants with active growth or heavy flowers or fruit need more water than dormant ones. Azaleas need water when they form flower buds in the late summer.

A slow, deep soaking is far superior to frequent light waterings. Trickle irrigation, soaker hoses, and slow soakings from sprinklers are all effective. Let the soil surface dry in between so that roots down deep can get the air they need for growth. Mature plants need more water per application than young ones, but the young plants, having no deep or extensive roots, are more desperate for regular attention.

Getting the Most from Mulches

Did you ever feel the earth in the summer? In the shade, soil is cool; in the sun, it can literally bake tree and shrub roots. Thick layers of pine straw, a popular and widely available mulch material, will keep soil temperatures moderated in the summer in addition to preventing the loss of moisture. If the mulch is thick enough, most weed seeds won't get the sunlight they need to germinate, and those that do come through will be spindly and easy to pull. Mulches around the trunks of young trees (particularly those that have spent less than four years in the ground) will help prevent the dreaded "lawn mower blight" that chews up the bark. Weed-eaters too are guilty of girdling young trees, and mulches can curb the weeds near tender trunks and stave off temptation to bring trimmers and mowers too close. The trunks of mature trees do not need as much protection. In fact, heavy mulches may favor rot. Pull mulches a few inches away from the collar of tree trunks.

> One of the best things about a garden, large or small, is that it is never finished. It is a continual experiment.
> *Margery Bianco*

Old hay, pine bark nuggets or chips, and even light-colored gravel are all effective mulches. I have begun using the peelings from a mill where poles are made. They are thin shavings, wide and long, and they pack down to make a nice, soft mat underfoot (when company comes, I soak the peelings with water so that they have a golden glow and give off a nice fragrance).

Plastic mulches are hot in the summer—so hot, in fact, that they are used for killing weeds and nematodes in gardens. Avoid them, even around newly planted shrubs. New fabrics have been developed which, when laid over freshly worked soil, will prevent weeds from coming through, will cool the soil, will allow water and fertilizers to penetrate, and will control erosion. A light dressing of ornamental mulch (pine straw or bark) will make the area attractive.

As organic mulches (leaves, grass clippings, and compost) decompose, they quickly lose their mulching qualities. They should be replaced frequently. When they decay, they add valuable nutrients, especially trace minerals, to the soil. A typical mulch should be kept at least three inches thick, but a depth of more than four or five inches may be harmful.

Planning for the Birds

I am a latecomer to birdwatching, and so far the few birds I have spotted in my yard have been ones with names I already knew or ones that are easy to identify. I've seen purple martins and egrets return after the winter. I've also noticed that the arrival of ruby-throated hummingbirds in town coincides with the departure of the gold and purple finches and the cedar waxwings. The permanent residents that stay in my yard year round include bluejays, redbirds, mourning doves, and a group of robins. They have affected my approach to gardening, prompting me to consider adding a few plants with berries as well as leaving some of the denser bushes for shelter.

Although well over 350 birds can be seen across the South in any given year, not more than a couple dozen types will be in any one yard at a time, whether in town or in rural areas. For the most part, these are the natives that stay around year in and year out, plus a few seasonal residents that spend part of the year farther north in the summer or cross the Gulf of Mexico for the winter (see table 1).

Although the various species need different foods and different types of nesting sites, most birds will be more attracted to the un-kempt landscape than to the neat and tidy one. One way of solving this problem is to keep wild areas separate and at a distance from cultivated areas. You may also want to modify the approach you take to yard maintenance and gardening so as to compromise between absolute neatness and the messiness that most pleases wildlife.

Consider leaving some dead branches on trees, for example, unless they present a hazard. Woodpeckers, nuthatches, and chick-adees are only some of the birds that feed on the insects concealed in dead wood. You might also give birds access to your compost heap, which harbors worms, bugs, and other foods. Try to offer adequate protection from predators. Use pesticides with caution— they can be lethal to species that prey on insects—and apply sprays only on windless days to prevent them from drifting. Dispose of containers and chemical remains safely.

When you add new plants to your landscape, consider choices that will benefit the birds in addition to performing well in other respects. Your aim should be to provide a highly varied habitat,

Table 1. Birds Commonly Seen in Central Mississippi

Permanent Residents

bobwhite, northern	sparrow, house
cardinal, northern	starling, European
chickadee, Carolina	titmouse, tufted
crow	woodpecker, downy
dove, rock (domestic pigeon)	woodpecker, red-bellied
jay, blue	woodpecker, red-headed
meadowlark, eastern	wren, Carolina
mockingbird, northern	vulture
owl, barred	

Migratory Permanent Residents

blackbird, red-winged	kestrel, American
bluebird, eastern	killdeer
coot, American	kingfisher, belted
dove, mourning	robin, American
flicker, northern (woodpecker)	shrike, loggerhead
grackle, common	thrasher, brown
grebe, pied-billed	towhee, rufous-sided
heron, red-tailed	warbler, pine
heron, great blue	

Summer Residents

bunting, indigo	martin, purple
cuckoo, yellow-billed	nighthawk, common
egret, great	swallow, barn
hummingbird, ruby-throated	swift, chimney
kingbird, eastern	

Winter Residents

duck, ring-necked	mallard
eagle, bald	sparrow, white-throated
finch, purple	warbler, yellow-rumped
goldfinch, American	waxwing, cedar
junco, dark-eyed	

Other Migratory Residents [a]

goose, Canadian	swallow, tree
goose, snow	tanager, scarlet
grosbeak, rose-breasted	thrush, Swainson's
pelican, white	warblers
teal	wren, marsh
swallow, bank	

Note: Permanent residents reside in Mississippi year round and nest there. Migratory permanent residents are also year-round residents in Mississippi and nest there, but their population is augmented in the fall by the arrival of migrants from the North. Summer residents reside in Mississippi from March through October and nest there; they winter elsewhere. Winter residents reside in Mississippi from October through March, more or less, and return in spring to breeding grounds elsewhere, where they nest. Migratory birds are strictly transitory.

[a] Usually temporary.

Source: Erskine Gandy, ornithologist, Mississippi Museum of Natural Science, Jackson.

with lawns, trees, hedges, shrubs, and other plants of different types and ages. It's particularly important to mix evergreens and deciduous trees and to offer good cover near feeders. If you plan a water garden, include areas for drinking and bathing, and allow enough space between plants so that the birds can move about and perch near the water's edge.

Mowed lawns supply blackbirds, thrushes, robins, starlings, and other species with a wealth of invertebrates. Weeds such as amaranth and lamb's quarters have seeds that are another important source of food (good not only for birds but also for people), as do various wild grasses, though many of them are very invasive and must be kept away from flower beds. Goldfinches like teasel and thistles. Other useful weeds include docks, sorrel, queen anne's lace, ragwort, and groundsel. A number of birds eat the seeds of dandelions. Flowering plants attract many insects and therefore also the birds that eat them; sunflowers are one good example. Hummingbirds are drawn to various red flowers. Plants that are good all-around selections include forget-me-nots, cornflowers, cosmos, asters, scabious, evening primrose, and ornamental thistles and grasses. Other fine possibilities are petunia, rocket, pinks, lobelia, candytuft, marjoram, honesty, lavender, foxglove, poppies, and larkspur.

Trees offer food of several sorts, shelter and nesting sites, and platforms on which to sing. Pigeons and jays eat acorns; blackbirds and thrushes eat the berries of mountain ash; beech nuts attract finches, chickadees, nuthatches, and woodpeckers. Oaks and willows are particularly rich in insects. Yew trees, which are poisonous to people and livestock (and were traditionally planted in cemeteries), have red berries on which titmice and some other birds feed. Pine trees appeal to chickadees and woodpeckers. Poplars may house as many as 100 insect species, and birches as many as 225 species. Other good trees are hawthorn, apple (a favorite food of waxwings), holly, shadbush, and dogwood. Small ornamental maples and conifers, on the other hand, have limited value. Table 2 lists some landscape plants that attract different birds.

Ivy provides cover and nest sites, a variety of insect foods, and berries. Among shrubs, privet is more appealing to birds than rhododendron. Other good choices include honeysuckle, blueberry, cotoneaster, roses, pyracantha, and fire thorn.

Species that appreciate special housing arrangements include

Table 2. **Landscape Foods Preferred by Familiar Birds of the Southeast**

BIRDS

PLANTS	Mourning and Ground Doves	Woodpeckers	Blue and Scrub Jays	Chickadees, Titmice, and Nuthatches	Mockingbirds	Catbirds and Brown Thrashers	Robins	Bluebirds and Thrushes	Cedar Waxwings	Orioles and Tanagers	Cardinals	Painted and Indigo Buntings	Evening Grosbeaks	Purple Finches	Goldfinches and Siskins	Rufous-Sided Towhees	Sparrows and Juncos
Autumn olive				u	◐	◐	◐	◐	◐		◐			○			○
Beautyberries					◐	◐	◐	○			○						
Cherries		◐	◐		◐	●	●	◐	●	◐	◐		●	●		○	
Crabapples		◐	○	u	◐	◐	◐		●	○	○		◐	◐		u	
Dogwoods		◐			◐	◐	●	●	◐	○	◐		●	○			○
Elderberries		◐	◐	u	◐	◐	◐	◐	◐	◐	◐	◐	○			◐	◐
Hawthorns		u	○		○	u	○		●								
Hollies	u	○	u		◐	◐	◐	●	◐	◐	○					○	u
Honeysuckles		u			◐	◐	◐	◐	◐					◐	◐	○	u
Millets	◐	○	u	u							◐	◐	u	◐	◐	◐	●
Oaks		●	●	●	u	●								○	u	◐	u
Plums		○	○		◐	◐	◐			○	○			○			
Pokeberries	◐	○			●	◐	◐	◐	◐	◐	◐						○
Pyracantha		u	○		◐	◐	○	○	◐		○				○		○
Sumacs		○	○	○	◐	◐	●	◐	○	u	○		◐	○			○
Sunflowers	◐	○	◐	●							●	○	●	●	●	●	●

Key: ● *Choice*   ◐ *Good*   ○ *Fair*   u *Used, amount not determined*

Note: Insects around plantings attract vireos, warblers, flycatchers, martins, and swallows. Grasses and weeds attract many seed-eating birds. Sugar-water feeders near certain flowers may attract hummingbirds. Other bird-attracting shrubs and trees stocked by many nurseries include viburnum, privet, ornamental evergreens, elm, and European white birch. Virginia creepers, grapes, roses, blackberries, and blueberries attract many birds but require special gardening attention. Groups of birds usually have similar plant food habits, although individual bird preferences and extent of use may vary. Actual plant use by birds varies with the season and situation.

Source: National Audubon Society.

bluebirds, purple martins, and owls. House wrens, on the other hand, nest in almost anything. You can grow one kind of simple birdhouse quite easily. Start by pressing some gourd seeds into warm moist soil in a sunny spot next spring. Water the growing vines early in the day, and when they die (they are usually killed by frost), pick up the gourds. Store them off the ground until they are

Ask Felder

Any easy solution to sparrows in martin houses?

Physically remove them as soon as possible. Some people keep the houses down until martin scouts arrive, but this is tricky. Try putting some cotton in the holes, with a long string attached so the cotton can be pulled out from the ground as martin scouts begin looking for suitable nests.

brown and cured. Then cut a two-inch hole in the side with a handsaw, and punch three holes in the bottom for drainage.

What birds need most is clean, fresh water no more than two and one-half inches deep. Shallow birdbaths are fine; an aquarium heater, installed and properly wired by an electrician, will keep ice from forming in the winter (don't use antifreeze; it's poisonous to animals). You can also make a birdbath from an inverted trashcan lid, setting it over an electric light so that the heat will prevent ice from forming. Whatever the container you choose, it should have gently sloping sides.

My mother has for years painted a plastic jug green, to help it blend in with the landscape, and punctured it with the tiniest pinprick of a hole. She fills the jug with water, screws the cap on (not too tightly), and hangs the whole thing out of sight in a tree or bush. As the water slowly leaks, a drop every few seconds, it is caught in a shallow basin below (usually a clay saucer). Birds see the ripples from many yards away, light beside the pool to drink, and sometimes even bathe.

A mixture of different seeds (millet, sunflower, and corn, for example) will attract several kinds of birds to a feeder; see table 3. Avoid cheap bags of wild bird seed, much of which is inedible filler. Instead, buy the ingredients separately and mix them your-

Ask Felder

How can I get different types of birds to come to the feeder?

First off, you don't expect to catch one of every fish when on the lakebank, and the same goes for attracting birds. Try sprinkling some bread crumbs around the feeder and ground to attract the "explorers," usually jays and sparrows. Once they signal the "all clear," other nearby birds will check out the scene.

Table 3. **Seeds Preferred by Some Common Birds**

BIRD	SEED
American goldfinch	hulled, niger, and oil (black) sunflower
Blue jay	peanut kernels; sunflower seeds of all types
Brown-headed cowbird	white and red proso and German (golden) millet
Brown thrasher	hulled and black-striped sunflower
Cardinal	sunflower seeds of all types
Chickadee	oil (black) and black-striped sunflower
Chipping sparrow	white and red proso millet
Common grackle	black-striped and hulled sunflower; cracked corn
Dark-eyed junco	white and red proso millet; canary seed
Evening grosbeak	sunflower seeds of all types
Field sparrow	white and red proso millet
House (English) sparrow	white and red proso and German (golden) millet; canary seed
House finch	oil (black), black-striped, and hulled sunflower; niger
Mourning dove	oil (black) sunflower; white and red proso and German (golden) millet
Pine siskin	sunflower seeds of all types
Purple finch	sunflower seeds of all types
Red-breasted nuthatch	black-striped and oil (black) sunflower
Red-winged blackbird	white and red proso and German (golden) millet
Rufous-sided towhee	white (proso) millet
Scrub jay	peanut kernels and black-striped sunflower
Song sparrow	white and red proso millet
Starling	peanut hearts, hulled oats, and cracked corn
Tree sparrow	red and white proso millet
Tufted titmouse	peanut kernels; black-striped and oil (black) sunflower
White-breasted nuthatch	black-striped sunflower
White-crowned sparrow	oil (black) and hulled sunflower; white and red proso millet; peanut kernels and hearts; niger
White-throated sparrow	oil (black), black-striped, and hulled sunflower; white and red proso millet; peanut kernels

Source: National Audubon Society.

self—or buy from a reputable dealer who carries quality mixes. The single best seed is probably sunflower, especially the black oil type (the most expensive kind, of course). It has a high calorie count, which is important to birds in cold weather. Some feeders—those made for thistle seed, for example—have features that accommodate certain kinds of birds and not others, thereby restricting the population served. By stocking feeders of different sorts mounted at different heights, you will attract a greater diversity of birds.

If you don't want to feed crowds of starlings, avoid offering food during the midmorning-to-afternoon shift, when they usually eat. To discourage squirrels, on the other hand, you must usually keep feeders well away from trees and other jumping-off points or mount the feeder five feet or more off the ground. Try placing a conical barrier at least a couple of feet in diameter beneath the feeder, or string several large phonograph records a few inches apart above the feeder on the line from which it is suspended. You can also skewer a series of pie plates, separated by short pieces of hose, onto the wires or lines. If your feeder is mounted on or near a window and you are worried that birds will fly into it, try closing the curtains or tape to the glass some fine nylon screen or the silhouette of a hawk.

One kind of feeder is especially made for hummingbirds. They are feisty eaters, and some incredible aerial battles will commence when more than one approaches. About one part sugar to four parts water is a good feeding mixture early in the season and can be diluted to 1:8 as the season progresses, but avoid using honey, which may cause a fungus to develop inside the beak. The sugar water that you provide will only supplement the diet of flower nectar and small insects that the birds must consume to stay in good health.

Some birds do not like to use feeders at all. To accommodate them, mix sunflower seed with millet and thistle and scatter some on the ground. You can also scatter breadcrumbs on the ground to attract initial explorers if your feeder has just been put up. Other foods that birds like, broken into small pieces, include pastry, cookies, cakes, cheese, fat, meat, dry fruit, corn, apples, grapes, oranges, unsalted peanuts, bacon rind, oatmeal, grains, corn flakes, and even broken bones (birds will pick at the marrow). Pulverized eggshells are a source of valuable calcium but may need to be concealed in other food.

The kiss of the sun for pardon,
The song of the birds for
    mirth—
One is nearer God's heart in
    a garden
Than anywhere else on earth.
        Dorothy Gurney

Suet supplies woodpeckers and other birds with fat. Commercially available suet mixes are great and last a long time even on the frequent hot days of winter. You can prepare your own suet mixture by melting lard and fat trimmings from meat (preferably beef) in a double boiler. Allow it to cool somewhat (so that seeds will not float), then add nuts, seeds, and other bird treats. Pour the mixture into cups, or cool it until it can be pressed into the wells on feeders. If you let it cool completely, then you can skim the surface fat (draining off the lower layer of oil), reheat it, and make much harder seed cakes. Another good food for birds is "poor man's suet"—peanut butter with seeds added to keep the butter from sticking to beaks. When the temperature rises about sixty-five or seventy degrees outdoors, fats in feeders are likely to turn rancid, and homemade suet mixtures should be replaced.

Aquatic Gardening

Water features have immense appeal in landscapes. Ponds, fountains, pools, and raised basins or tubs may all be used to enhance even the smallest gardens. A simple clay saucer set among plants and filled with water can be used with great effect and will attract birds. Then, too, depending upon your needs, budget, and space, you might plan a simple splashing fountain or a stream with a waterfall.

Garden ponds have come a long way since Joseph Paxton designed the first modern-day greenhouse in 1849 in Chatsworth, England, specifically for the culture of the newly discovered *Victoria amazonica*. That giant lily, whose leaves can be six or more feet wide, caused quite a stir. Lily pools are no longer considered expensive additions; modern materials make possible a simple, low-maintenance oasis.

Garden pools may be preformed or lined (plastic and similar materials are easier to work with than concrete). The first step in planning a pool is choosing a spot for it so that it will look good from all possible angles. Most aquatic plants require six or seven hours of sunshine for peak performance (less sun simply means fewer big flowers). You will also need to allow space for flooding surface water from heavy southern rains and to conceal "the works." Will hoses or electrical lines be exposed? Does the surrounding paving or other pool-side material hide the liner adequately (sunshine may eventually ruin liner material, and space between the water level and the pool rim is aesthetically disturbing)? By extending flagstone or precast pavers a couple of inches over the lip of the rim, you can thwart the sun's destructive influence, and the resulting shadow can make the water look cooler.

Most garden pools are at least eighteen inches deep. Part of the reason is that the crown of water lily plants (where they protrude from the top of the soil) should be between twelve and eighteen inches down, so the garden should be at least a few inches deeper to allow for the height of the pot. Of course, if you wanted a pool with greater depth, you could simply elevate the plant containers on bricks or blocks. Other plants, such as pickerel rush and Louisiana iris, don't like to be more than two or three inches below the surface, so it's useful to build them a shelf around the perimeter. Fish like water to be at least two feet deep somewhere, especially if they are to overwinter and the pond ices over. (When winter comes, attempts to thaw the pond with warm water are more likely to injure the fish than a freeze will. It's better just to break the ice a little.) In other words, your pool should probably be between eighteen and thirty inches deep.

Gravel on the bottom, especially smooth gravel, may make a new pond look nice but will probably cause maintenance chores later. Plant debris and fallen leaves tend to sink and become scummy, and gravel only complicates the chore of cleaning.

Water noises, even subtle ones, are soothing, pleasant, and relaxing. Fountains aren't the only sources of wet sounds, either; you can make or buy spouts which bubble, gurgle, splash, trickle, spray, or just ripple the surface of the pond. A recirculating pump (available at garden centers and at some hardware stores as well as by mail) should be able to displace the total volume of water in the pond every three hours or so. In the absence of a pump, you will need to replace the water from time to time as it gets swampy.

When you install a pump, it is more than a good idea to have a licensed electrician or plumber do the hookups. Outdoor power outlets and conduits and such are not to be trifled with, especially when water is involved. Insist on having a ground fault circuit interrupter.

Aquatic plants add color and special effects (tropical, serene, or exotic) to the landscape. Upright plants such as pickerel rush, Louisiana iris, equisetum, water canna, cyperus, and even cattails will all supply vertical accents in large ponds. In smaller pools they must be used sparingly. These are, for the most part, plants for shallow water and bogs and should be kept on shelves around the edges or set upon bricks so that their crowns are just below the water's surface.

Herbaceous perennials—everything except the equisetum—must be pruned of dead foliage after frost. Freezing weather rarely harms the hardy lilies and bog plants. Whether or not plants remain alive during the winter depends on their type and on the thickness of ice. Normally a pool has enough reserve water to keep them from freezing, but the contents of small containers may freeze solid. Most lilies will tolerate having their tops but not their roots frozen. With hardy plants, unless the water freezes more than an inch or two, there is little to worry about. Water gardens may look bleak in the winter, though.

Lilies and lotus need some space as well as depth for their best growth. They, like the other plants already mentioned, should be planted in wide, shallow containers in mostly heavy garden soil. Potting soils and peat are not needed for these aquatics; in fact, such soils may harm them. A little fertilizer pushed into the earth (13-13-13, 8-8-8, or something with a similar analysis) every couple of months during the growing season will help produce larger foliage and more abundant flowers. Commercial lily fertilizers, tablets available from supply shops or by mail, may simply be inserted in the soil around plant roots. Although fertilization once a month is usually recommended, that is a maximum dose. If you prefer, cut the tablets in half, or use them half as often, especially in small ponds where the plants perform well enough to suit the gardener. Don't add algaecides—they'll hurt both fish and plants. Instead, simply remove algae from time to time. You can try to keep it from returning in full force by having a third or so of the pond surface covered with lilies. You'll want to remember, though, that algae isn't as harmful as it is unattractive.

For more specific tips on planting aquatics, follow the directions that you receive from the supplier. You may, for example, be advised to allow the plants to remain at shallow depths for three weeks and to lower their crowns gradually to a foot or more below the water surface.

Floating plants (water hyacinth, water lettuce, and duck weed) are self-supporting and derive their nutrients from the water around them. Some attractive tropical plants (wandering Jew, coleus, and Sander's dracaena) may be used with interesting seasonal effect in ponds and fountains.

When I was most tired, particularly after a hot safari in the dry, dusty plains, I always found relaxation and refreshment in my garden. Lone female that I was, this was my special world of beauty: these were my changing styles and my fashion parade.

Osa Johnson

The works of a person that builds begin immediately
to decay; while those of him who plants begin to
improve. In this, planting promises a more lasting
pleasure than building.

William Shenstone

2

Choosing and Caring
for Trees and Shrubs

If possible, select landscape plants that will have more than one
season of interest. Some ground covers have winter color that differs from their summer greenery; some flower in the summer.
Shrubs may bloom only once, but fall colors or berries can provide
an extra touch. Trees may have not only good foliage and attractive flowers or berries but also an interesting bark and growth
habit.

In addition to considering light and other conditions, you must
know what effect you want the plants to have in the overall landscape. Do you need a hedge as a screen? If so, how tall should it be?
There may be two dozen plants from which to choose, but some
eventually grow much taller than others and will require heavy
pruning if they are to remain small. Wouldn't it be best simply
to create a hedge that you know will remain somewhat the size
you want?

Before you buy, ask how large the plant gets. Shape is important to consider, too, especially if you want a treelike, rounded, or
conical form, natural (wild-looking) appearance, cascading or
weeping or spreading habit, or other special effect. You may want
to group similar plants so that their normal shape is compounded.

33

Or you may need an accent. Not all fast-growing or large trees make decent shade, so it is important to know the eventual form before you plant.

Does the plant keep its leaves year round, or is it deciduous? Consider whether it has a coarse texture (large leaves or bold branching habit) or a fine texture (dense or airy but with a light effect in the landscape). Are fall colors noteworthy, or could they clash with existing plants or color schemes? Do flowers appear at a welcome time in the shape and size you need? Could thorns or bees ever become problems?

The plant's long-term survival depends upon its preferences and its hardiness in your area (heat and cold tolerance and moisture requirements). The farther a plant moves from its preferred setting (soil, water, and temperature ranges), the more care it will need. For this reason I personally prefer many of the native species over imports (with some superb old-fashioned exceptions). Visit nurseries and botanical gardens; study the catalogs sent out by mail order firms. The selection available by mail may be larger than that available locally, but you will have to weigh this advantage against the drawback that you will be unable to inspect before you buy. Botanical gardens give you a chance to see how well various recommended species are growing locally.

The most important factor for success with landscape plants, apart from the choice of something appropriate, is soil preparation. Be sure to provide adequate drainage. Try to supply enough water for the first summer at least. Nursery stock is usually in small containers and will dry out quickly if its roots can't penetrate the soil. Add organic material (peat, pine bark mulch, or compost) to the backfill, but use plenty of the native soil as well. I shoot for about 60–70 percent of the original earth (clay in my case) in my backfill, with the rest a blend of organics and perhaps some clean, sharp sand. Replacing the soil completely with fresh topsoil will only cause root problems later. Do not put fertilizer into the hole with new plants; most nursery stock has already been fertilized enough for one season, and fertilizer can seriously burn tender young roots if it touches them.

Container plants, even ones that are hardy, are more likely to have their roots freeze in the winter. Group them together, and mulch the pots and surrounding area when a hard freeze is predicted. Alternatively, you can bury them up to their rims in soil for

The best place to seek God is in the garden. You can dig for him there.

George Bernard Shaw

the winter. Fertilize existing trees and shrubs with all-purpose plant foods (the granular material can damage trunks, so keep it away, under the spread of branches) during March and April. A basic rule of thumb is to use a quart (two pounds) for every hundred square feet of area. Water it in well.

Mulches keep down weeds and conserve moisture by preventing fluctuations in soil temperatures. Pine straw or bark is widely available and should be applied in a three-inch thickness. Add more mulch as the old layer settles.

Principles of Pruning

People feel differently about pruning. A friend and sometime horticultural confidante of mine disagreed with me last winter about some badly neglected cleyera along the front of my home. I wanted to cut the plants low to rejuvenate them; she ridiculed me, saying that I should instead shape them into small, multitrunk specimen trees. Several days afterward I did half of the plants each way.

Those that I sawed off at a height of eighteen inches were reduced to stumps four or five inches in diameter. They sat forlornly by my doorstep for nearly two months before producing a rash of tiny maroon buds. Less than four months later, the new growth was tip pruned, and now it, too, is branching out. The shrubs are compact, as thick as can be, and less than three feet high. The hidden stumps are healing nicely, and I can see my front windows.

On the other side of the sidewalk, fronting the taller half of my house, the tree-form cleyera are nine or ten feet high, full at the top, with beautiful, glossy foliage. The once-hidden azaleas and ground covers, now interplanted with a perennial border, are showcased beneath a light, informal canopy. As this example shows, overgrown shrubs need not all be treated alike when it comes to pruning.

Most of the trees, shrubs, and ground covers used in southern landscapes are termed "broadleaf," as opposed to "needle leaf," plants. Broadleaf plants tolerate beastly treatment in the jaws of clippers and usually recuperate quickly from heavy pruning, whereas needle leaf plants will not usually do so. Some broadleaf plants, however, have what appear to be narrow leaves (yew is one example). All have the ability to flower, although the blossoms may be so inconspicuous as to escape human notice.

Needle leaf plants, as the name implies, all have very thin leaves and are conifers. They include cedar and other junipers, pines, arborvitae, hemlock, cypress, and the few spruces and firs that are planted by some southerners. Conifers, or needle leaf plants, will not tolerate the heavy pruning often given to other landscape plants. Their growth habits are often destroyed in attempts to shape them up, and any branches or limbs lopped off at arbitrary lengths very occasionally produce new growth from within the dead zone (the leafless area in the center of the plant).

Needle leaf plants should be trimmed little, if at all. Pruning should be limited to the removal of injured or diseased branches, the thinning of excessive growth, the training of a top branch to replace a broken main stem, or the removal of as much as one-half of the length of new growth to promote compactness or to help cover bare spots. Such tip pruning, if carried to excess, will make the outside leaf area thick and dense, aggravating the dead zone beneath and causing massive leaf drop.

It is best, then, to leave the natural shape of conifers alone. At most, to prevent them from getting leggy or scraggly, you might remove entire twigs or branches cleanly from their points of origin. Again, avoid cutting branches at midpoints.

Broadleaf plants, on the other hand, may be shaped up or out and may be thickened or thinned or even made to resemble animals or furniture. My mother's althea (rose of sharon) was pruned to the ground when it was hit by a pickup truck under the influence of a drunken driver, yet it came back pretty as ever and even bloomed weakly the following summer. The trick to pruning broadleaf plants, whether they are vines, trees, or shrubs, is to have, before you start, a basic knowledge of exactly what you want to achieve.

Broadleaf plants are of two general types: evergreens, which keep their leaves in the winter (holly, azalea, privet, and honeysuckle), and plants that drop their leaves until spring (rose, forsythia, crape myrtle, and pear). Both are treated roughly the same as far as objectives are concerned; it is a little easier to prune the deciduous plants because you can see better what is happening.

Two major groups of plants, then, are the needle leaf plants, which don't respond well to routine pruning, and the broadleaf plants, of which there are many different examples that respond well to many different sorts of pruning.

My shrubs need pruning all the time. Is there anything I can do to slow them down?

Ask Felder

While there are chemical growth regulators (liquid hormones which slow down growth or cause dwarfing) which work fine on many plants (including even lawns), your best bet will be either to prune the hapless plants up into small trees or to remove them and replace with plants which are genetically adapted to be the size you want.

The most common reason for pruning is to control the size of plants. Shrubs are often trimmed to keep them from getting too big for their allotted space. Trimming also keeps ground covers flat or in bounds, helps espaliered vines stay within their designs, keeps hedges flat, and eliminates unsightly sprouts. Routine shearing or clipping may be a problem when plants have been improperly selected in the first place. Many a homeowner has inherited a large shrub where a small one should have been planted. Although chemical growth regulators work well on many plants (even lawns), your best bet is usually to prune or to replace the vigorous plant with one of more desirable shape and growth habit.

It is wise, where possible, to limit the amount of formal pruning for tight shapes, if just to cut down on the high maintenance they require. In my town a quarter mile of healthy abelias surround a football stadium. They would be gorgeous if they were allowed to grow freely and to flower all summer and fall. Instead, the caretakers have decided to make them a long, flat-topped hedge which must be clipped four, five, or more times each season just as the plants begin to bloom. Why not a soft, blooming hedge that would need a clipping only once every couple of years? In too many instances, plants are regularly sheared into balls or squares or long green worms needing constant attention, when the same landscape effect would be achieved if they were left mostly to their own devices.

Pruning to control size is best done in the late winter or early spring, but it often needs to be done throughout the growing season. It is generally a good idea through most of the South to stop pruning after mid-August so that tender new growth does not sprout in the fall and get caught by early frosts. Wait until after frost to neaten up plants for the winter, but remember that spring-blooming shrubs and vines (deutzia, Indian hawthorn, Carolina jessamine, or yellow jasmine, and spirea) bloom on the growth from the previous summer and fall. Wait until after they bloom in the spring before pruning, or you will risk losing the floral display.

A second very common reason for pruning is to train plants or to change their shapes. Shaping or training should be done in the late winter or early spring, before plants waste energy on growth that will need to be removed later. Some pruning of this sort may continue into the summer if necessary. In Georgia I recently saw a display of topiary—in this case, vines grown into fantastic shapes on wire cages. There were monkeys hanging from trees and hippos in the pond; there was even a giant Statue of Liberty with a torch of salvia. In front of my own office stand a pair of Foster hollies in the shape of spaceships. The privet dinosaurs at Disneyworld are a famous example of topiary art.

> Unlike most other works of art, a garden requires of its owner something more than mere appreciation.
>
> *Louise and James*
> *Bush-Brown*

Most fruit trees and vines must also be trained to grow into the desired final shape. It is best to start from day one, beginning when the plants are first set into the ground. The thinning of branches and selective shaping of young limbs and shoots can force a young tree or shrub to become stronger and more florific or fruitful and can give it greater visual appeal. Pruning can also improve air circulation, helping control disease while also eliminating crossing, rubbing, or wild branches.

Overgrown, leggy plants may be encouraged to become small trees by the selective removal of lower limbs and branches, or they may be cut back severely so that they start over. Drastic pruning is a fearful thing to do unless you remember that some plants actually need it every year (roses, fruit trees, and clematis are examples), and other, more vigorous plants (such as privet) love this treatment from time to time. Red-top photenia, holly, ligustrum, azalea, forsythia, abelia, spirea, and many other broadleaf plants will benefit from occasional cutting back.

A third reason for pruning is general maintenance, which includes the removal of broken or dead limbs or branches, the elimination of suckers and of diseased or insect-infested plant parts, and various sorts of safety measures, such as the removal of overhanging limbs and thorny branches near walks. This pruning may be done at any time of the year, especially if broken or diseased wood could otherwise damage or spread to other parts of the plant. Some variegated plants, especially privet and euonymus, may develop branches which "revert" to all green. This growth is more vigorous than the variegated parts and should be removed completely as soon as it is noticed.

If a young tree develops two main trunks, one of them should be removed. Older trees with many trunks may not be worth treating. Suckers, or "water sprouts," are nuisances on apples, pears, and older shrubs and should be removed at their point of origin, especially if they arise from below grafts on roses and fruit trees.

A fourth broad reason for pruning, to aid in transplanting, is now the subject of debate. It has long been held that a plant, when it is dug up and replanted, should have a few limbs and leaves removed so that the aboveground portion balances the cutoff root system. This pruning reduces stress until the roots can begin their regrowth and can cope with the heat of summer. Recent research, however, indicates that plants need the stored food in the limbs, as well as the hormones produced in shoot tips, to help them put forth new roots. It is therefore now considered preferable to remove a few limbs and leaves only after the plants have had a chance to settle into their new soil and to begin growing new roots.

This light pruning should remove about a fourth of the foliage of the transplant and may be either light shearing over the entire plant or the selective removal of a fourth of the twigs or branches, depending upon the desired effect.

Techniques and Timing

Tip pruning, to make growth more dense and to force new shoots on the ends of branches, is often called pinching because it involves removing just the last few inches of growth. Tip pruning should be done selectively to maintain the natural shape of the plant. It is very easy to tip prune to just above a leaf or bud that points in the direction in which you would like the new growth to go; this technique, known as directional pruning, can be used to keep upright plants tall, squat plants flat, espaliered plants going the right way, and roses full.

Shearing, the method used to keep edges neat and thick, is simply a light form of tip pruning on a large scale. Lawn mowing is shearing. It is important to clip just the new growth and to do so with sharp tools so that diseases can't enter broken tips. Since shade kills the inside or lower branches of shrubs, it is best to trim hedges so that they are narrower at the top than at the bottom and so that sunlight can reach all the leaves. Shrubs become leggy as a result of improper shearing.

To espalier is to prune plants flat against walls or fences. This technique is suitable for vines, shrubs (such as pyracantha), fruit trees, and even large trees. At my alma mater several four-story magnolia trees grow flat against high-walled buildings and require only the regular removal of outward-growing branches so that all new growth is directed back toward the walls. Routine tip pruning and directional pruning are all that is needed to keep espaliered plants in line.

Topiary art involves training vines, shrubs, and small trees into shapes and special forms, then keeping them in place with shearing and directional pruning. Such gardening makes plants grow as they would not naturally. Various degrees of skill are required to train and maintain fruit trees and vines, to make trees from large shrubs, and to bonsai plants, or keep them exactly the same shape and diminutive size for hundreds of years. I once saw a group of mature oak trees which had been trimmed regularly into twelve-foot lollipops. "Poodle" plants, very expensive, are another example of topiary art.

Rejuvenation involves severe pruning and is an important way of reasserting control over big, old, unthrifty plants. It is a drastic measure that should not be undertaken unnecessarily, but it certainly works well. The nandina and camellias in front of my house, some over nine feet tall, were whacked back to knee height in late March, and by late May they had all put out new foliage and buds—growth that emerged from stumps up to five inches across. I tip pruned the new growth when it was about four inches long so that it, in turn, could branch out rather than becoming tall sprouts. Within four months of dramatic pruning and subsequent tipping, every plant had become a thick, lush, healthy, *small* shrub. It will be easy to keep the plants under control now with annual tip pruning and shearing.

At the new home of my grandmother Wilma, the yaupon and Chinese hollies crowded the sidewalk and porch so badly that we could hardly enter the house. While she was packing to move into the house, I cut everything but the bark off those bushes. Weeks later the plants began sprouting, and now they are handsome and manageable.

Rejuvenation is best done in the late winter or early spring to give the plants plenty of time to recover and shade themselves from the hot summer sun. It takes about five or six weeks after warm weather arrives for a heavily pruned shrub to put out new growth (boxwoods may take somewhat longer). Note that pruning has a localized effect; the new growth will nearly always appear within three or four inches of the cut. If you want a layered effect, for example with nandina or crape myrtle, be sure to cut some limbs high, some low, and some in between.

Heavy pruning of this sort can be successful on large trees as well, but it usually ruins their overall appearance and in the end causes many weak sprouts and the eventual death of the tree. It is better to cut trees down rather than maim them.

By cutting large limbs from trees and shrubs in a special way, you can prevent the tearing and splitting of bark along the trunk. Start by making a shallow incision an inch or two deep on the underside of the limb to be removed, out from the trunk. Then saw off the limb *beyond* the undercut. The limb will fall from the tree without ripping the remaining bark. The stub should then be removed to prevent rot from setting in.

Unless you are removing broken or diseased limbs from a plant, it is a bad idea to do any pruning in the late summer or early fall. Otherwise you will stimulate new growth, which may take a few weeks to emerge, and there may not be enough time for hardening off in the warm days of fall to enable the plant to withstand winter freezes. All other times of the year are fine if a few points are kept in mind. For example, spring-blooming plants (dogwood, azaleas, climbing roses, and so on) should be pruned in the spring after they finish blooming. Summer and fall or winter bloomers, such as crape myrtles, roses, althea, hibiscus, winter honeysuckle, and camellia, may be pruned in the winter, in the spring, and after flowering (until late summer). Summer pruning actually stimulates new growth and flowering for crape myrtles and roses. In general, it is a good rule of thumb to prune all plants except for spring bloomers in the late winter (February at the earliest), to prune the spring bloomers right after flowers begin to fade, and to finish everything (including hedge shearing) by mid-August or so. Any plant needing pruning later should be made to wait until a killing frost has sent it into dormancy.

One group of plants unusual in its pruning needs consists of spring bloomers with fall berries. Hollies and nandinas bloom first

A garden is the one spot on earth where history does not assert itself.

Sir Edmund Gosse

thing in the spring and begin forming berries then. If you prune them in the winter, you lose the berries. The solution is either to tip prune only the new growth of the current season, finishing up by midsummer, or to remove or prune branches selectively, leaving some intact each year, and sacrifice only a few flowers and berries during each season. Remember, when cutting holly for Christmas, to leave some of the past summer's growth so that you'll have berries the next year.

When you prune spring-flowering shrubs and trees, don't worry about the tender new growth that is already appearing—you would cut that off anyway. You will actually be stimulating more vigorous new growth which can be better managed later. You can rejuvenate shrubs either by cutting them severely and letting them put forth new shoots from the base or by selectively removing shoots and branches from deep within the plants to preserve the natural shape. Avoid a flat-topped effect by cutting at different heights and lengths.

Prune landscape shrubs, especially junipers, cedars, arborvitae, and hemlock, in February. Do not prune these conifers as severely as you would hollies or ligustrum. Instead, use light shearing to thicken the new growth in the spring unless you want to keep the natural shape. The broadleaf plants (cleyera, bloomed-out camellias, photenias, and so forth) can be pruned in February, too, as can boxwoods, which take a little longer to put out new growth.

At the same time you can take hardwood cuttings of rose, althea, crape myrtle, forsythia, spirea, and other deciduous shrubs. Insert ten-inch cuttings of last summer's growth so that only two or three inches protrude from the ground. As the cuttings leaf out in the spring, roots will begin to grow. Water and mulch during the summer, and transplant to permanent locations in the fall. I place three or four cuttings directly where I want a shrub and treat the area as if it were a new planting. Established shrubs will benefit from light fertilizing with a balanced plant food in February; broadcast about half a cup per square yard under the branches (not on the trunks) and water it in.

A few last tips on pruning are in order. If large cuts are made, especially on trees or big shrubs, go ahead and use some of the commercially available pruning paint (if not to keep out moisture and diseases, which are big risks in the South, then for cosmetic reasons until the wounds heal). Never leave short stubs when lopping off parts of plants. Cut branches flush with limbs, and cut limbs flush with trunks. Stubs even an inch long will invite decay and rot in the heart of your plant. Before pruning hedges or thick bushes in the summer, kick them to check for wasps. Call an insured professional horticulturist or tree surgeon if you cannot reach the part you wish to prune while you are standing on the ground; to attempt to prune it yourself is to invite an accident. Remember that heavily pruned plants need extra water and mulch in the summer to prevent stubs from cracking and to guard against root damage from the hot sun.

Trees and Their Care

Trees are the most basic element of any landscape. They set the stage, and every other plant is dominated or controlled by their types and locations. Nor do they remain static; young ones become large, often changing shape, and older ones die. A properly selected tree can provide more than a lifetime of pleasure and enjoyment, rewarding its owner with cool shade, fall colors, and an interesting profile in winter.

There is no list of "best" trees for the South. There are too many possibilities, and no two gardeners would place the same ones in a given landscape even if they agreed beforehand on the effect to be achieved. Most people decide what kind of tree they want and simply force it into place. A better approach by far is to decide what effect is desired, bearing in mind degree of shade, type of specimen, soil, proximity to utility lines or pipes, and the sorts of plants you may want to grow underneath eventually.

Evergreen specimens suitable for planting in the sun include several hollies, the native wax myrtle, juniper, and tree-form privet and ligustrum. Deciduous trees for full sun include sumac, Bradford pear for spring flowers and fall colors, the several flowering fruit trees (peach, plum, cherry, and crabapple), crape myrtle, and goldenrain tree.

Some of my favorites naturally include the various magnolias, especially the miniature Little Gem and the huge-leaved *Magnolia macrofolia,* often called cowcumber. And what could be more impressive than the huge flowers, glossy leaves, and fist-sized fruit clusters of our own native *Magnolia grandiflora?*

One other native hard to beat for light shade and gracefully

Ask Felder

The ground under my oaks and one pine is washing away, and roots are coming to the top of the ground. I've given up on grass, so what are some good ground covers for that much shade? And should I haul in some good dirt to cover the tree roots?

If you haul in topsoil, you may actually "smother" your valuable trees! They breathe through their roots, you see, and that's why they are so shallow, so they can get air. You can use natural leaf mulch to slow the erosion until groundcovers get established. English ivy is very popular (it's common because it does so well), as are the different types of Liriope, the spreading Mondo grass, vinca (major and minor), and ajuga (in better soil than you apparently have). Refer to chapter 3 for more information on groundcovers and why grass won't grow back in the shade.

fine texture is the river birch, with its shaggy bark accenting the multitrunk effect favored by many landscapers. Still another superb native that is grouped for greatest effect is the conical bald cypress, noted for lime green new growth in the spring, in contrast with its reddish, shredded bark and its rusty fall colors.

Two of the best oaks are the willow oak (often erroneously called pin oak), which has leaves shaped like your little finger, and the water oak, which has thumb-shaped leaves that are fat at the end. Both are relatively fast growing. Black gum has perhaps the most intense red fall colors, followed closely by sweet gum and sourwood (with its drooping sprays of summer flowers). Ginkgo, one of the oldest flowering trees on earth, still amazes me with its slow change from pale green to yellow and its sudden rain of leaves. The fastest tree I have ever grown was a tulip poplar that I set into the ground as a knee-high seedling. Only two and a half years later it was nearly twenty-two feet tall!

Flowering trees in the landscape are generally small—for example, crape myrtle, cherry, almond, crabapple, hawthorn, dogwood, pomegranate, redbud, and witch hazel (this last is really a large shrub). They often have attractive berries and fall coloration as well, especially the flowering dogwood, crabapples, and ornamental or flowering pear. Most are used as understory trees beneath or near larger plantings. One of the very best for flowering in the shade is the native flame buckeye, with spikes of brilliant red in the late winter, followed by tan nuts in the late summer (buckeye

What are some of the fastest growing shade trees I can plant near my patio? Also, how close can I plant them to my new house?

First of all, be aware that most of our hot summer sun comes from the west-northwest (morning, east-northwest), rather than from the south. Place shade trees as close as you want to houses and patios, but consider the effect roots may have on thin paving material or bricks. Many horticulturists recommend against planting trees too close to the house, more for safety from falling limbs later than because of root damage to foundations. I see no real reason why you shouldn't plant trees up to ten feet from the house, as long as they have room to develop properly and are given routine pruning and watering care.

As for "fast" varieties, it is wise to remember that the fastest-growing often are the shortest-lived. Use river birch, ash, honeylocust, red or silver maple, and tulip poplar; the fastest oaks for the landscape in general use are willow and water oaks—the former has willow-like leaves (sometimes erroneously called pin oak), while the latter has thumb-shaped leaves (bigger towards the end).

sheds its leaves prematurely, becoming one of the first plants in the landscape to show off its structure). An inedible fruiting tree worth considering if space permits is the osage orange (sometimes called horse apple), whose grapefruit-sized, lime green fruits fall to the ground in September.

On Arbor Day, observed nationwide in February, the Soil Conservation Service, Forestry Commission, or Cooperative Extension Service often makes available free tree seedlings. February is a fine month for setting out bare-root or container trees if the soil has been well prepared (no easy task in February) and if the plants are watered when they are set out.

You can plant some trees and shrubs as nature does. Take the red fruits from within the magnolia cone, for example, just as they start to hang out by the thread, and take dogwood berries when the birds begin to eat them at full ripeness. Then rub the seeds from their fleshy red packages under running water. Hormones within the seed covering inhibit germination, so it is very important to clean the seeds thoroughly. When they are stored in the refrigerator in a plastic bag filled with damp peat, they will last until spring, although they are actually able to germinate right away after being cleaned.

Don't use string trimmers near the trunks of young trees, or you will certainly girdle them. Girdling wounds, like the nicks caused by lawn mowers, are almost impossible to repair and usually bring about an untimely death. Also avoid cutting or bumping into bark. Mulch near the trunks to keep down grass and weeds until the trees are several years old—or use commercial tree trunk wrapping material.

Bagworms may appear in June on cedars, arborvitae, junipers, and hemlock. These creatures look very much like shaggy little Christmas tree ornaments. They are the larvae and females of a moth, and they cover themselves with fine webbing into which leaves have been woven. Bagworms can kill needle leaf plants within a few weeks if they are not picked off or sprayed with any of the several recommended herbicides.

A black film often begins to develop on the leaves of crape myrtles, gardenias, hollies, pecans, and other shrubs and trees as the result of insects and mites. This sticky material, called sooty mold, is easily rubbed or washed off but will reappear as long as the bugs feeding on plant sap are not controlled. As they suck juice from the undersides of leaves, their sugary excrement falls onto whatever is below (leaves, cars, or outdoor furniture), and mold develops there. To control it, spray for insects, adding a little liquid dish detergent to help the spray material spread and stick as well as to loosen the film.

When lightning strikes a tree (or, for that matter, when a car does so), little can be done apart from cutting away loose bark and perhaps covering the bare areas with pruning paint (pine trees need no paint; they seal themselves well with pitch). Trees, like people, may be killed by lightning or may show virtually no ef-

---

Ask Felder

What are some good small trees I can set out by the end of my driveway in the sun?

Evergreen specimen include several hollies (Foster's hybrid, yaupon, American, and tree-form Burford), the native waxmyrtle, juniper, and tree form privit and ligustrum. Deciduous trees include sumac (beautiful fall colors), bradford pear for spring flowers and fall colors, the several flowering trees (peach, plum, cherry, crabapple), crape myrtle, golden rain tree, and many others. Good soil preparation is crucial to their survival way down at the end of a driveway away from the hose.

fects. Much depends on the strength of the bolt and the prior condition of the tree. Some trees are blown open and live for decades; others die instantly with little or no trace of the cause. Damaged trees are not dangerous until rot sets in, which it may not do for many months. Have a forester examine the tree and estimate the damage, then forget about it.

Drought and sudden freezes will all too often manifest themselves in split bark near the base of trees and shrubs, a symptom that you should be able to spot in March. Plants with this type of damage will usually brown out in midsummer. Some can repair much of the damage and may survive for many years, but heartrot decay will cause a decline. To assess the extent of the damage, scratch the bark lightly with your thumbnail or a knife. If the tissue underneath is not green but brown, tan, or black, that part of the plant is dead. Sometimes the upper parts are still green but the trunk is dead, in which case the plant may put out new growth in the spring but may die in the summer. The hardier shrubs, such as nandina, camellia, holly, euonymus, and protected ligustrum, will have scorched leaves from drying winter winds and will usually shed the damage when growth begins in the spring.

Landscape plants often suffer severe damage in December and early January from sudden drops in temperature, especially after prolonged dry weather. Mulch, water thoroughly at least once every couple of weeks, and wrap the trunks of young trees with tree wrap or with strips of burlap. Antiwilt sprays, available at most garden centers, will protect the leaves of broadleaf evergreens from drying winds.

Lichens, scaly, gray-green growths, are a beacon of plant stress, a warning to humans that help is needed. They are a combination of harmless algae and innocent fungus growing together in a symbiotic mass that appears only on weakened, dying limbs and trunk.

Some of the other plant hitchhikers in the landscape are more likable. Not the least noteworthy is Spanish moss, or *Tillandsia usneodes.* It is a member of the bromeliad family (which includes the pineapple), a cluster of plants that drape our trees and have a true flower, although admittedly one that resembles the wiry, curling leaves. There is even a cylindrical fruit—a capsule full of airy seeds that forms at the base of the flower. Spanish moss is not a parasite (it doesn't get succor from its host plants) but an epiphyte, like the orchids: it receives its nutrients from the rain and from air. A second nonparasitic plant often found on trees is the resurrection fern, which usually grows on large limbs.

Shrubs and Their Care

Some commonly sold shrubs are not reliably hardy in the Deep South. Rhododendrons and lilacs, for example, usually do poorly where winters are not cold. Pittosporum and oleander often fare better in the South. Even some hardy plants, such as ligustrum, Burford holly, and live oak, however, are occasionally damaged or killed outright from sudden, severe weather following warm, dry spells.

Two native shrubs, both deciduous, are worth considering for their seasonal changes and interest. One, the American beautyberry (often called French mulberry), has long, stiff branches which serve as foils for tight clusters of brilliant magenta berries by late summer. The large, oval leaves usually fall prematurely to reveal the color. Another native shrub is the exotic staghorn sumac, with its deeply divided leaves and unparalleled crimson colors in the fall. The staghorn sumac holds its cluster of red berries high well into the winter, when other plants simply droop. A new introduction has a very deeply divided leaf for a fine-textured effect in the landscape.

Roses come in many varieties; there are bush roses, miniature roses, climbers, hybrid teas, huge Old World roses, and rambling roses, each with its own hundreds of cultivars and each with its own growth habit and role to play in the landscape. George Washington's birthday is the traditional day for pruning roses except for the spring-blooming climbers, which should be pruned after blooming. Cut back last year's growth of hybrid teas, floribundas, grandifloras, and other roses to within a couple feet from the soil line. Remove dead or broken canes and clutter, and cut out any blackened, diseased plant parts. If a bush is dead or dying, examine its roots for galls or dark growths; the disease can reinfect new plants set out in the same spot unless new soil is supplied. February is the ideal month to replace or plant roses.

Pruning promotes more vigorous new stems and blossoms and keeps plants compact. Cut to just above a leaf that has five leaflets; the lower you prune, the longer it will take for the new break to come out, but the stronger the stem will be. Spray in spring and early summer for black spot, and add an insecticide from time to time to control aphids. Thrips are a problem in buds, so look for tiny cigar-shaped insects down between the petals. If they are still there in June, spray with an insecticide recommended for roses. Rose aficionados often believe that roses need to be fed every five to six weeks. They contend that frequent feeding promotes strong stems, improved flowers, and green foliage. At the American Rose Society in Shreveport, however, the roses are fed lightly just twice a year, in March and in July or August. The Society waters deeply every week or ten days and sprays for insects and diseases with the same frequency. Its 20,000 roses are of course gorgeous.

The winged euonymus, another deciduous plant, is noted for almost excessive red colors in the fall (it was supposedly the burning bush of biblical times). The oakleaf hydrangea prefers partial shade and holds its large terminal clusters of summer flowers well into the winter. The flowers make nice additions to dried arrangements. Hydrangeas may be made to bloom either pink or blue, according to the pH value of the soil. If you work in a pint jar or more of lime, the soil will become more alkaline, and the plant's roots won't be able to absorb as much elemental aluminum—so the flowers will be pink for several years, or until the soil becomes acidic again. If you work in half a cup of sulfur, the soil will become more acidic and the roots will be able to absorb more aluminum, which will cause the flowers to turn blue the following seasons.

The aucuba, a shade-loving ornamental shrub, has rare but demoralizing problems growing in our area. Black leaves are the most common. Even in the winter, aucubas can get sunburned in just a few hours. The damage will appear the following spring or summer. Late spring freezes can also be a source of trouble. The leaves of aucubas also turn black when they are allowed to become too dry. Deep water regularly, especially if the plants are young and tender. Pinch off any blackened leaves, and lightly prune damaged stalks to promote healthy new growth.

The palmetto is the only truly hardy palm for the middle South. My greatgrandmother Pearl used it well around the old home, and I have seen it stand up for years in hot, dry commercial plantings surrounded by paving.

Azalea, ligustrum, holly, euonymus, Asiatic jasmine, forsythia, and many other plants are easy to root. Gather sprigs in the morn-

I have grown wise, after many years of gardening, and no longer order recklessly from wildly alluring descriptions which make every annual sound easy to grow and as brilliant as a film star. I now know that gardening is not like that.

Vita Sackville-West

ings while they are still firm and fresh. June is a good month to start cuttings, since the new, tender branches will have hardened a little. Cut branches that are four or five (maybe six) inches long, strip them of most leaves, and stick them into peat, sand, and perlite mixed in equal amounts. Rooting powders are helpful. Be sure to keep the cuttings moist and in a bright but shaded area until they root (five or six weeks in most cases). A plastic tent draped over some coathangers or other frame will keep the humidity high, and the cuttings will stand a better chance of surviving. If pruning is done early in the day, the clippings may be rooted to create new shrubs.

Equisetum, commonly called horsetail, is a chest-high, pencil-thin, leafless stem found growing in thick reedy groups which spread by underground rhizomes like bamboo. It is invasive and should be controlled, but it is so unusual that it may be worth considering for your landscape. It does well in boggy areas and is useful in flower arrangements. You may also plant bamboo, of course—several good varieties are available—but it should be contained so that it does not get out of control.

One of my favorite all-purpose evergreen shrubs, the cleyera, has few pests, is easily pruned, and turns a beautiful bronze in winter. The native Carolina cherry laurel, an amazing small tree, may be pruned into a neat hedge or allowed to screen large areas. It is a versatile plant and can reach thirty feet or more in height. In my opinion it makes the very best hedge in the least time. Being native to our part of the world, it withstands our weather and pests. It can become weedy from an abundance of black seeds every year, but it is easily pulled up or transplanted when it is young. I heartily recommend it, especially in preference to the disease-plagued red-top photenia, which is not on my list of favorites (although I do enjoy an occasional specimen of the larger, more spreading Chinese photenia, or serrulata, and its showy heads of spring flowers and winter berries).

The fast-growing, attractive, inexpensive photenias are subject to a fungus called *Entomosporium.* Since it can infect old leaves as well as new, it has no real season. It can hit at any time of year, and it often kills. The control is threefold: first prune the plants severely, removing twigs as well as leaves (twigs carry the fungus, too). Then clean up the area thoroughly to remove any infected debris. Last, spray the trunks and limbs with a fungicide, and repeat the sprayings for several weeks.

Gardening can become a kind of disease. It infects you; you cannot escape it. When you go visiting, your eyes rove about the garden; you interrupt the serious cocktail drinking because of an irresistible impulse to get up and pull a weed.

Lewis Gannit

Other dependable, less frequently used shrubs include the native deciduous azaleas (there are several excellent varieties, from the bright red plumleaf and the fragrant wild honeysuckle, or pinxterbloom, to the bright, woodsy flame azalea). These should be planted in good, peaty soil, shaded from afternoon heat, and watered regularly (even during dry, windy winters). Many are hardy throughout the South. Consider the early-blooming Kurume hybrids or the somewhat tender, mostly large Southern Indians. If you're buying plants to supplement those already in your yard, take a blooming branch by a large nursery when its plants are flowering to compare varieties.

Azaleas and other acid-loving plants sometimes have trouble absorbing iron from the soil, even when it is present in sufficient amounts. You can tell by looking closely at off-color leaves to see whether the veins are still green. If they are, green the plants up quickly with a liquid iron chelate, available at garden centers, or correct the problem with acid-forming azalea fertilizers or even by adding sulfur to make the soil beneath the plants acidic. Take any unusual diseases or insect damage to your nursery or county agent for identification before treating with chemicals. Quick and accurate diagnosis makes it possible to choose the most effective controls.

There are hollies of all types and sizes and descriptions (my favorite small holly is the dwarf yaupon, with its gray bark and bluish leaves; I also love the heavily fruitful, thin-leaved Foster's hybrid and yaupon, American, and tree-form Burford). To see the many different types of hollies, walk the holly trail at Callaway Gardens in Georgia. I personally also enjoy viburnums (there are many), spirea, forsythia, the summer-flowering altheas, and rabbiteye blueberries. Shade plants with unusual shape and pendulous clusters of flowers include Japanese andromeda (*Pieris*) and mahonia, which has blue berries.

The roots of plants do most of their growing for the year in the fall months, and they need moisture to be healthy and aggressive. Many shrubs need a deep soaking in October to prevent undue winter damage (in the case of broadleaf shrubs mostly caused by drying winds and drought, not actual freezing, unless there are sudden severe cold spells). Mulches conserve moisture and keep the soil warm longer into the winter, helping roots stay active and vigorous. Use five or six inches over the soil, and keep it moist if the plants are close to the house (bone-dry mulches present a fire hazard). Be sure to water the root zone in the soil, not just the mulch. Pine straw is probably the best mulching material in wide use, although wood chips (and the pole peelings I use) pack down nicely and last a long time.

Fall is a good time to plant new shrubs and ground covers; the plants will have a head start over those that you set out the following spring. Water is the critical factor in the survival of many half-hardy, young, or shallow-rooted shrubs (ligustrum, azalea, pittosporum, and sweetshrub), so be sure to use plenty to supplement the sparse rainfall.

November and December are good months for transplanting, too. Dig carefully, and take as many roots as possible (shallow roots are more important than deep ones). Dig a trench around the root zone of each plant, then undercut the root ball before carefully lifting and moving. Set the plants into the new soil (which should already have been dug and amended with peat or other organic material) at the depth at which the plant originally grew or slightly higher to allow for settling. Stake trees and large shrubs so that they do not blow over in hard winds; slip wires through a piece of hose so that they cannot damage the bark. Water the plants thoroughly to settle soil around the roots (poke the soil to remove air pockets, but don't stamp on it when it is wet). Mulch heavily to prevent roots from drying too quickly or from freezing.

You can bring spring indoors by cutting limbs from forsythia, jasmine, pussy willow, winter honeysuckle, and flowering quince. Give the stems a broad, angular cut to provide a large surface area for absorbing water. Immediately place them in lukewarm water, and they should begin blooming within a few days. Replace the water, and recut the stems weekly until flowering subsides.

Nothing is more pleasant to the eye
than greene Grasse kept finely shorn.

Francis Bacon

The Well-Kept Lawn

Lawns are complex organisms consisting of thousands of indistinct pieces of turfgrass, each trying its best to survive under often difficult circumstances. Sunlight, the energizer for grasses, provides the power of life. Water, reasonably friable soil, fertilizer, and routine mowing are all essential to the vigor of each individual grass plant and to the overall health of the lawn.

While modern man developed turfgrass in order to enhance his environment, our insistence on having spacious lawns has become something of a national mania. Grass is being cultivated everywhere. In addition to lawns' strong horizontal visual appeal, they reduce heat in the summer and unify the landscape and neighborhood, creating a relaxing, parklike atmosphere even around workplaces.

The advantages, however, have their price. An attractive, neat, well-kept lawn requires some basic knowledge about grass and a willingness to do certain chores regularly.

Types of Grasses

We in the Deep South can choose among many types of turf. The various types often exhibit striking differences in growth habits

53

and cultural needs. By deliberately choosing one with which you are familiar, or learning a little about what you already have, you can take care of it more easily.

We hear a great deal about grasses which aren't grown in the deepest South. Bluegrass, fescues, and ryegrass, known as cool-season lawn grasses, grow best in areas which stay relatively cool (60–75 degrees Fahrenheit). They are of European origin and perform best in the North (down to the northern ranges of the South), where summer temperatures are more moderate. Cool-season grasses must be watered frequently and mowed high, or they will thin out and will need reseeding often. They are not as vigorous as other grasses, tending to form clumps more than to spread out. In general, cool-season grasses are not recommended for zone 8 except in unusual situations, and then they must be given careful attention.

Recently some interest has been shown in growing certain varieties of tall fescue, including Falcon, Rebel, and others, in shady areas of landscapes in the Deep South where traditional grasses run into difficulties. In the shade of deciduous trees, where sun can invigorate the fescue in the winter yet summer foliage can reduce some of our intense heat, these turf-type fescues may indeed offer us some hope that we will once again have grass in the shade. It's worth noting, however, that these grasses prefer to be farther north and must be mowed as high as possible. In addition, be prepared to water frequently during hot spells. Foot traffic is hard on fescue; expect to reseed thin areas.

Our most popular grasses by far are known by turf experts as warm-season grasses. These include Bermuda, centipede, St. Augustine, and zoysia. While they have been very popular on lawns and athletic fields across the South for many years, they are not native to our climate and need occasional help in coping with our soils and weather. Often their performance, even their winter hardiness, depends upon their being fertilized correctly, mowed at the recommended heights, and watered, especially during prolonged drought (even in the fall and winter if drying winds are a problem). The acidity or alkalinity of your soil can play an important role in your lawn's ability to use fertilizer efficiently and to develop strong, deep roots.

Bermudagrass, imported nearly two centuries ago, is one of the most vigorous southern lawn grasses. It is popular as a fast-growing

It is apparent that no lifetime is long enough in which to explore the resources of a few square yards of ground.
Alice M. Coats

dense turf which starts quickly from seed and will green up with just a little attention to fertilizer and water. It not only resists wear and tear but also recovers quickly from damage (for these reasons it is used extensively on high school football fields and in other high-traffic or recreational areas as well as along roadsides). Bermuda, a dark green type, withstands close, frequent mowing and several light applications of fertilizer during the growing season; in addition, it can tolerate weed killers. Its major drawbacks are that it won't grow in even moderate shade, it may invade ground covers and flower beds, and it suffers from cold damage during severe winters in the northern areas of our region. Hybrid Bermudagrasses cannot be started from seed and are generally used for specific situations, for example on golf greens, where a very close, thick, fine-textured grass is needed and will be well tended.

Centipede contrasts with other warm-season grasses. It is gaining in popularity because of its low maintenance requirements. It is both slow growing and extremely sensitive to overfertilization (once a year is fine; more frequent fertilization or heavy doses will actually kill it). This grass is acid loving, so limestone should not be applied unless it is indicated by a soil test. Centipede may be started from seed, although sprigs, plugs, or sod will give faster results. Many people are initially put off by the high cost of centipede seed, but since a mere four ounces of seed will give good coverage for 1,000 square feet of ground, in the end it is close in cost to the seemingly less expensive Bermuda, which takes a full pound for 1,000 square feet. Centipede should be mowed fairly high, at a height of about two inches, and must have a slow, deep soaking every couple of weeks or so during extremely dry, hot weather to be at its best.

Centipede's biggest problem lies in the fact that it is not normally a deep green color. It is a yellowish green, and since some people tend to overfertilize to green it up, it often dies from complications. Centipede prefers to be fed only once a year, in May or June (though it's possible to put on an additional very light application again in August if the lawn is watered regularly or is on sandy soil). Although centipede will tolerate shade, it prefers full sun—again, with regular watering.

St. Augustine is a very popular coarse-textured deep green grass for the South. It is easily started from sprigs or sod (seed is not available for this grass) and quickly forms a thick turf which grows well in full sun yet will tolerate more shade than any other type of warm-season turfgrass. It is not easy to start in the shade, however; it merely tolerates shade over a period of years.

St. Augustine is susceptible to winter damage, especially when it is overfertilized or when it is subjected to sudden, severe changes in the weather. It is also prone to insect damage, particularly from chinchbugs and soilborne white grubs. Chinchbugs are small, ant-sized members of the stinkbug family and actually inject poison into the grass while they are feeding. They may be controlled quickly with liquid or granular insecticides, including diazinon.

Even though St. Augustine does not tolerate wear and tear, it is a fast, vigorous grower and recovers fairly quickly from damage when it is managed properly. Mow St. Augustine high, lime as necessary, fertilize lightly once or twice during the growing season, and the lawn will stand a good chance of being lush, attractive, and pest free.

What a man needs in gardening is a cast-iron back, with a hinge in it.

Charles Dudley Warner

St. Augustine comes in a variety of cultivars, each of which has advantages and disadvantages. Some are insect or disease resistant; others have better cold hardiness or tolerate more shade. Color and density vary from one cultivar to the next.

Zoysia is probably the most beautiful turfgrass available. It is deep green and extremely dense in growth and tolerates quite a bit of shade if it is already established before the shade becomes heavy. Zoysia is not available from seeds, so it must be started from sod or plugs. Since it is a thick-growing sod, it is usually a relatively weed-free grass. In fact, the very fine-textured zoysia is so tough and dense that it is often difficult to clip with a regular rotary mower unless it is shorn regularly and the mower blade is kept very sharp.

All varieties of zoysia will withstand foot traffic to a certain extent, being very thick and durable. Unlike Bermuda and St. Augustine, however, zoysia grows very slowly, so it takes a longer time to become established and to recover from being worn thin. The two most popular cultivars, Emerald and Meyeri, are very cold resistant. An unexpected beauty of zoysia is that at first frost it turns a beautiful tan, making quite a nice contrast with its rich summer mantle. It takes longer than the other lawns to green up in the spring. Mow zoysia with your mower blade set at medium height, and keep the cutting blades sharp.

Carpetgrass, being very similar to centipede, is not used as widely across the middle South because of its weak root system and lack of tolerance for drought and cold. Its lack of popularity is also attributable to its habit of sending out many seed heads seemingly right after it has been mowed.

Establishing a Healthy Lawn

Established lawns may need complete renovation if careful attention was not paid to proper grading, soil preparation, and fertilization in the beginning. Planting a lawn need not be hard or expensive as long as a little time is spent on planning. Planting turfgrasses at the wrong time of year can be an expensive, frustrating route to failure.

To get a good start on a new yard, or to renovate a poor lawn, first remove debris from the area, including brush or dead roots, bricks, shingles, stones, scrap lumber, or mortar chips. Look for poorly drained low areas or steep slopes which may be problem areas to mow or to maintain in years to come. Try to grade the area so that water drains away from buildings (and be considerate of neighboring lawns and yards). If much grading is needed, or if the topsoil has been removed or eroded, you may need to have some clean, coarse sand or good topsoil tilled or disked into your native soil. If your soil is very sandy, add clay-loam and a little organic matter (peat, compost, and so on) to help hold moisture and nutrients for the roots of the grass. Avoid simply piling a layer of new topsoil, however thick, over the unprepared surface of your original soil, or your lawn may end up with root problems later.

It is wise to have soil tested before adding lime or fertilizers. There is simply no other way to tell whether your soil needs additional nutrients or lime. Anyone making an educated guess, even one based on a lot of experience, is merely guessing. Centipede is acid loving but only to a point, and the other grasses simply do not grow good, strong roots or use fertilizers efficiently except when the soil falls in a fairly narrow pH range (the measure of a soil's acidity or alkalinity).

Add any recommended fertilizers and lime before tilling or disking the area for the last time. The final tilling will incorporate the additions into the future root zone of the lawn, where it will be most readily available later. Use a spreader for accuracy.

Immediately before spreading seeds or setting out sod or

plugs, till or disk the area thoroughly. This tilling will enable the tender new roots of the grass seedlings and sod to penetrate quickly into the soil, where they will be cool, moist, and protected from summer drought and winter damage. If you are renovating a lawn or are adding more grass to a thinned-out area, be sure to break the ground a little to help the new grass roots off to a strong start. Rake the area smooth, and either broadcast the grass seed or plant the grass pieces so that their roots don't protrude above the soil level.

Seeds are much easier to spread when they are mixed first with some clean sand. Broadcast half of the seed-sand mixture across the yard in a north-south direction and the other half east-west. The change of direction helps ensure even coverage. Use at least the recommended amount of seed; to determine the square footage, simply measure and multiply the length and width of the area. After seeding, lightly rake the area to mix the seeds with a little soil. Do not rake to a depth greater than about an eighth of an inch or so. If practical, roll or pack the area so that the seeds come firmly into contact with soil and so that erosion will be reduced later.

Southern horticulturists frequently suggest planting between spring, after the soil has warmed up, and later in the summer, so that the grass roots have a chance to establish themselves before winter sets in. In other words, warm-season grasses should be planted between early May and late August, although there is some room for variation.

Once grass has died out in the heavy shade, no matter how long it may have grown there, it will be virtually impossible to start again. You may till the area, lime and fertilize it perfectly, put down sod, and water it with great care, but chances are over-whelming that grass won't be able to grow enough good roots to survive a typical winter in zone 8.

Overseeding for the winter, something too few people under-stand, is best done only on Bermudagrass lawns. The other turf-grasses may be smothered or may become diseased if the over-seeded grass is allowed to grow too tall in the spring. The best choice of grass for winter color is ryegrass. There are two major kinds. Annual ryegrass is fairly inexpensive and is used more than anything else, but it tends to lose color and to die out under ex-treme winter conditions. It also burns out early in the spring. Perennial ryegrass, despite its name, lasts only for one season. Perennial ryegrass is more expensive, yet it germinates better than annual ryegrass and holds up better in both hot weather and cold. Perennial ryegrass is used where lower maintenance and better color are preferred.

To overseed, you must mow your Bermudagrass close in late September or very early October. Sow the ryegrass seeds and rake or drag them in (pull a piece of rug or fence over the area to make sure that the seeds contact the soil rather than staying caught in the Bermudagrass), and water thoroughly. Fertilize lightly in November and again in February (but do not use so much fertilizer that you make the Bermuda tender). Mow regularly as necessary throughout the winter. In the spring, as the Bermuda begins to green up, mow the ryegrass closely so that it won't interfere with the summer lawn. This close mowing and the hot days of spring will kill the rye. Wait until late April or early May to fertilize the summer lawn.

Whether or not you decide to rake leaves each year is up to you. The main reason for doing so is aesthetic. If the leaves become knee deep and are packing to the point where they smother the grass, then you should remove at least the top few inches so that the grass can breathe. If you want the humus and mulch to filter into grass and tree roots, on the other hand, you could mow the leaves. Don't remove the leaves in autumn simply to help the grass, though; they insulate the soil and protect roots from drying winter winds. They also return valuable nutrients to the soil.

Watering

How you water the newly seeded area vitally affects your lawn. Since seeds have no roots at first, they don't require a lot of water. It is vital, however, that they not be allowed to dry out during the critical first two or three weeks. Water very lightly and frequently (not enough for erosion but just enough to keep the seeds moist for fast germination). After the seedlings begin to grow, you can gradually increase the amount of water and decrease the frequency. In other words, water lightly and frequently at first, then gradually begin watering deeper and letting the soil surface dry between soakings. By midsummer, a thorough weekly soaking should be enough. Figure 1 shows how water affects grass.

Figure 1. *Effect of Water on Grass Roots.*

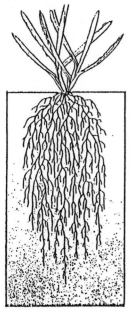 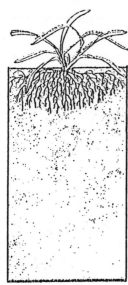 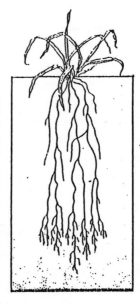 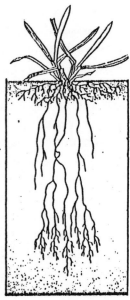

1. Ideal Situation

Adequate air-pore space, with moisture at all depths. As moisture is lost, it is replaced.

2. Saturation

When soil becomes saturated with moisture, movement of air is blocked. Grass blades tend to become limp. Roots cease to penetrate and remain near the soil surface.

3. Lack of Moisture

As plant dries out, growth is stunted and tips turn brown. Feeder roots near the surface are the first to succumb and gradually die back to lower depths. Roots thrive only at lower depths where moisture may be available.

4. Light Watering

Plant obtains slight temporary relief, with shallow roots absorbing moisture at the surface. Normal surface drying with inadequate deep rooting leaves plant in depleted condition and can result in severe damage.

Courtesy of O. M. Scott and Sons.

If sod, sprigs, or plugs are being used, be very sure that you water deeper than the roots of the grass, then allow the area to dry almost completely before soaking it again. In this way you will encourage a strong deep root system and one better able to withstand drought and heat in the summer and sudden freezes in the winter. Keep in mind that, although roots need moisture to grow, they also need air. More than a slow, deep soaking every week or two, depending on the weather, may encourage diseases and shallow roots.

Mowing

The mowing of a lawn is in essence a defoliation process which weakens and stresses individual grass plants. The overall mass of grass will usually recover unless it is abused time and time again. Even an untrained eye can spot a lawn that has been mowed properly, since it generally looks much better than its neighbors. It is very important to have a sharp mower blade. A dull blade beats the grass, leaving rough tips that die back a fraction of an inch and look scorched. On the other hand, if you have the blade sharpened after every few mowings and have a spare to use while it is in the shop, your lawn will stay crisp and green.

Each type of turfgrass has its own preferred cutting height based on its particular growth habit, but the amount of rainfall or irrigation and fertilizer will affect the frequency of mowing. Coarse-textured grasses such as St. Augustine and centipede are usually mowed higher than the fine-textured Bermudagrasses and zoysias. Midsummer heat, as well as lack of water, will cause lawns to grow more slowly and to require mowing less frequently. Large amounts of fertilizers, especially when coupled with regular irrigation, will cause more growth and will therefore make necessary more frequent mowings. Shaded lawns should be cut a little higher than normal.

If your lawn consists of two or more different types of grasses (or mostly weeds), as often happens, your mower height should be set to suit whatever type of lawn you prefer, so that at least that type of grass will get what it needs.

Since shearing the grass when it has gotten too high puts tremendous strain on it, you should follow this general rule of thumb: never remove more than a third of the leaf area with each mowing. Rather than cutting the lawn on a regular schedule, cut whenever the lawn needs it, depending on its rate of growth. Another odd rule is that lawns in the shade should be mowed a little taller than lawns in the sun. The extra allowance provides an additional area through which the grass can collect energy from the sunlight—which is very important for root growth and winter hardiness.

Thatch Removal

Over a period of many years, lawns may develop a deep layer of old stems, roots, stolons, and partially decayed leaves. This spongy residue is known as thatch. A little thatch is good for moderating soil temperatures and moisture, but too much can cause problems. With your finger, measure the distance through your grass that the roots must travel before they enter the soil. If the thatch layer is half an inch thick or more, then it may cause problems. Deep thatch can harbor insects and diseases; grass roots can dry out or sustain winter damage if they have to stretch through too much thatch; and thatch may catch fertilizer and absorb most of your natural rainfall or watering, keeping moisture from the soil.

Prevent thatch accumulation by mowing at regular intervals (leaf clippings, unless very long, don't cause thatch), and use fertilizers sparingly, since overfertilization causes grass to grow and build up too fast. Remove thatch when it gets more than an inch deep by renting a dethatcher, a special mower with vertical blades that clip down, cutting and thinning and flipping the dead thatch onto the surface of your lawn.

Rake away the debris, water the lawn deeply, and your grass will quickly return to normal. Dethatching is best done before spring greenup. It can set your lawn back severely if it is done during the spring transition. Summer dethatching is fine as long as the lawn is watered to help it recover. To avoid winter damage, do not dethatch in the late fall or winter. Mechanical dethatchers provide temporary relief from heavy buildups, but in the long run the best preventive measure is proper care.

Soil Aeration

Aeration, often overlooked but also important for your lawn, is achieved by simply punching many holes three or four inches deep into the soil to help air and water penetrate. It will help roots breathe, especially in clay soils, enabling them to go deeper and to branch out. You may aerate a lawn at any time of year.

Commercial aerators, run like lawn mowers or rolled behind small tractors, either punch holes with spikes or pull thumb-sized plugs of soil out of the ground. The holes will last a few weeks or through a few waterings but can be made to last for many months, even years, by topdressing with sand immediately after the aeration. Sand, when spread out by itself on the soil surface, has little real value in lawn care (except that it helps a small amount of thatch to decompose), but it can make aeration of the soil more or less permanent, as little fingers of sand form and penetrate into the root area of the lawn.

When using sand on the lawn, flower bed, or garden, always avoid river sand, which may contain not only weed seeds but also microscopic nematodes from fields under cultivation. Nematodes feed on grass roots and are all but impossible to kill or control once they are present. Pesticides strong enough to be effective yet safe for use around homes appear on the market and then disappear as the Environmental Protection Agency deems proper. To avoid problems it's best to use clean, coarse sand, sometimes called builder's, or sharp, sand.

Pest Control

Weeds, insects, diseases, and weather-related damage are continuing problems for some lawns, yet others never seem to be bothered. The level of fertility, mowing height, the frequency and timing of watering, and even the type of grass all play important roles, interacting with one another in preventing, promoting, or reducing the severity of problems. By understanding your particular type of grass and treating it its own way, you are less likely to need pesticides. Chemicals are last resorts in controlling pests. Pesticides are not cure-alls; they are valuable tools for temporary relief until the lawn can be restored to good health.

Your nurseryman provides lawn medicines which treat only symptoms of a larger problem, especially where weeds and diseases are concerned. You should identify not only the specific problem but also the source or cause in order to deal with it and prevent its return. The pesticides we have available nowadays are very specific in their actions, providing only temporary effectiveness. Choose carefully, and use the preparation according to package directions.

As with insects, diseases, and other nuisances, your nurseryman has the recommended control material for your specific problem and your particular type of grass. All pesticides these days are required to state on the label, in plain English, exactly what the contents are supposed to do. The label must also say what type of turfgrass the pesticide can and cannot be used on. The precautions, included on the label, are enough to scare anyone away but are handy when you need to know about the possible impact on nearby plants, pets, and people. If you choose the chemicals properly and use them according to directions, they are safe and effective.

Insects can be killed, perhaps for good but occasionally only until another infestation appears. Lawn pests will always be with us, and we must be prepared to deal with them as they appear. There are no preventive measures, only controls for use after the fact. Many very good materials are on the market and are available in every nursery, hardware store, and even supermarket. In many cases they are exactly the same materials used by professional lawn care companies. The various sprays and granules are formulated for use exactly according to directions; using them stronger or weaker will give erratic control at best and may damage or weaken your lawn and your own health.

Spray material, whether applied from premixed aerosol cans (expensive), from pressure sprayers, or from hose-end sprayers, is very effective against foliage-feeding armyworms, chinch bugs, and adult fleas. Good coverage is essential in controlling insects, and sprays are simply much better at reaching the insects where they hide than are dusts and granules. You can add one teaspoon of liquid dish detergent in each gallon of diluted spray material to help the liquid spread out and stick on. In most cases with insect control, it is wise to repeat the sprays after a week or ten days to make sure you kill newly hatched insects before they can reach maturity.

The most common insects found in southern lawns include armyworms (especially in Bermudagrass); chinch bugs (worst on St. Augustinegrass); white grubs (which feed heavily on grass roots, out of our sight); webworms; and, in sandy areas, mole crickets. Fleas and the fire ant are also serious pests. All of these insects can be controlled, but methods of applying insecticides differ, depending on the pest.

Diseases of the lawn (table 4), unlike insects, cannot be killed. They can only be controlled and kept from spreading. Many different fungi exist in the lawn, never causing diseases. Without some of them, in fact, we would be overwhelmed by undecayed leaves

Table 4. **Profile of Diseases of Warm-Season Grasses**

DISEASE	Jan.	Feb.	Mar.	Apr.	May	June	July	Aug.	Sept.	Oct.	Nov.	Dec.	CONTRIBUTING FACTORS
							Period of Occurrence						
Brown patch													Cool-wet weather
Slime mold													Warm-wet weather
Dollar spot													Wet weather, heavy dew and low nitrogen
Fairy rings													More mushrooms and puffballs in wet weather
Gray leafspot													Warm-wet weather and high nitrogen
Helminthosporium leafspot													Humid weather in late summer

Source: Cooperative Extension Service, United States Department of Agriculture.

and organic debris. The beneficial fungi keep nature under control. Some fungi, however, can disfigure and destroy the turf-grasses. When conditions are right, these fungi cause diseases. Not knowing what the problem is, and knowing just a little about the cause, could foil any attempted cures and could also make matters worse.

Two very common serious examples are brown patch of St. Augustine and melting out of Bermuda. The fungi that cause these two diseases exist just about everywhere in the South, like cold germs and mosquitoes. They become diseases, however, only under certain conditions. Brown patch, caused by a fungus called *Rhizoctonia,* is most severe when days are warm, nights are cool, and the grass is wet. These conditions occur most often in the spring and late fall. As hundreds of individual grass plants turn brown or die, the disease spreads in a circular or curving pattern, leaving rings and patches of yellowed or dead areas in the lawn. Large swaths of lawn are often killed.

Spring comes and the grass grows by itself.

Tao Te Ching

To control brown patch, use a fungicide spray as a protective film over the grass plants, like a raincoat or shield. You may need to repeat the spray every couple of weeks during the wet season, since the fungicides may wash off or may lose effectiveness after two or three heavy rains. Once the night temperatures begin to warm in the late spring, the fungus usually stops causing the disease, so continue the sprays from the first sign of the symptoms until the weather changes. In the fall, sprays will help keep the grass protected until it goes dormant. Granular fungicides will help protect roots, but foliar sprays are easy to apply with a hose-end sprayer. Whichever method is used, be sure to treat the entire infected area and its perimeter.

To keep brown patch from being its most severe, avoid watering late in the day or at night. The disease is worst on wet, cool nights. Water in the morning or early enough in the afternoon for the grass to dry completely before dark. A good, deep soaking every week or two, by the way, is much better than light sprinklings every few days and will help reduce the spread of brown patch.

One of the very worst things you can do where brown patch is a problem is to fertilize heavily or before the recommended dates. Brown patch is severe on lush, tender lawns early in the season, so avoid applying nitrogen fertilizers until the night temperatures have warmed the soil and your lawn is well established for the summer.

The other major lawn disease, melting out, is caused by a fungus with the intimidating name of *Helminthosporium.* "Melting out" describes how this fungus makes the lawn appear as tiny spots spread up and down leaves and the fungus kills the plants. Like brown patch, this disease is at its worst on wet lawns, so again, avoid watering late in the day or at night. Fungicides will control melting out, but you should keep your grass in good vigor with light fertilization. If your mower has an attachment for catching leaf clippings, you can remove many of the infected leaves to help keep the disease from spreading. By watching when you water, fertilizing lightly during the growing season, and using fungicides, you can easily curb melting out.

Other lawn diseases include various leafspots, which may be controlled as necessary with fungicides and proper watering; microscopic root-feeding nematodes, for which there is no surefire measure at this time; slime mold, which is a fairly harmless but ugly blue-gray material on leaves that can simply be washed off with a hose or swept off with a broom; and fairy ring, which causes arching curves of dead grass a foot or so wide, with apparently healthy grass growing in behind. Fairy ring, which sometimes has mushrooms growing in its curves, stays in the same spot year after year, moving a few inches or so each season like a slow ripple on the surface of a pond. There is no fungicide cure for fairy ring. All you can do is aerate the soil to help air and water penetrate the fungal mat. The fairy ring will eventually grow off your property and become someone else's problem.

Weed Control

If your turfgrass is vigorous and thick, it will naturally have fewer weeds. It can also resist the harsh weed killers you may need to use from time to time. On the other hand, if you kill the weeds in a thin, weak lawn, more will simply come back to replace the first crop, and you will have wasted your time and further weakened your turf. Weed control, then, is an ongoing process of watering, lightly fertilizing, mowing at the right height for your type of grass, and using weed killers only as a means of keeping problems from getting out of control.

Chemical weed control in the lawn is particularly frustrating. The culprit may be hard to identify, there are dozens of herbicides on the market, and you will probably worry about hurting the grass. Knowing the kind of turf you have will considerably narrow your choices of herbicides. What will kill weeds in one type of lawn may kill another type of grass. If you have St. Augustine or centipede, for example, you may use certain herbicides which will kill Bermuda, and vice versa. If your lawn is a mixture of grass types, you must simply decide which one you prefer to have in the end or avoid using materials which may damage any of them.

Lawn herbicides are made to attack specific types of weeds at certain times of the year. It does not matter what the name of a particular weed is; you can control it as long as you can tell whether it is a member of the grass family or a broadleaf weed. All weeds may be classed in one of these two broad groups. Grassy weeds, including crabgrass, goosegrass, and annual bluegrass, are true members of the large grass family. They don't have what most of us call "flowers"; instead, they have slender stalks with seeds. Some herbicides will kill only grassy weeds, but they are formulated for use only on certain types of turf. You must know what kind of turfgrass you have before selecting a herbicide.

> All gardens are the product of leisure. It is no good looking for gardens in a society which needs all its energies to survive.
>
> *Derek Clifford*

All weeds other than true grasses are called broadleaf weeds and are lumped together for purposes of control. They include dandelions, henbit, onion and wild garlic, clover, and a multitude of round-leaf weeds. The chemicals used to control all broadleaf weeds can usually be applied safely on most grasses as long as care is taken to use the sprays exactly according to the directions for the one particular type of turf.

Weeds which live only one season but reseed themselves for the next year, such as crabgrass and chickweed, are called annual weeds. They are fairly easy to kill but are all too often replaced by more of the same from hidden seeds in the soil. Perennial weeds, on the other hand, live for several years, usually dying down to a root or bulb, and spring back stronger than ever the following season. Hard-to-kill perennials include nut grass, wild onions, Bermudagrass (when it grows as a weed in another type of lawn), wild strawberries, dichondra, and dandelions. Perennial weeds require direct applications of herbicides during their most active stage of growth for control of the entire plant, roots and all. Some will need retreatment for complete control.

Postemergence materials, most often sold as sprays, are simply herbicides used to kill existing weeds while they are actively growing. For the herbicide to be effective, the weeds to be killed should be putting on new leaves, not going to seed or showing stress from drought or cold. You must get good coverage of the leaves of these weeds without putting an overdose of the herbicide onto your turfgrass or tree roots.

Preemergence materials, whether sprays or the more commonly available granular materials, should be applied before the targeted seeds sprout. In other words, before your weeds even begin to grow, you must already have identified the problem from the year before and must have selected the best herbicide. Preemergence herbicides have little or no effect on existing weeds; they prevent seeds from sprouting.

For summer weeds, preemergence materials should be put out in the late winter or very early spring, before the seeds germinate. Weeds that we notice in late February and March, on the other hand, begin germinating the previous October and November, so apply preemergence controls for them in the late summer or early fall.

Fertilization

How and when you feed your lawn is crucially important. While there are numerous examples of attractive lawns that get no care at all or are overfertilized out of season, there are many more instances of weedy, thin, diseased, and winter-damaged lawns. From Texas and Louisiana through Mississippi, Alabama, southern Georgia, the Carolinas, and Virginia, researchers and turf professionals agree that too much fertilizer applied at one time, or the wrong type, especially when applied at the wrong time of year, aggravates existing weed problems, makes lawns highly susceptible to diseases, and promotes winter damage. It also wastes money. Early applications of nitrogen-based lawn foods (widely sold in combination with small amounts of weed killers) are especially notorious for increasing lawn problems.

In addition, since southern turfgrasses don't really benefit from early applications of fertilizer, money is washed away when fertilizers leach through the soil right past dormant grass roots—unless the fertilizers are waylaid by hungry weed roots, which grow actively in cold soils. The so-called winterizers have enough nitrogen in them to keep our turfgrasses active and succulent in the fall, right when they should instead harden off to survive the winter. Nurserymen and chemical fertilizer companies make tremendous profits from fertilizer sales (a survey made in the mid-1980s showed that 40 percent of the retail garden center profits came from fertilizer sales alone).

On the other hand, too little fertilizer, or none at all, can keep the grass from having a strong root system, causing it to suffer more winter damage and keeping it from recovering from stress as quickly as it could. This problem doesn't usually become readily apparent, since weeds fill the spaces and make the lawn look green (weeds also make it need mowing more often than the original turfgrass).

A little food every now and then may be all your turfgrass needs to stay healthy. Too much, especially at one time, can burn roots or cause other damage. Some of the generic all-purpose garden and agricultural fertilizers (13-13-13, ammonium nitrate, and so on) are too strong, too harsh, and temporary at best when applied to lawns. At most they cause a sudden flush of tender, succulent growth that needs mowing almost every week.

By far the best fertilizers for use on southern lawns are those formulated especially for turfgrasses, those containing mixes of both fast-acting and slow-release nitrogen materials. Typically they are higher in nitrogen (indicated by the first number on the bag under "guaranteed analysis") and are usually blended with much smaller amounts of phosphorous and potash (the second and third numbers, respectively, in the analysis). While nitrogen is very important for green growth, it stays in the soil a fairly brief time. It dissolves and leaches away during rains and irrigation, and it is carried out to the curb with collected grass clippings. Too much nitrogen at one time will burn or even kill grass. Commercial lawn foods, however, which are available at nurseries, have a type of nitrogen which lasts for several weeks, even months, making them much better from the lawn's point of view (and a better buy in the long run if they are used sparingly).

Some types of grass, particularly centipede, are damaged from too-high concentrations of phosphorous (the middle number on the bag). Too much phosphorous, among other things, causes imbalances in other nutrients, keeping grass from being green and healthy. Since phosphorous tends to last for a long time (up to two years or more in some soils), the use of generic garden fertilizers such as 13-13-13 or 8-8-8 causes the buildup of far too much, leading to subtle problems which are hard to diagnose but add trouble. Avoid using these fertilizers, especially every year.

Potash, or potassium, is used by lawns in many important growth processes, but we usually apply it primarily for its winterizing effects. When it is absorbed by turfgrasses, potash acts like an antifreeze in grass tissue. It is most easily absorbed by lawns during the active-growth season, when nitrogen levels are adequate. Unfortunately, commercial lawn winterizers are formulated with too much slow-release nitrogen to be applied after early September. Since potash, somewhat like phosphorous, tends to last a while (except in very sandy soils), a little potash applied every year or two will usually winterize the lawn adequately. Most nurseries sell muriate of potash, a very strong material which can be used quite cheaply at a couple of pounds per 1,000 square feet of lawn every two or three years as a supplement to the small amount found in commercial lawn foods.

Some minerals are needed in very small amounts by lawns and other plants. These micronutrients, or trace minerals, perform important functions and, when absent, cause stunting. Iron, an often overlooked nutrient, is used by turfgrasses, particularly centipede, carpetgrass, and St. Augustinegrass. While many soils have natural iron, it may be hard for the grass to absorb, especially if the soil is acidic. A soil test can indicate whether iron is present and whether lime is needed to sweeten the soil so that the iron will become available to roots. Some commercial lawn foods have iron added in small amounts. Iron chelate and other iron sources are also available at nurseries and garden centers (these provide only temporary benefits and may burn the lawn unless they are used according to directions).

Lime is not a fertilizer. It is a material used to neutralize soil acids and to help plants absorb fertilizer. Many soils in the South are acidic, as indicated by soil tests; the relative amount is charted on a fourteen-point scale, with amounts under 7 being acidic and amounts above 7 being alkaline. This pH scale is used universally to determine whether a soil's pH is too high or too low for good plant growth. Most grasses prefer to root in slightly acidic soils, although they will tolerate some variation. Centipede, however, is

I believe that a leaf of grass is no less than the journey-work of the stars.
Walt Whitman

the most acid loving of all. It will grow very poorly unless the pH is fairly low. Find out whether your lawn needs help before embarking on any kind of fertilizer program.

Agricultural limestone, either dolomitic or calcitic, is often available at nurseries in granular or powdered form, the latter being somewhat difficult to apply on windy days. If your soil test indicates a need for lime, apply it evenly across the yard, and water it in or brush it off the grass leaves. If you need more than fifty pounds per 1,000 square feet, do split applications a few weeks apart. Avoid, if possible, putting lime down at the same time as fertilizer; wait until after a few waterings between the two.

Slag, while having the same basic effect on soil pH as lime, works much faster but doesn't last very long (a year or so at most). It also contains other by-products, including some plant nutrients which may create an imbalance in your lawn. For the money, ground limestone allowed to work for three or four years is preferable to slag.

Once lime needs and other deficiencies revealed by a soil test have been corrected, maintenance is a relatively simple matter. Use the special commercial lawn foods, available from retail garden centers, to get the very best value for your money. They give superior results over a long period of time rather than quick flushes and burned roots.

If you are on a budget or think that regular fertilization only increases the chore of mowing, follow the recommended times for fertilizing but decrease the amount applied. For example, if a ten-dollar bag of commercial lawn food says it will cover 5,000 square feet of lawn, you can make it cover 10,000 square feet—and still have a healthy lawn with good color cheaply. Avoid using blends of fertilizers and weed killers if the instructions call for application before midspring (late April or May), or you may damage the lawn. Winterizers containing nitrogen should be applied no later than very early September to avoid winter damage.

Don't fertilize the lawn in the fall. This advice comes from researchers in Texas, Louisiana, Mississippi, Alabama, Georgia, South Carolina, and North Carolina. Floridians and southern Texans can get by with it, as can northerners who have fescue or bluegrass, but lawns in the Deep South will remain too tender for too long if they are fed nitrogen in October or November, and they will be more likely to suffer damage from freezes and drying winds later in the winter. In addition, winter weeds, which are beginning to grow in October, love fertilizer.

Centipede Avoid liming unless soil pH is below 5.0. Use a slow-acting high-quality lawn food one month after the grass greens up in the spring (usually May). Centipedegrass normally needs no other treatment in the mid-South for an entire year; in southernmost areas, or in very sandy soils, use half the recommended amount in May and half in August.

Every third year, substitute a commercial winterizer—even in the spring—to provide potash. Supplemental iron may be used sparingly. Avoid using phosphorous-rich garden fertilizers on centipedegrass lawns.

St. Augustine Lime if necessary every few years. Use a slow-release commercial lawn food one month after spring greenup begins (it is safe to do so in May) and again in late August. Every three years substitute a commercial lawn winterizer to provide potash (as the regular May or August feeding). Use half-strength rates if the lawn is shaded half the day or more. Supplemental iron may improve the color somewhat.

Bermuda and Zoysia Lime if necessary. Use a slow-release commercial lawn food in late April (three weeks or so after spring greenup), again in midsummer, and once more about September 1. Substitute a lawn winterizer as one of the three regular feedings every two or three years.

Hybrid Bermuda, if irrigated, may need an additional feeding in the summer. Shaded zoysia should be fed at half strength.

Lawn Substitutes and Ground Covers

Turfgrasses can create very strong horizontal planes in the landscape. Trees, shrubs, flower beds, walks, and ground covers help add interest. Ground covers, used more extensively in the past two or three decades to break up expanses of lawn and paved areas into visually smaller sections, have the extra advantage that they reduce the need for expensive lawn maintenance. They can mask bare patches of soil, provide erosion control, supply contrasting textures and color, or create a strong, unifying effect in the landscape, tying together many spotty plants. Some make fine evergreen covers for perennial beds where a little winter backbone may be needed.

Table 5. **Quantity of Ground Cover Plants Required for Areas of Varying Size**

Planting Area[b]	Spacing[a]					
	6″	8″	9″	12″	18″	24″
100	400	225	178	100	45	25
200	800	450	356	200	90	50
300	1,200	675	534	300	135	75
400	1,600	900	712	400	180	100
500	2,000	1,125	890	500	225	125
1,000	4,000	2,250	1,780	1,000	450	250

[a] inches in both directions.

[b] square feet.

Source: Cooperative Extension Service, United States Department of Agriculture.

Ground covers are particularly useful, however, in areas where turfgrass is impractical or won't grow. Steep banks and hillsides, small enclosures or hard-to-mow areas, and the area around the tender bases of young trees and shrubs are all primary candidates for the ground covers that thrive in sun. Especially around mature trees, where conventional turfgrasses have failed and cannot be started again, the shade-loving kinds come into their own, with often subtle and sometimes surprising effects. Some of these versatile plants may be a little slower than turfgrass to establish themselves, but they usually become both attractive and interesting while remaining functional and low in maintenance. Table 5 shows how much space to allow per plant when you set them out.

Sun-loving ground covers (table 6), usually evergreen and less than a foot or two in depth, need good soil preparation in order to establish strong roots, especially where erosion control is desired. Mulches of hay, pine needles, and material such as burlap and the recently developed plastic landscape fabrics will check erosion and inhibit weeds until root growth and good coverage of foliage take over. Weeds may still be a problem the first year or so, but in spite of their unsightly looks, they do help control erosion until the ground covers are established. Herbicides are available for eradicating the weeds in the long run.

Shade-loving ground covers (table 7) often help make drab landscapes eye-catching and attractive. They not only create visually powerful lines but also add the evergreen texture in mass plantings that often gives depth to otherwise flat panoramas. Ground

Table 6. **Evergreen Ground Covers for Sunny or Bright Areas**

GROUND COVER	REMARKS
Asiatic jasmine	plant 18″ apart; spreads rapidly; ever-green vine
Bearberry cotoneaster	plant 3′ apart; spreading shrub to 10″ tall, covers large area; attractive red fruit in winter
Creeping phlox (*Phlox subulata*)	plant 12″ apart; excellent low-growing cover for rock walls, hot areas; brilliant flower display in spring
Honeysuckle (*Lonicera japonica*)	plant 3′ apart; excellent summer-flowering evergreen for erosion control; vigorous (may become invasive of nearby plantings)
Juniper ground covers	
Andorea juniper	18″ tall, 6′ spread; gray-green foliage turns purple in winter
Bar Harbor juniper	12″ tall, 8′ spread; blue-green foliage turns rust-plum in winter
Blue Rug juniper	6″ tall, 6′ spread; bright blue foliage, hugs ground
Japanese Garden juniper	2′ tall, 8′ spread; dark blue-green foliage, stiff and dense
Shore juniper	12″ tall, 6′ spread; soft blue-green foliage
Liriope muscari (monkey grass)	clump forming, spreads slowly; plant 12″ apart for quick cover; spikes of blue flowers in summer; many varieties available, including variegated
Liriope spicata (lily turf)	similar to *L. muscari,* but spreads quickly; foliage thinner and longer
Mondo grass (*Ophiopogon*)	9″ high, very thin leaves, spreads rapidly in good soil; "little monkey grass"
Sedum	4″ tall, spreads slowly; light green foliage with yellow spring flowers
Wintercreeper (*Euonymus fortunei*)	18″ tall, spreading vine; green foliage turns red in fall; variegated form available

Source: Cooperative Extension Service, United States Department of Agriculture.

covers are also useful in dense shade, for example, under magnolias, live oaks, and mature trees where traditional turfgrasses have failed.

Favorites of mine for the South include many of the low-growing spreading junipers, all of which prefer full sun for thick-

Table 7. **Evergreen Ground Covers for the Shade**

GROUND COVER	REMARKS
Ajuga (carpet bugle)	low growing, spreading; spires of purple flowers in spring; foliage colors include green, bronze, and maroon; not drought tolerant
Dwarf bamboo (*Sasa pygmaea*)	12″ tall, mat forming, and aggressive; should be contained
English ivy	popular, easy to grow; several varieties available with various leaf shapes and sizes; will climb trees, walls, etc.; spreads well
Holly fern	evergreen fern, 20″ tall; forms slow-spreading clump; plant 12″ apart to cover
Hosta (plantain lily)	summer perennial, to 18″; clump forming, slow to spread; many cultivars available, including variegated; summer spikes of flowers, divides easily
Liriope muscari (monkey grass)	clump forming, spreads slowly, plant 12″ apart for quick cover; variegated forms available; does not flower freely in heavy shade
Liriope spicata (Lily turf)	similar to *L. muscari* but spreads quickly; foliage long and narrow
Mondo grass (*Ophiopogon*)	very thin leaves; "little monkey grass"; one of the best ground covers for dense shade; spreads quickly; may be mowed once or twice a year for turflike effect
Pachysandra (Japanese spurge)	15″ tall; plant 18″ apart; spreads moderately in good soil; variegated form
Vinca major (bigleaf periwinkle)	24″ tall, vigorously spreading upright vine; large blue flowers in early spring; variegated form
Vinca minor (little leaf periwinkle)	12″ tall, excellent ground cover, better suited for confined areas than *V. major;* blue or white flowers in early spring; variegated form available
Viola (sweet violets)	winter and spring perennial, many cultivars available with blue, white, rose flowers in late winter and early spring; needs rich, woodsy soil
Wild strawberry	considered a weed but an excellent ground cover; 4″ tall, spreads with runners; yellow flowers, red fruit

Source: Cooperative Extension Service, United States Department of Agriculture

ness. Some, including Andorra, Bar Harbor, Blue Rug, Sargent, and Waukegan, are prostrate and will spread over a large area without growing more than eighteen inches tall (some remain under twelve inches). Many have foliage that changes color in the winter; you will want to take into account their appearance at all seasons. Others, a bit taller and more likely to be upright or arching while still spreading over large areas, include Compact Pfitzer, Blue Pfitzer, San Jose, and the Japanese garden juniper (*J. procumbens*). All prefer a moist, well-drained soil and full sun.

For the shade I like nothing better than the spreading liriopes and mondo grass. It is rugged enough to take the foot traffic of many children and has a patina of white flowers in the late summer after being mowed in June.

Mass plantings of the evergreen holly fern are very effective for heavy shade, as is pachysandra, a northern plant that is often hard to find. I have found that pachysandra does poorly in even moderate sun this far south unless it is watered regularly, but excessive moisture seems to predispose it to leafspots and crown rot.

Vines—vinca (major and minor), ajuga, and English ivy, for example—can be used as ground covers to soften harsh lines in the landscape or as barriers or dividers on trellises. They are most often used as specimens on fences or arbors, to shade, screen, or add interest. Vines may also be the answer to narrow spaces with little soil, since they can either sprawl across paving or be trained upright. Some vines do well in hanging baskets. Most have good flower, fruit, or fall color effects.

Some vines have tiny, disklike adhesive tips or aerial roots which may damage wood or house paint. Such vines—English ivy, Virginia creeper, Boston ivy, trumpet creeper, and fig vine—should not be used on brick, stone, masonry, or trellises separated from wood siding. Ivy may get so thick on wood and other materials to which it clings that the humidity and the rootlets may rot the wood. Pressure-treated wood is not as subject to rot. Vines which climb by twining or by means of tendrils are safe for use anywhere; examples are bittersweet, clematis, honeysuckle, wisteria, muscadine, Confederate jasmine, Carolina jessamine, and smilax.

The native trumpet honeysuckle (*Lonicera sempervirens*) is known for its long, trumpet-shaped flowers, which are coral red outside and yellow inside. It flowers all summer long with watering. It is not invasive like the naturalized Japanese honeysuckle, but pruning may be necessary to keep it under control. It has few pests, and hummingbirds love it. Virginia creeper has five leaflets and fine fall colors. Boston ivy, which is deciduous, has three leaflets and turns a brilliant red in fall. Fig vine may be killed to the ground by severe winters, but it usually returns. Bittersweet is noted for its heavy production of bright berries on female vines; a male must also be planted. Confederate jasmine is intensely fragrant when it blooms in the summer.

I also enjoy evergreen smilax, commonly found in the woodlands, in spite of its thorns. It does well when allowed to grow on a wire up and across the porch, especially in the shade. Many forms are available in the wild, with quite a variety of leaf sizes, including a variegated kind.

Poison ivy, never popular as a cultivated vine because of its noxious oil and the difficulty of keeping it in one spot, has white berries and beautiful fall colors that make it valuable in some distant situations (away from people, where it can be enjoyed from afar).

Moss, that ubiquitous green stuff found mostly in older, shaded lawns, is a fascinating group of plants that are lovely in their own right and are usually blamed unfairly for the lawn's demise. Mosses grow in conditions that are highly unfavorable for turfgrass: compacted soil with poor internal drainage, acidic soil needing lime, and heavy shade. To reinstate grass, you must aerate and lime the soil (thereby promoting root growth) and trim enough limbs to allow more sunlight to penetrate to the ground. More often than not, moss is the better choice for the area. It may be easiest to add a rock or two and a shade-loving ground cover or specimen plant and call the area a moss garden.

No great thing is created suddenly, any more than
a bunch of grapes or a fig. If you tell me that you
desire a fig, I answer you that there must be time.
Let it blossom, then bear fruit, then ripen.

Epictetus

4

Fruit in the Landscape

Most of us like the idea of growing fruit trees in the yard, but southerners' hopes of the promised bounty are all too often dashed by insects, diseases, poor soil, bad weather, and ignorance of the fruit plant itself. To grow a variety of fruits at home successfully, you will need to plan ahead and to benefit from the experience of others while modifying things somewhat to accommodate both your own life-style and the needs of your plants. Researchers across the South have made considerable headway in developing vigorous hybrids. The new strains preserve the best traits of the old while being stronger, more pest-resistant cultivars that bear more heavily and are better adapted to southern soils and weather.

While some fruit-producing plants may be grown in the South and will be attractive in the landscape, there is no guarantee that they will be fruitful here. Many people grow banana plants with never a banana, cherry trees with no cherries, potted lemon and avocado plants which won't hold flowers, and almonds that produce small crops after intervals of years. These plants properly belong in other climates—farther north where months of cold keep them dormant all winter, farther south in tropical paradises, or in California, where fruits of all descriptions flourish.

79

Pineapples, citrus, and other unusual types of fruit plant may be grown potted and protected indoors or in a greenhouse. Cherries, grapes, raspberries, and certain other varieties of fruit cannot be grown at all. Warm weeks in the southern winter cause some of the more cold-hardy plants to burst wide open from hot bark in January. Furthermore, southern winters lack solid freezes, which some fruit varieties require to break dormancy in the spring.

A number of fine plants are nevertheless easily grown, producing an abundance of delightful fruit that is relatively pest free and appealing to the eye. They are good choices for four-season performance as well as offering downright good eating. Blueberries, muscadines, grapes (of the right sort), some of the "tame" blackberries, figs, pomegranate, Japanese persimmon, strawberry, one raspberry, and even the elusive jujube are fruit plants that thrive in the southern landscape.

Choosing Varieties

It is most important to select varieties that will be good for your area. A good plant will die in bad soil. You can neglect to prune it. You can overfertilize, underspray, never water, or mow it down with the weed-eater. Neglect can keep a good plant from doing its best, but a bad variety can never be made to produce good fruit.

Some fruits won't grow in the Deep South. The reason is usually that we have too much or not enough cold weather but sometimes that the humidity or the stress from insects or diseases is too high. The ever-popular Bartlett pear, for example, is fine to eat but is very susceptible to fire blight, a fatal disease that is prevalent in the South. Concord grape, one of the best juice berries on earth, sets poor bunches susceptible to rot in high humidity which often fail to develop properly because of high temperatures.

Muscadines come in many combinations of color (clear, bronze, red, deep purple); size (some are as large as plums); vigor; productivity; and sugar or flavor content. Some have thick skins; some are crisply edible and make fine hull pies; some have enough free juice to be good for wine or jelly; and some are best eaten fresh. Some vines are self-pollinating; others have only female flowers and require pollen from a nearby male (a self-pollinator will pollinate others nearby if pollination is needed).

The oldest cultivated bronze muscadine, known for a couple of centuries as the scuppernong, is still available. It is female (it needs a pollinator nearby) and will produce about sixty or seventy pounds of sweet berries per vine on a twenty-foot wire. New varieties such as Carlos, however, are also bronze yet are self-pollinating (you need only one vine for production) and are sweet, with more juice and less pulp, while being easier to harvest. They produce over 100 pounds of berries in the same twenty feet that are needed for the traditional scuppernong.

Varieties suited for the Gulf coast will usually not do well 200 miles north, and vice versa. The reason is that fruit plants to bud out in the spring require a certain number of "chilling hours"—the cumulative amount of time each winter when the temperature is between freezing and 45 degrees.

If a tree needs, say, 850 chilling hours to bloom in the spring, it will bloom the first warm week that comes along after that time has elapsed (whether spring is here or not). If it gets only 525 chilling hours during the winter, it probably won't bloom at all the next spring or summer. Conversely, a variety which requires only, say, 500 chilling hours may, when grown in a 750-hour area, satisfy its needs early and bloom out on a warm day in midwinter only to be blasted by cold weather before spring. Chilling hours are very important.

Luckily most fruit plants will do all right if their needs for cold weather are at least approximately met. Plant only those varieties recommended for your area, and know the average chilling hours for your part of the state. Apples, pears, peaches, nectarines, plums, and cherries all have specific chilling requirements (cherries generally need far more than they can get in the Deep South, and so they rarely produce fruit here). Pecans, blueberries, grapes, and other fruit have low requirements, so we have few problems with this aspect of their culture. Nurseries often sell varieties for which people ask year after year, regardless of whether or not they do well in our area.

Some plants shed pollen at the wrong time, so that their own flowers cannot pick it up. Such plants must have another, different variety of the same fruit type before fruit will set. Apples, pears, pecans, blueberries, and some muscadines need pollen from other plants nearby (again, different varieties, not just another plant of the same). As a rule of thumb, peaches, nectarines (which are simply fuzzless peaches), grapes, brambles, figs, plums, strawberries, and many muscadines are self-pollinating. One of the most frustrating things about ordering plants from mail order firms (and frequently also from local retail stores) is that no one can explain with conviction which varieties need to be cross-pollinated. Ask nursery sales staff to show you the order book where it says which plants need another variety for pollination. If you need two varieties for cross-pollination, be sure the two are within eyesight of one another (no more than fifty or sixty feet apart if possible), so that bees and wind can spread the pollen from one to another.

It is also very important to consider disease resistance when you choose fruit varieties for the landscape. Apples and pears are susceptible to fire blight, and sprays are usually ineffective except as preventive measures. Blight-resistant varieties, which may nevertheless become infected in bad years, at least don't die. Grapes intended for planting in the North are not good for the South primarily because of diseases.

Dwarf or semidwarf varieties are worth considering even for home orchards with lots of room. These plants, for the most part, are the varieties of regular trees made smaller; dwarfing is achieved by grafting the desirable fruit variety onto dwarfing rootstocks to produce a general slowdown of whatever is grafted above. In other words, a Golden Delicious apple limb, grafted onto a dwarfing rootstock, will still make normal fruit on a more compact tree. In genetic dwarfing, such as that found with some peach trees, the plant naturally grows more compact, but such plants too are usually grafted onto a dwarfing rootstock to help them cope with southern soils and climate. In odd instances you may read of a fruit variety which has been grafted twice to give the specific fruit both a better rootstock (resistant to nematodes, for example) and a dwarfing interstock. Such twice-grafted trees are, understandably enough, quite expensive to produce, and they therefore cost more.

Dwarf trees, about eight feet tall, and semidwarf trees, a yard or so taller, quickly grow much taller if they are not pruned regularly. These plants require the same care as ordinary trees. The only difference is their eventual size. Pruning and other chores are every bit as important with dwarf trees as with trees of regular height.

Site Selection and Culture

To succeed with fruit in the landscape, you must first and foremost allow adequate space. Select the site, bearing in mind the entire fruit plant—mature, in or out of production. A thorny blackberry vine should not be in the way during social gatherings in the fall or winter, when it will be formidable despite the absence of leaves. Construct the muscadine arbor so that the vine may easily be pruned every winter. Will your young trees really have enough elbow room five or ten years from now? January, February, and March are the best times to set out fruit plants, especially bare-root trees, which are badly affected if they are not planted when they are still dormant. Once a tree or vine has leafed out, even if it is on sale at a nursery, you are well advised to bypass in favor of a container-grown plant. Container plants may be put in the ground at any time of year as long as you do a good job of soil preparation and are willing to water as often as necessary.

In the South, as elsewhere, most fruit vines need a fence or trellis for support. Fruit trees generally require room to grow. Most brambles must be contained to prevent them from crossing the neighbor's driveway. All demand sunshine for peak production. None will grow well in heavy clay or very sandy soils unless attention is first paid to soil preparation. All must have water, at least in the first season or two (and occasionally from then on). Some fertilizers will be needed, although a little is better than a lot.

When the cool of the evening sets in, fall or spring, hot air rises, and cool air flows downhill, settling into low areas just as water would. This cool air, early on frosty mornings, can kill tender flower or fruit buds. You should therefore avoid planting tender spring-blooming fruits (or other trees or shrubs, for that matter) in low areas of the landscape. Likewise, it's a good idea to protect them from blasts of cold arctic winds (especially figs, loquat, and kiwi).

> In gardening, one's staunchest ally is the natural lust for life each plant has, that strong current which surges through everything that grows.
>
> *Jean Hersey*

Since frosty air flows downhill, it will also form banks against evergreen hedges and buildings, just as water does against dams. Fruit trees placed just uphill from thick shrubbery or retainer walls will certainly suffer more from frost damage to tender buds than they would if they were planted where cool air could flow on past. Where hedges may cause problems, consider pruning to create gaps near the bottom so that cold air can drain from the area.

Fruit trees cannot stand wet feet and rarely survive when planted in low, wet areas or in heavy soils. They need to breathe, which they do through roots. If the soil stays moist for weeks, or if water stands in a puddle for a day or so after heavy rains, then you should either avoid planting there or build low, wide "turtle backs" to raise the crowns of trees and vines a few inches.

Soil preparation is important to most plants, and fruits are no exception. A small amount of organic peat, compost, or cheap potting soil will improve almost any soil, whether clay or sand, when it is blended in. Blueberries are exceptional in that they absolutely require the addition of generous amounts of peat moss before being planted.

When setting out fruits, never allow the roots to dry, even for a few minutes. Even a moderate wind may kill delicate feeder roots in an alarmingly short period of time. Do not put fertilizer into the planting hole, or you will risk severe root damage (wait a few weeks before fertilizing, and then do so only lightly). Prune the plant one-third or more to get it off to a strong start and to begin shaping it.

Fertilizers and lime should, of course, be used when the results of soil tests are known. Generally speaking, and apart from the specific prescription for your soil that a test will make possible, it is best to go light with fertilizers of any type, since fruit trees and vines need only tiny amounts at a time. Complete plant foods—containing nitrogen, phosphorous, potash, and micronutrients—are best, especially for fruit grown in sandy soils or containers. Excess food, even too much manure, can necessitate much pruning at year's end, reducing the amount of fruiting wood and even causing winter damage.

Blueberries are the exception among fruiting plants when it comes to fertility and liming. These shallow-rooted bushes have a different sort of root; they have no root hairs (which usually do the actual work for roots), and so they may be terribly damaged by even moderate amounts of fertilizer. They are also the only plants we grow for fruit that truly prefer acidic soil and therefore need

---

Ask Felder

How much fertilizer should I put around my grape vines each year?

Most grape vines, like other fruit trees, need only a scant handful of fertilizer to get them started, with a gradual increase every year until they reach their mature size and production. Usually this is just a pound or two (a pint is a pound of fertilizer) in the spring, and perhaps a little extra in early summer if the plants seem off-color. Too much fertilizer does not increase fruit; it increases vine or tree growth in competition with fruit and leads to more pruning chores later. And remember: never mix fertilizer into planting holes, or get it directly on trunks.

no lime. Be very careful when using commercial fertilizers, or heavy amounts of any fertilizers, around blueberry plants. In fact, no fertilizer at all is recommended the first year.

Mulches will moderate the temperatures around roots, an important benefit in southern summers. Pine straw or other organic material will allow air and water to penetrate the soil while keeping at least some of the weeds under control. It is a good idea to keep mulches away from direct contact with tree trunks, since field mice love to hide there in the winter (they gnaw bark).

Be sure to give plants a slow soaking regularly and let the soil nearly dry in between times. Trickle or drip irrigation is by far the best and most effective way to supply the moisture directly to plant roots. A system can easily be set up so that a simple timer cuts the flow on and off automatically. A soaker hose is another possibility.

Once fruit plants become established, they need only occasional waterings, especially during early spring when they are budding (if the month is dry) and again as the fruit swells. Extreme drought can, of course, damage fruit trees, as it does all other landscape plants.

Pest Control

Fruit grown in the South is often rotten or wormy; the trees may also show evidence of twig blights, stem borers, bird attack, leafspots, and root rots. There will probably come a time when your plants, in order to produce mature, edible fruit, will need to be sprayed with insecticides or fungicides to protect them from a life-threatening plague. Once insects and diseases have attacked fruit, little can be done for the crop. The word, in fruit pest control, is "prevention." You must spray plums and peaches from blossom almost until harvest to prevent insect and disease attack. Do not spray insecticides on trees where bees are active, however, or you will kill the pollinating bees. Ruined fruit may be merely disappointing, or it may be aggravating, but fruit trees and vines often die needlessly from diseases and insects. Dormant oil, applied in February when no freeze is expected for two or three days, will control overwintering scale insects. A timely application of dormant oil or insecticide, fast work with pruning shears to remove disease, and the replacement of bad varieties with pest-resistant ones will all eventually be necessary. Your nurseryman or extension agent can help you recognize and understand the signs of disease and improper care.

Pruning for Productivity

Incredible as it may seem, most fruit plants require routine pruning, either at planting time, to give them the right start, or annually, to keep them producing.

Pruning accomplishes several important things. It balances the tops of new plants with their weak roots, to help them off to a rousing start and to make them sturdy. New plants should be cut back by one-third to one-half so that, when they are set into the ground, the plants are forced to produce strong vigorous shoots which will bear the load of the tree, vine, or shrub for many years. This early pruning also promotes sturdy limbs close to the ground and shapes young trees and vines so that, as they mature, they remain manageable and small enough for easy harvest and care; it makes for a much heavier crop earlier in the life of the plant; it eliminates cluttered branches or unfruitful suckers from the plants; it encourages the formation of more fruit buds; it removes diseased, broken, or insect-damaged tissue; and it thins the fruits so that what is left is larger, more likely to be disease free, and of better quality. In all cases water sprouts must be taken off, too. They are unproductive and sap strength from the fruiting wood— and they can quickly grow thick and tall, causing the trees to be too cluttered to prune easily later. Cut them flush with the limb from which they arise, and don't be surprised at how often they seem to reappear. Failure to prune causes fruit plants to be unhealthy, unproductive, subject to pestilence and storm damage, impossible to harvest, and short-lived.

Ask Felder

The pears and apples in my yard keep sending up long, tall shoots near the trunk. Should I cut them off?

By all means remove those watersprouts! They are unproductive and sap strength from the fruiting wood—and they can quickly get thick and tall and make the trees difficult to prune later. Cut them flush with the limb from which they arise, and don't be surprised at how often they seem to reappear.

It is best to wait until late winter, just before bud break if possible, to prune trees and grapevines. Pruning at that time will remove some flower buds and potential fruit, but it is still recommended for tree fruits, which need to be thinned anyway. Pruning then is not recommended for blueberries and blackberries. These two, like raspberries, are best pruned in the early summer.

When a muscadine or other fruit tree has been left unpruned for very long, it becomes unmanageable and unfruitful. In order to bring it back under control and into production, you must sacrifice a year's crop by pruning severely to get it started again. Luckly, the root system is probably strong, so any heavy pruning will result in a very fast recovery. This type of drastic pruning should be done in the winter, when the vine is dormant and free of leaves so that you can see better what you are removing. It is best to choose two or three main trunks or limbs of the vine and remove all others, leaving only a few short stubs of smaller growth protruding from the remaining arms. The results will certainly look dramatic, since you will no doubt have cut off the vast bulk of the vine or tree. Through the spring and summer, be sure to thin any excess or unusually vigorous sprouts to keep the vine from overgrowing. Train new shoots into the framework you want, and keep the vine in that shape from then on with routine winter pruning.

Fruit trees can sometimes also be bent. A piece of wood with a nail driven into each end (clip off the heads) can be used to shift a young limb from a narrow, weak angle to a wide, fruitful one. By using such spacers to make apple and pear limbs grow parallel to

---

Why do the peaches on my tree stay so runty and hard, when those from our farmer's market are the same variety and yet are big and juicy? Do I need to fertilize more?

Ask Felder

Commercial growers know that thinning the fruit will increase the size and quality of those left. They shake, beat, and hand-pick most fruit off when it is still very small (marble size) to allow only one fruit every four or five inches on each limb. (If you aren't comfortable doing this, just imagine how commercial growers must feel, seeing thousands of little peaches and apples lying on the ground!) To get the best effect, again, thinning must be done early. Your fruit will be sometimes two or three times heavier and both bigger and sweeter if thinned early. Try it on half a tree one spring, and the results will make you wish you had done the whole tree!

the ground or nearly so, you can strengthen them and make them produce more fruit buds.

There is also a magic tip for growing giant fruit. After flowers have set and the fruit is marble sized, if you see that your trees will bear heavily, knock some of it off. Such thinning reduces numbers but will not reduce the weight of the harvest. It will increase the size, color, sugar content, and overall quality of the fruit left on the tree. Since most trees set much more than they could possibly bear to maturity, most fruit will naturally fall off during "June drop" (which can happen in May, June, July, or even August). It is also natural for trees to die from heavy loads. Years of heavy crops are often followed by barren years ("alternate bearing," as it is called in the industry). Thinning will improve the harvest left on the tree more than enough to make up for the loss.

Thinning should be heavy and early, or the benefits will be lost. Most experts recommend that about 70 percent of the apples, pears, peaches, plums, and nectarines be removed from the limbs early in the season. Thin by hand picking or by whacking limbs with a piece of rubber hose hanging a few inches off the end of a pole. Leave about a hand's width (four or five inches) between remaining fruit—more on apples and pears, less on peaches, plums, and nectarines. Early-bearing varieties usually need more thinning than others because early fruits, being generally smallish anyway, stand to benefit most from the increased size which thinning promotes.

Timing the Harvest

With fruit, it's feast or famine. Once the harvest is upon us, there is usually too much at one time to be dealt with, and lots goes to waste. Fruit should be left on the plant as long as possible, but sometimes it is more important to pick before birds do so or before bad weather or rot sets in.

Generally speaking, you should harvest at the firm ripe stage, when sugar content is high and flesh is firm but the skin yields slightly when it is gently squeezed. Most fruit will deteriorate rapidly in our heat and humidity, so be prepared to cool, can, freeze, or eat as soon as possible after harvest (blackberries and red raspberries will be gone in a matter of hours if they are not cared for; apples and pears can last for weeks with few ill effects). Some va-

Ask Felder

The pears keep rotting on my tree just as they are supposed to get ripe. What can I do to save my pears?

Pears, if left on the tree to ripen, often rot. Harvest them when still firm but give a little under pressure, then store them indoors while they finish ripening. Some fruits, especially peaches and grapes, will not continue to ripen once pulled, but pears and apples will.

rieties of muscadine have a tendency to tear when they are pulled from the vine right at the stem; these types will not store as long as those with dry stem scars (this characteristic may influence your choice of variety). While few fruits become sweeter after harvest, some continue to ripen off the plant, and others do not. Vegetables in the South are in a similar situation.

Winter Damage

Winter injury to southern fruit trees is not, in most cases, caused by cold weather alone. It results from fluctuating temperatures, especially changes which occur over a period of only a few hours. Warm, sunny days, followed by cold nights, often cause tissue to be killed. Also, as springtime nears with warming day temperatures, flower (fruit) buds swell and are often killed by the late frosts that are common in the South. Many home gardeners as well as commercial fruit growers have lost an entire year's fruit as a result of "normal" weather in the spring.

Sudden, deep winter freezes (near zero) have killed many a fruit tree and vine in the South, even those that are fully dormant and even in the best commercial orchards, yet many home gardeners are surprised to find bad weather so harmful to plants. Figs, blueberries, and brambles can regenerate from roots, but trees and vines usually sustain severe trunk damage and cannot be saved. Winter damage often appears quite suddenly in the middle of the summer, when plants brown out in only a day or two as a result of the cumulative stresses of winter damage that prevent them from supplying adequate moisture to leaves and fruit during the hot summer weather.

Another common but hard-to-diagnose winter problem confronting southerners is known as sunscald. Sunscald affects the lower trunks of trees, which are normally shaded by summer foliage, when direct sunshine keeps the south or southwest side warmer longer than the other sides of the bark. At night, freezing temperatures will kill the tender patches of bark. Painting the lower trunks of young trees with white latex paint or whitewash will help them reflect the hot sunshine until the trees age and develop tougher, thicker bark. White commercial tree wrapping material will also do the job, as will aluminum foil.

Excess fertilizer, particularly in midsummer, promotes succulent vegetative growth which not only inhibits the formation of fruit buds and increases the amount of pruning needed but also intensifies winter kill of twigs and buds. Pruning too early in the winter has been shown to cause more winter damage, particularly on fruit trees.

Landscaping Considerations

Home fruit production and landscaping goals can and should be considered together. Some exciting plants for use in home landscapes look good year round and may also produce abundant crops of delicious fruit with few pest problems. Other plants may be less suitable because of insects, diseases, or poor fruiting in this climate. With the selection of a sunny, well-drained planting site, good soil preparation, and routine watering and feeding, most fruit trees, shrubs, and vines will at least live and remain attractive in the garden design. A little more effort, mostly in choosing the best varieties of fruit for your specific part of the state and in pruning and watching for pests, will give you better yields.

Recommended Fruits

The fruit varieties suggested below are by no means the only good ones; many, many others have proven quite productive, attractive, and hardy. To learn what is available, compare the lists obtained from a local university (call your county agent) with the recommendations of leading reputable mail order fruit firms (see "Additional Resources").

Apple Lack of consistent cold weather may cause delayed blooming, poor fruit set, and lack of good red color. Two or more varieties are needed in almost every case for pollination and will increase fruit set even on "self-fruitful" varieties. The spur type is more fruitful but not necessary for good crops. Trees should be spaced twenty feet or so apart (more or less, depending upon whether they are dwarf or standard type, upon the amount of pruning done, and so forth). Train the plants into a modified up-right shape, cutting the central leader and suckers to prevent leg-giness and allowing the limbs to spread nearly parallel to the ground. Fire blight, mites, and bitter rot should be anticipated.

There are several possible reasons for a tree's failure to set fruit even when it is blooming; it may be too young, blossoms may have been damaged by late frost, or pollination may not have occurred. Most apples are not able to pollinate themselves and so will not set fruit unless pollen is available from nearby plants of a different va-riety. Bees spread pollen also, and the absence of bees may cause problems for some plants.

Apple and crabapple trees may develop rusty spots on their leaves—an infection which spreads from nearby cedar trees. This "cedar-apple rust" starts out as gelatinous growths on cedars, lasts a month, and will cause infected apples and crabapples to drop leaves. Heavy infections can be prevented in subsequent years with fungicide sprays.

A plant is like a self-willed man, out of whom we can obtain all which we desire, if we will only treat him his own way.
Johann Wolfgang Von Goethe

Better varieties: Golden Delicious (an excellent pollinator for other varieties), Mollies Delicious, Stayman Winesap, Granny Smith, Yates, Lodi. For low-chilling areas only: Einshiemer, Sara, Anna.

Blackberry   Bushes that give incredibly large berries on very productive upright canes need no trellis but must be contained to prevent the spread of underground rhizomes. Prune once a year after the harvest (in June or early July) to remove old canes, and tip prune new ones for a heavier harvest the next year. Set in rows, allowing three feet between plants and eight feet between rows. Good garden soil is not necessary. The fungus disease known as double blossom is a major problem.

Blackberries fruit each year on canes grown the preceding summer. After fruiting, remove all canes that had berries (they will only become brambles if they are allowed to remain), and cut the remaining new ones back to knee height to promote growth dur-ing the rest of the summer. Blackberries don't need mulches but will benefit from water after pruning.

Better varieties: Avoid thornless varieties (they need to be trellised and are not as productive for most people). Good choices include Brazos (tart), Cheyenne, Comanche, and Rosborough.

Blueberry   Blueberries are very showy, upright shrubs with gorgeous fall colors, interesting bark in winter, attractive flowers in spring, and heavy fruit in early summer. Space them six feet apart in rows or on eight-foot centers. A blueberry will grow to ten feet or more if it is not pruned as a shrub in midsummer (do not prune after early July, or some flower bud formation will be lost in early fall). Tip prune suckers when they become knee or waist high in spring to encourage branching for next year's fruiting. Blueberries absolutely require the addition of plenty of peat moss with native soil (a fifty-fifty ratio is best), a heavy mulch of pine straw, regular watering during summer, and no lime or fertilizer (provide tiny amounts of azalea-camellia food after the first year, but the use of generic garden fertilizers may cost you some plants). Blueberries are very good in the sunny landscape. Bird netting anchored with clothespins will help curb the worst pest.

   Better varieties: Two or more are needed for the best fruit set. Tifblue (by far the best), Woodard (spreading habit; not as upright as others); Delite.

Crabapple   Small to medium trees with spreading growth habit, crabapples are noted for texture and for their transitional value in the landscape. They produce very showy spring flowers and tart, edible fruit that is suitable for jellies. Their culture is the same as for apples and pears except that less pruning is required (and then only after spring blossoms have faded). Crabapples flower best in sun but tolerate light shade.

   Better fruiting varieties: These are generally self-fruitful. Callaway (none better); Dolgo.

Fig   Figs, grown for thousands of years, are large, suckering shrubs that are susceptible to winter damage in southern areas unless they are protected. The shallow roots require water, mulch, and very light fertilizers. The fruit ripens from July to early September. Premature drop is a problem in hot, dry summers. Figs have few major pests other than birds. The sap is irritating to some people during harvest. Light pruning is helpful in late winter to remove suckers and to improve the low-growing shape.

   Figs should be mulched heavily with leaves or pine straw to prevent winter injury. Plants with winter damage will usually send up sprouts the following summer, and these will become new fig trees or shrubs. It is a good idea to remove all the old, dead wood, thin out the suckers to a manageable handful, and tip prune those at knee height so that they bush out for the rest of the summer and are stronger in years to come. Some varieties, especially Brown Turkey, may make a small crop the first summer after freeze damage. If they do not, just protect the new sprouts with a mulch, water them, and hope for better luck next year.

Better varieties: Celeste (somewhat more cold tolerant), Brown Turkey; Alma.

Grape   Grapes are not generally recommended because of their high susceptibility to diseases of the fruit, leaves, and roots. They are excellent for landscape effect but no more so than muscadine. Most grapevines, like other fruit trees, need only a scant handful of fertilizer to get them started (never mix fertilizer into planting holes or allow it to touch trunks). Increase fertilizer gradually every year until the vines reach maturity and full production. Usually you will then need just a pound or two of fertilizer (a pint is a pound) in the spring and perhaps a little extra in early summer if the plants seem off color. Too much fertilizer does not increase fruit; it increases vine or tree growth in competition with fruit and adds to the chore of pruning later. Grapes require a trellis or arbor and growing space of fifteen to twenty-five feet. They are often infected with black rot, which causes fruit to develop spots and quickly to shrivel into raisinlike mummies.

Better varieties: Blue Lake, Miss Blue, Lake Emerald, Mid South, Miss Blanc, Fredonia (the best substitute for Concord), Champanel (great for arbors). Not recommended: Concord, Niagara, Thompson Seedless (not well adapted to our climate for good fruit production, but try it if you think you have good luck).

Kiwi   Kiwi vines need a trellis or other support. Male and female plants are separate (one unfruitful male services several females) and take several years to become heavily fruitful. The kiwi needs protection from sudden early frosts and hard freezes (below 10 degrees Fahrenheit); cover the vines with plastic, and mulch the bases with straw. Home-grown seedlings are of indeterminate sex and are rarely very productive; use grafted, named varieties for best results. Pick fruit before frost and store it wrapped in plastic in the refrigerator. Let fruits ripen at room temperature as needed.

Better varieties: A nonfruiting male will be essential. Hayward.

Loquat   The loquat, a very attractive, small evergreen tree, grows to twelve feet or more and has large, coarse leaves that are useful in landscapes. It is susceptible to freeze damage in severe winters or in northern areas of the Deep South. A relative of the apple and the pear, the loquat may suffer from blight in some years. It requires little pruning, pest control, watering, or fertilizer. The thumb-sized fruits, borne in clusters, don't always survive late frosts. They are good for jelly and may also be eaten fresh, although some people find the seeds objectionable.

Better varieties: Early Red, Champagne, Oliver, Advance.

Muscadine   Muscadine is the best grape for the South. There are now many varieties from which to choose. The plant needs an arbor or a twenty-foot fence for the vigorous, heavy-fruiting vine. Muscadine has good fall colors and few major pests. It requires heavy annual pruning for best production and growth. The self-fertilizing varieties will pollinate nearby females. The juice varieties are best for wine and jelly as well as juice because of their heavy yield, short harvest time, high sugar content, and proportionately larger quantity of juice per berry than "fresh-eating" types.

Muscadines do bleed quite a bit after being pruned, especially on warm days and when they are pruned late in the winter. This bleeding has not been shown to hurt them at all, but it may be wise to water the plants during unusually dry springs after they have been pruned. You can prune from late December until after the new growth comes out somewhat in the spring. I prefer to use pruning as an outdoor exercise on warm afternoons in January or February just to get myself out of the house.

Better varieties: L = light color; D = dark; J = juice. Self-fertile: Carlos (L, J); Dearing (L); Magnolia (L, J); Doreen (L, J); Noble (D, J); Cowart (D); Chief (D); Southland (D); Magoon (D); Bountiful (D). Female (needs one of the above to help set fruit): Hunt (D, J); Scuppernong (L); Thomas (D); Higgins (L); Creek (D); Fry (L); Jumbo (D); Hunt (D); Topsail (L).

Peach   Small peach trees have many problems when they are grown in heavy or poorly drained soils. They may be grown as little as twenty feet apart with close pruning (even dwarf fruit trees will grow tall and straight, like pines, if they are not shaped and trained with regular pruning). The generally self-pollinating fruit ripens in May, June, and July and must be sprayed for brown rot in humid weather. Prune to an open vase shape early in the tree's life, and maintain the shape by regular heavy pruning. Trunk borers are a serious problem, but gumming on the trunk may also be caused by root diseases from heavy rains or prolonged drought. Nectarines are peaches without the fuzz; little dependable varietal information is available on nectarines.

Better varieties: It is very important to choose on the basis of average local chilling hours. A lower number of hours means earlier blooming; "early" means that buds and crop will be killed by frost. A high number means later blooming (too high for your area means no blooms at all). Clingstone is best for canning; Freestone is better for eating fresh and slicing.

Pear Most southern-grown pears are oriental types (most others are not adapted to our climate or are not resistant to southern diseases). Summer and fall fruit grows on upright trees which need twenty-five feet (even the semidwarf) of space in which to spread out under heavy fruit load. Pear trees are pruned upright like apples. It is very important to spread young limbs parallel to the ground for training. Some fruits have grit cells and are best used for canning and preserves. Fruit should be picked before ripening and stored indoors so that it ripens without rot. Trees do well in poor soil; rich soils cause excess shoot growth. Plants may be very badly damaged by bacterial disease spread by bees from wild pears and by rain splash; sprays are usually ineffective unless they are used as a preventive measure. Choose blight-resistant varieties. Some are self-fertile, but cross-pollination increases fruit set. The chilling factor must also be considered when plants are ordered by mail from remote nurseries.

When pear branches turn brown on the tips and the half-grown fruit shrivels, your pear is infected with "fire blight." Pears that become infected by fire blight may die from it if they do not receive treatment. Even blight-resistant varieties may be infected in some years, although they usually throw off the disease, suffering only minor twig dieback. Since the disease is bacterial, there are no effective cures, only prevention. You must do as good a job as you can in pruning out the infected twigs, cutting them at least a couple of inches or more below the blighted areas to get all the disease out. Dip clippers in household bleach and water (half and half is fine) to disinfect between cuts, or the bacteria may be spread even more. No amount of spraying will cure an infected tree.

Beginning the next spring, during the bloom period, you can

I'm still devoted to the garden . . . although an old man, I am but a young gardener.
Thomas Jefferson

use the streptomycin sprays commonly sold for fire blight control. These sprays do not kill the bacteria; rather they leave protective films on flowers, new twigs, and leaves during the early spring, when the bacteria are spread by bees and splashing rains. Streptomycin does not hurt bees (which are mostly responsible for the disease spread), and it is important to put two or three sprays on the trees, beginning when they blossom.

Better varieties: All are blight resistant. Orient (not self-fertile but good for fresh fruit); Kieffer (not self-fertile; a hard pear that is good for canning); Moonglow (excellent pollinator for others; good for eating and canning; not good for areas with less than 700 chilling hours); Garber; Starking Delicious (good pollinator); Ayers. Bartlett should not be planted because of its exceptional susceptibility to fire blight.

Pecan and Walnut   Pecans and walnuts are large trees needing plenty of sunshine and room to develop. They mature in several years and produce nuts in the fall. They are usually not suitable for use as shade trees near patios, houses, or garages because they are heavily infested with insects (aphids and mites) which drip sticky excrement onto everything below. Pecans are wind pollinated and require more than one variety for cross-pollination (use an early pollen variety with an early nutlet variety). Heavy rains at pollen shed (April) may prevent pollination and may cause crop failure. The fungus disease called scab is serious on many varieties and is very difficult to control (use resistant varieties). If knots or galls are a problem in June, use a protective spray the following April.

Pecans will fall from the tree in November and should be picked up as soon as possible and air dried indoors on paper to reduce internal moisture-related fungus. Leaving them in the rain, or storing them wet, often makes the meat rancid or faulty. Bag shelled pecans and put them in the freezer for long-term storage. They will keep for several weeks or two to three months in the refrigerator.

Better varieties: All are resistant, but not immune, to disease. Pecan: Elliot, Cape Fear, Owens, Cheyenne, Candy, Davis. Avoid the high-disease varieties Stuart, Success, Mahan, and Schlev. Black walnut: Thomas (grafted trees yield in five years or more).

Persimmon   Oriental and Japanese persimmons are superb specimen trees that grow to twenty feet or so and produce a heavy crop of fist-sized attractive red or orange fruit in October. The fruit is delicious but slightly astringent if it is eaten before it is fully ripe. Fruits will ripen off the tree and can be refrigerated overnight to reduce the bitterness. Some varieties are seedless or nearly so. Trees will drop fruit when exposed to heat, drought, or flooding, and so mulches and water must be supplied.

Better varieties: Tane-nashi (orange); Tamopan (very large and orange, with an interesting acorn shape); Fuyugaki (red and not astringent even when green); Eureka (red and a heavy producer); Hachiya (orange-red and a very attractive tree).

Plum Wild varieties are often good and adaptable to local conditions. Japanese varieties may freeze in severe winters; most may suffer late frost damage to blossoms. The plum is a small tree for the landscape. It often looks and fruits well by itself (the Japanese varieties produce much better with cross-pollination than alone). Allow eighteen feet or more of space per plant, and prune upon planting to encourage an open shape (much as you would peaches). Remove suckers, and lightly prune late each winter to prevent the tree from fruiting only every other year and from weakening. Blackknot bacterial disease may be severe. There is no way of controlling it apart from pruning out infected limbs or removing trees (all varieties found in the nursery trade are susceptible). Chilling is an important factor to consider in choosing among the cultivated varieties.

Better varieties: Methley (self-fertile; best pollinator for others; red with purple skin); Bruce (excellent for jelly); Santa Rose is too susceptible to black knot to be worth trying; Ozark Premier (large fruit that is light in color; needs 800 chilling hours); Morris (bright red, best for upper South).

Pomegranate The pomegranate is a many-seeded fruit produced on medium-sized suckering shrubs that grow as tall as ten feet. The large red flowers are very attractive. The fruit is susceptible to the same diseases as peaches (mostly brown rot); the plant should be pruned for better air circulation. During pruning, remove mummified infected fruits. Spray plants as you would peaches. The pomegranate requires a long hot summer for fruit development.

Better variety: Wonderful.

Raspberry The only raspberry recommended for the South is Dormanred, which was developed at Mississippi State University. Prune it as you would blackberries. It will set fruit after mild winters and will survive hot summers. The fruit is red, and the vines must be tied onto a wire trellis. Try other varieties, but be surprised if they perform for more than a couple of years.

Strawberry   Strawberries are best treated as two-year crops in garden rows, since disease and pests build up quickly in old-fashioned strawberry beds. Dig and replant in the fall.

Water is essential to strawberries during fruiting. A slow soaking every week is preferable to frequent light sprinklings. Netting material helps control bird pests. Water plants and curb weeds in June in order to have healthy plants to move in the fall. Some gardeners prefer to thin out old plants in June, leaving six-inch spaces for new plants to fill during the summer and fall. A light fertilization will help strawberries after they finish bearing. Strawberries are hardy and do not need mulch in the winter.

Better varieties: Florida 90, Cardinal, Tioga.

Other Possibilities   Many trees, shrubs, and vines for the landscape have edible fruit, and it would be impossible to list them all, much less to do them justice. The few described below have outstanding potential in southern landscapes. I omit such tender subtropicals as kumquat, satsuma oranges, and avocado, since they generally need some protection from frost and are therefore best treated with seasonal effect in containers. The plants I include below may generally be depended upon to fruit in most years.

The banana provides a decidedly tropical effect, with extra-large leaves arising from a herbaceous suckering base. It needs a protected place in order to develop clusters of exotic purple flowers, followed by small, extra-sweet fruit. It has few pests but requires water in summer and a heavy mulch after the frost has killed foliage.

The quince, related to apples and pears, is a small, upright tree (very similar in appearance to crape myrtle) with colorful patchy bark and aromatic, pear-shaped fruit that ripens in late summer. The fruit is not edible fresh but makes wonderful preserves.

The rugosa rose, a densely spined, deciduous, suckering shrub that grows up to five feet tall (with a habit of spreading which should be contained) has somewhat showy flowers all summer, followed by very colorful, large orange-and-red fruits that are treated like edible rose hips.

Pawpaw trees, which may grow up to twenty-five feet tall, are natives with large, oval leaves that turn yellow in fall. Their two-inch maroon flowers appear in very early spring and are followed by oblong fuzzy brown fruits with a bananalike aroma and a creamy texture when they ripen in the late summer. They are self-fertile.

The Chinese jujube, an attractive, upright tree with interesting bark and glossy leaves, is hard to find in nurseries but is certainly most satisfactory in the landscape. It has smallish, oblong fruits which ripen in August, when the skin begins to develop dark spots. The fruit has a single seed inside like a giant olive and flesh that tastes like a combination of pear and apple. This very unusual but hardy tree grows about thirty-five feet tall.

With a garden there is hope.
Grace Firth

Mayhaw trees, also native to the South, are small, slightly thorny trees with showy white flowers an inch or so wide that bloom just before and during leaf break in early spring. Mayhaws (for which the Pilgrims' *Mayflower* was named) are members of the haw-thorn family and are one of the few fruit trees which prefer to grow in a low, seasonally wet area. They will tolerate some shade. Mayhaw fruits ripening in May or early June greatly resemble large crabapples and make one of the finest jellies to be had.

Elderberries are somewhat weedy yet showy medium-sized shrubs noted for their coarse compound leaves and large, flat cymes of white flowers from May to July, followed by equally flat heads of attractive purple berries which make excellent jelly and wine. Elderberries are easily propagated from roadside divisions but must not be confused with the poisonous berries of poke-weed, which hang in long, loose racemes.

Mulberry trees, often thirty feet tall or more, include fruiting species as well as ornamentals. The white mulberry, planted in co-lonial times during efforts to establish a silk industry, has become fairly widespread (it seems weedy to some folks) and produces great quantities of staining purple fruits in midsummer that are en-joyed mostly by birds and children.

Chinese chestnuts are tasty nuts enclosed in extremely spiny husks. Trees are small with decorative white, taillike flowers in June or so. Two or more varieties are best for cross-pollination.

Sumacs, including several species, turn brilliant, fiery colors in the fall and produce spear-shaped spikes of reddish berries (ex-cept for the poison sumac, which has white berries); when ripe, the acidic berries may be rubbed and soaked in cold water to produce a tangy syrup, which may be strained, sweetened, and used as a refreshing, lemonadelike drink. It is delicious mixed with other mild juices such as cranberry. A very attractive plant in the landscape, this thicket-forming tree is either male or female (hence the seed spikes on some plants but not on others).

Trifoliate orange, a very thorny deciduous shrub of medium size, has cloverlike leaves of three leaflets each. It has commonly been used as the rootstock of satsuma and other citrus plants and is often the only surviving part of the graft after heavy freezes. It is very hardy but not very showy except that it has numerous white flowers in spring and decorative orange fruit in the fall. The oranges are up to three inches in diameter and are distinctly sour though not poisonous. Spider mites are a problem.

Purple-leaf plum makes a strong showing all summer, with deep purple foliage on a somewhat rounded, small tree. Its pale pink flowers (single or double) often precede edible red fruits in midsummer.

Filberts, or hazelnuts, are deciduous plants that form dense thickets and, under favorable pollination conditions, in late summer produce curious leafy sheaths enveloping edible nuts. The filbert is not a very attractive plant for the landscape except when it is used as a border or low screen.

The prickly-pear cactus (Indian fig, or *Opuntia*) is our only native cactus. It comes in several varieties that have round flat, often dinner-plate-sized leaves covered with small clusters of very troublesome spines. Spreading three-foot-high clumps of leaves form the bodies of these evergreen plants. To start a plant you need only insert a leaf partway into the ground. Prickly pears do best in a well-drained soil that is not kept moist. Several imported species have hardier leaves or showier flowers that may be red, orange, or yellow in spring. Fruits two or three inches long appear in summer and are covered with extremely small spines. They should be handled with care (wear gloves). The fruit has tasty red pulp with many small seeds and may be roasted or eaten raw (somewhat messy but interesting).

One to rot and one to grow,
One for the pigeon, one for the crow.

Traditional

Vegetables Year Round 5

There are times in the southern summer when the humidity and heat are insufferable, and there are warm days in the winter when the mercury suddenly plunges and the wind grows bitter and biting. In spring, bone-dry gardens become rolling rivers and quagmires under four-inch downpours. Weeds, insects and other creatures, and diseases often reign supreme, regardless of the time of year. On the other hand, there are nearly twelve months of gardening weather, each with many days well suited for working the soil and planting seeds, roots, or transplants. There is nice weather for harvesting crops just about year round.

We southerners can produce an incredible variety of edibles in backyard gardens, from mirliton and sweet potatoes, which need a long, hot growing season, to staples such as beans, corn, tomatoes, and peppers. By planning ahead and understanding our fickle weather, we can truly plant and harvest something almost every week of the year.

Without being grueling or even moderately difficult, outdoor gardening can provide physical exercise, increased contact with other people, and a source of relaxation and enjoyment.

It is amazing how few southerners take advantage of our un-

101

usually versatile growing season. The soil is prepared, rowed up, planted, and weeded once or perhaps twice before being abandoned to the elements and pests. As a result, a great potential harvest that could be had with a minimum of effort is lost. A little planning ahead can certainly keep a garden not only productive but also attractive and reasonably easy to maintain.

We actually have four gardening seasons in our area: winter, late spring, summer, and early fall. By selecting those vegetables and herbs and flowers that do best in cool or cold weather for planting in the winter and fall, we can take advantage of some of the best outdoor weather on earth for working outdoors. Onions, garlic, and other vegetables can be successfully grown in the winter with few problems. Where plants can be protected, the list becomes even more impressive. Then again, such long-season vegetables as tomatoes, squash, southern peas, and peppers can be grown through the summer and into the fall.

In addition, we can quite easily replant more crops in rows or beds from which we recently harvested vegetables. At Callaway Gardens in Georgia one day in June, I watched while people dug up some potatoes and carrots to make a point on the television program "Victory Garden." As soon as the cameras had left, the fellow who tended the demonstration garden turned the fresh soil, added a bit of compost (an important step every time you plant), and immediately planted leeks and some pumpkin seeds. Not two hours had passed, in other words, before the row was once again on its way toward production. Such replanting greatly increases the productivity of your garden, but to do it you must arrange to have seeds on hand when you need them.

Here is how the system can work. You may of course substitute or add vegetables as your tastes dictate. In January and February, set out onion transplants, Irish potato seed pieces, and seeds of English peas, turnips, carrots, lettuce, and other greens (some may need a plastic cover or mulch if the weather is severe). In March and April, transplants of broccoli and cabbage may be set out, along with seeds for corn and beans if the soil has warmed enough. When sowing, make sure the soil stays evenly moist, and sow several times to ensure a longer harvest. By May, the early vegetables—turnips, peas, and potatoes—will become mature, and their space in the garden will be useful for tomatoes, peppers, egg-

plant, and squash. Plant tomatoes in rich soils full of organic matter and a touch of lime, water thoroughly every week (not necessarily more often), mulch the soil surface to conserve moisture and moderate soil temperature, stake the plants to keep the fruit off the ground, and spray regularly to curb diseases (spray as needed to eliminate insects).

In June, the garden will be in full swing, with minimum insect and disease pressure. Weeds will still be small and easy to pull or hoe, and mulches can be laid down to cool the soil, to conserve moisture for the coming summer, and to discourage weed seeds from germinating. You should, at this point, have okra (if you like it), southern peas, squash, sweet potatoes, cucumbers, melons, and a few flowering periwinkles and salvia and marigolds for color.

After the garden is up and growing, additional nitrogen fertilizer is usually called for. Nitrogen alone is needed, so avoid using all-purpose or balanced fertilizers. Calcium or ammonium nitrate, or nitrate of soda, are most widely available; cottonseed meal (slow as it is to show effects) will also do. Apply very small amounts alongside the garden rows (a pound per 100-foot row is the maximum) or a few inches from the bases of plants (one teaspoon per plant, no more). A little is good, but more may be harmful or may cause extra greenery to be produced at the expense of fruit. Most vegetables need a sidedressing or two, especially corn, beans, squash, tomatoes, leafy greens, and peppers. Avoid sidedressing sweet potatoes, southern peas, and peanuts.

July and August, despite the extreme heat, are the two months which begin the fall gardening season. At this time some of our very best harvests of the year are made possible. We often set out transplants or seeds too late for autumn harvest only to watch them die from freezing weather. But we can avoid that obvious pitfall. By knowing the date of the average first killing frost for your area, you can count back the number of days a vegetable needs to mature and plant accordingly. Jack-o'-lantern pumpkin seeds which may take 100 days to grow and produce pumpkins should be planted—and cared for—a little over 100 days before Halloween. The same philosophy also applies to fall broccoli, peas, tomatoes, and other vegetables with predictable maturation dates. The figure for days to maturity that appears on seed packets is only a general guideline and is subject to variation because of our climate, but it

My good hoe as it bites the ground revenges my wrongs, and I have less lust to bite my enemies. In smoothing the rough hillocks, I soothe my temper.

Ralph Waldo Emerson

Table 8. **Light Requirements of Common Plants**

Requires Bright Sunlight

beans	eggplant	potato
broccoli	okra	pumpkin
cantaloupe	onion	squash
cauliflower	peas	tomatoes
cucumbers	peppers	watermelons

Tolerates Partial Shade

beets	kale	radish
brussels sprouts	lettuce	spinach
cabbage	mustard	sweet potatoes
carrots	parsley	turnips
collards		

Source: Cooperative Extension Service, United States Department of Agriculture.

will help you compare different varieties and time successive harvests. Tables 8 and 9 indicate some of the conditions needed to grow different crops.

Tomatoes and peppers set out in late July or early August will have just enough time to make decent crops by frost, but keep in mind that vegetables planted in August will need watering and weeding, and insects may become troublesome. Chile peppers, which require warm soil and plenty of mulch and water for best production, may be frozen or dried for storage as edible ornaments and for later use.

Ever wonder what variety of corn makes those perfectly formed tiny ears you see in salad bars and on Chinese dishes? There isn't a special kind. Just harvest the little ears on regular corn as soon as the silks start to show, before pollination. The cobs will be only about three inches long and completely edible, raw or briefly cooked. Good varieties, then, are those that bear more than one ear to a stalk.

Conserve moisture for seed germination by covering the seedbeds with mulch, compost, or boards until the seedlings emerge (table 10 indicates the approximate number of days to emergence). Mulch will also help prevent the soil from crusting. September transplants of broccoli and cabbage will have time to mature before frost in late October or early November; in fact, fall-harvested vegetables often turn out to be better than those pulled in the heat of early summer. When crisp nights arrive in the fall, such cool-season vegetables as turnips, mustard, and collards develop a sweet flavor they lacked before. The bitterness of summer-grown greens is lost as well. Plan your planting in the late summer or fall so that harvest dates come between the first average frost and the predicted killing freeze for your area. While light frost has little effect on tender greens other than enhancing flavor, and even freezing weather will not kill spinach, kale, or collards, prolonged hard freezes will often slow or stop their growth. Plan to replant if necessary, since most of these can make another stand during the warm spells we usually get in January and February.

October and November are excellent months for making compost piles. Compost piles are more than stacks of leaves; they are living, breathing organisms full of life in many forms. In order to produce the desired end result, you must start with some soil, add a pile of organic debris, and cultivate the mixture. Ideally, layers of organic matter should alternate with layers of topsoil. A layer of sticks separating the heap from the ground will let air filter in from below.

The various ingredients decompose at temperatures near 150 degrees, producing rich, dark humus. Nature does the job slowly, but we can speed things up by understanding the process. Bacteria, worms, fungi, and a myriad other tiny creatures in the soil eat the leaves, clippings, eggshells, coffee grounds, and other fruit or vegetable detritus that you supply (see table 11). Do not add meat. The worms and microorganisms deposit nitrogen-rich droppings and provide pathways by which water, oxygen, and nutrients can

---

I add manure and compost to my garden every couple of years or so. How long does it last, anyway?

Ask Felder

Dirt continually disappears in the south. You should add organic material (peat, compost, leaves, etc.) to your garden every time you plant, as a constant renewal of that which is lost to bacteria and fungi in our warm, moist soils.

To further renew and enrich the soil, winter cover crops may be grown—planted in October and turned under in March or April. Give the soil time to warm in the spring, well after the air temperature entices you to garden; few benefits come from planting summer crops too early. When sowing seeds, make sure the soil is kept evenly moist and sow several times to ensure a longer harvest.

Table 9. **Vegetable Crop Information**

CROP	TYPE OF PLANTING	DAYS TO FIRST HARVEST	PLANTS OR SEED PER 100' ROW	DAYS TO GER- MINATE
Asparagus	perennial (crowns)	2nd season	75	—
Asparagus	seed (transplant)	4th season	2 oz.	10–20
Rhubarb	perennial (crowns)	2nd season	30	—
Beans, snap	seeded	50–60	½ pound	5–8
Beans, lima	seeded	65–75	½ pound	5–8
Beets	seeded	55–65	1 oz.	7–10
Broccoli	seed or transplant	60–80*	½ oz. or 75	(6–8)
Brussels sprouts	seed or transplant	85–95*	½ oz. or 100	(6–8)
Cabbage	seed or transplant	65–80*	½ oz. or 75	(6–8)
Chinese cabbage	seeded	80–90	¼ oz.	5–7
Cantaloupe	seed or plants	80–90	½ oz.	7–12
Carrots	seeded	70–80	1 oz.	10–12
Cauliflower	seed or transplant	95–140*	½ oz. or 75	(6–8)
Cucumbers	seed or plants	60–65	½ oz.	5–8
Eggplant	transplants	75–90*	50 plants	(8–12)
Garlic	sets	140–160	3 lbs.	—
Horseradish	roots	Fall	75–100 roots	—
Kale	seeded	60–90	1 oz.	6–9
Kohlrabi	seed or transplants	60–75	¼ oz.	(6–8)
Lettuce (seed)	seeded	45–50	½ oz.	6–8
Lettuce (plants)	transplants	35–45	100–200 plants	(6–8)
Head lettuce	seed or transplants	60–85*	½ oz. or 75	6–8
Onions (sets)	sets	100–120	2 qts.	—
Onion (plants)	transplants	100–120*	300 plants	—
Okra	seeded	50–60	1 oz.	6–12
Parsnip	seeded	Fall	½ oz.	10–12
Peas	seeded	60–80	1 lb.	7–10
Peppers	transplants	65–80*	50 plants	(10–14)
Potatoes	tuber pieces	70–90	10 lbs.	—
Pumpkin	seeded	110–130	1 oz.	7–10
Radish	seeded	25–30	1 oz.	4–6
Rutabaga	seeded	90–120	½ oz.	5–10
Salsify	seeded	140–150	1 oz.	8–12
Spinach	seeded	40–45	2 oz.	9–12
Squash, summer	seeded	50–55	1 oz.	7–10
Squash, winter	seeded	50–55	1 oz.	7–10
Sweet corn	seeded	80–100	¼ lb.	6–8
Sweet potatoes	plants	130–140	75–100 plants	—
Swiss chard	seeded	50–60	1 oz.	9–12
Tomato	transplants	70–85	30–60 plants	(7–10)
Tomato	direct seeded	80–95	¼ oz.	7–10
Turnips	seeded	45–65	1 oz.	5–10
Watermelon	seeded	80–90	1 oz.	8–12

Note: Numbers in parentheses represent seeding information for hotbeds; allow six to eight weeks in hotbeds.
*From date of transplanting.

Source: Cooperative Extension Service, United States Department of Agriculture.

OPTIMUM TEMPERATURE (°F)	DEPTH OF PLANTING (IN.)	AVG. SPACING IN THE ROW (IN.)	AVG. SPACING BETWEEN ROWS (IN.)	FROST RESISTANCE
—	8	18	48	hardy
65–75	1	3	6	hardy
—	1	36	36–48	hardy
70–85	2	3–4	36	tender
75–85	2	4–8	36	tender
50–60	½	2–4	18	half hardy
(50–60)	(½)	18–24	36	hardy
(50–60)	(½)	12–18	36	hardy
(50–60)	(½)	12–18	36	hardy
55–70	½	10–12	36	hardy
75–85	1–1½	48–72	48–72	very tender
55–70	½	2–3	18	half hardy
(55–70)	(½)	18–24	36	half hardy
75–85	½–1	10–48	48–72	very tender
(75–85)	—	18–24	36	very tender
—	1	4–6	18–36	hardy
—	3–4	12–18	36	hardy
50–60	½	2–4	36	hardy
(50–60)	(½)	5–6	18–24	hardy
50–70	¼	2–4	18–24	half hardy
(50–70)	(¼)	2–4	18–24	half hardy
60–70	¼	12–15	18–24	half hardy
—	1½–2	3–4	12–24	hardy
—	1½–2	3–4	12–24	hardy
75–85	½	18–24	36	tender
55–70	¼–½	3–4	18–24	half hardy
50–65	2	1–2	12–24	hardy
(75–85)	(½)	18–24	36	tender
50–60	4–5	8–12	36	half hardy
75–85	1	72–90	72–90	half tender
50–60	½	2–3	12–18	hardy
50–60	½	4–6	18–24	hardy
55–70	½	2–3	12–18	half hardy
55–70	1	2–3	12–18	half hardy
75–85	1	36–48	48–72	very tender
75–85	1	60–72	96	very tender
70–80	2	14–18	36	tender
—	—	12–16	36–48	very tender
55–70	½–1	6–8	18–24	half tender
(75–85)	(½)	24–48	36–48	tender
75–85	½	24–48	36–42	tender
60–70	½	3–4	12–18	hardy
80–90	1–2	72–90	72–90	very tender

Table 10. **Days from Planting to Emergence under Good Growing Conditions**

CROP	DAYS	CROP	DAYS
Beans	5–10	Onion	7–10
Beets	7–10	Peas	6–10
Broccoli	5–10	Parsley	15–21
Cabbage	5–10	Pepper	9–14
Carrots	12–18	Radish	3–6
Cauliflower	5–10	Spinach	10–12
Corn	5–8	Squash	4–6
Cucumber	6–10	Tomato	6–12
Eggplant	6–10	Turnip	4–8
Lettuce	6–8	Watermelon	6–8
Okra	7–10		

Source: Cooperative Extension Service, United States Department of Agriculture.

Table 11. **Composition of Compost Materials**

MATERIAL	NITROGEN (%)	PHOSPHORUS (%)	POTASH (%)
Banana skins[a]	—	3.25	41.76
Cantaloupe rinds[a]	—	9.77	12.21
Cattail reeds	2.00	0.81	3.43
Coffee grounds	2.08	0.32	0.28
Corncob ash	—	—	50.00
Corn stalks, leaves	0.30	0.13	0.33
Crabgrass (green)	0.66	0.19	0.71
Eggs (rotten)	2.25	0.40	0.15
Feathers	15.30	—	—
Grapefruit skins[a]	—	3.58	30.60
Oak leaves	0.80	0.35	0.15
Orange culls	0.20	0.13	0.21
Pine needles	0.46	0.12	0.03
Ragweed	0.76	0.26	—
Tea grounds	4.15	0.62	0.40
Wood ashes	—	1.00	4.00–10.00

[a] Ash (dry-weight basis).

Source: Cooperative Extension Service, United States Department of Agriculture.

permeate the pile. The faster the bacteria eat, the faster the compost forms. To move quickly, they need nitrogen.

If you add nitrogen fertilizer, cottonseed meal, or grass clippings to the pile, you will be making the most important ingredient available. Add a little lime or wood ash so that the heap does not become too acidic, stir in some water, and toss and turn the pile to aerate it. A compost heap may be started in a structure as simple as a ring of chicken wire held upright by wooden stakes, or it can be square or rectangular, with three permanent walls of brick or stone and removable wooden planks on one side to provide access. If you have two adjoining bins, you can turn the compost by simply shifting it from one to the other.

October and November are also good months for digging fall potatoes and for planting garlic cloves and cover crops of vetch or clover. Pansies can be set at the ends of rows.

December brings seed catalogs, holiday gift lists, and the beginning of yet another gardening year. Plan ahead for these various seasons, ordering seeds and plants, and having tools and soil prepared ahead of time. Take the tiller and any other power equipment to be tuned up, and have blades and tines sharpened. Before summer comes you will also want to check your hoses and irrigation setups for leaks.

Unless the garden is really big, most home gardeners should hire someone once a year to till it rather than investing in a rototiller. A power tiller is an expensive machine, and it is actually possible to overcultivate the soil with one. A more useful tool for the practical-minded gardener is a flat-bladed file with a wooden handle. This one gadget can take the work right out of hoeing and digging by keeping garden implements razor sharp. A sturdy shovel (or a flat-bladed spade, which I prefer), a hoe, a garden rake, and a hand trowel are the best equipment. Raised-bed gardeners will find a turning fork invaluable. A good garden sprayer for insecticides and fungicides (and a separate one for herbicides) is not a large investment and will help you control pests much better than the dusts that used to be shaken over plants.

In garden tools, you get what you pay for. Those of high quality last longer, are easier to use, and actually feel better in the hand. Look for stainless steel blades or tines and white ash or hickory handles for strength and flexibility as well as comfort and shock resistance. Tools made from a single piece are usually more durable than those made from welded parts. Proper care is also important in prolonging the life and usefulness of garden tools. Clean and oil blades to prevent rust. Linseed oil will protect wooden handles.

Site Selection and Soil Preparation

Water—or the lack of it near the garden—used to be a terrible problem in the South. Nowadays, however, irrigation systems and equipment available are often much less expensive to install and run than the older methods of flooding rows or dragging hoses. Trickle, or drip, irrigation has been immensely simplified with the introduction of long-lasting tubes that won't crack in the sun or during freezing weather and are easy to use. Soaker hoses, too, are proving their worth, especially in wide rows and raised beds. Overhead sprinklers, while easy to set up and move about as needed, do more than just water the garden. They also wet vegetable leaves, promoting the development of diseases, and they unnecessarily and wastefully water weeds and furrows. Flooding the furrows between rows is far more beneficial to plant roots, although it is somewhat messy and cumbersome.

The need for irrigation notwithstanding, it is true that sunshine is most important for success with vegetables (although leafy vegetables and root crops will produce with much less solar energy than do fruit and seeds). In deciduous shade, where winter sun can be found, many otherwise outshaded gardens may succeed. Many a summer shade garden for flowers has borne fine onions and broccoli and peas before the trees leaf out in the spring. Most vegetables to be productive need a minimum of six hours of direct sunshine.

While it is difficult to grow onions from seed here in the South because of fluctuating temperatures in the winter, nothing is more frustrating than to have onions bolt (flower) without making bulbs. Winter-planted slips or bulbs (the smaller the better) stand the best chance, but a trick is involved. As the days grow longer, bulbs begin to swell. For them to grow large, you must allow them to grow nearly on top of the ground, perhaps even pushing the soil away from them. Be careful not to damage the very shallow roots, however. A constant supply of moisture will help the onions stay mild and sweet. Mulches will protect them from sunscald if the weather is hot.

The successful garden has sun, water, and, ideally, a sandy-clay-loam soil that is well drained and on a nearly level site. It's also wise to situate the garden so that it does not compete with trees and shrubs for moisture, nutrients, and sunshine.

Soil preparation for southern gardens is nothing new, but the familiar techniques can easily be improved upon. The idea of sowing seeds onto open, flat ground is fine in some situations and for a few crops, but raised rows can help the garden drain somewhat better during rainy spells, warm up a little earlier in the spring, stay warm longer in the fall, and remain easier to work year round. Wide rows three or four feet across combine the benefits of both flat ground and raised beds. They take better advantage of space and resources, and they enable you to interplant different crops and to grow plants closer together so that they shade weeds and make the most out of fertilizer and water.

Old hands at gardening have long known that fertilizers help make plants grow and produce better. Chemical fertilizers (granular and liquid), organic composts, manures, and several other sources of plant nutrients have been used and abused for years. People argue their pros and cons interminably. While chemical fertilizers are unquestionably fast acting and strong, organic materials such as manure, cottonseed meal, and composts are slow to become useful to plants and are often low in actual fertilizer value. To use any type of fertilizer wisely, you must understand how it works. The amount of fertilizers needed depends on the needs of the vegetable and the type of soil. Too much fertilizer may overload heavy clay soils or burn roots of plants in poor sandy soils. Some plants, especially peas and peanuts and sweet potatoes, make their own nitrogen with the aid of bacteria in the soil—and too much supplemental feeding will cause tremendous plant growth and poor fruit or root growth.

There is no simple recipe for fertility. By using small amounts of fertilizer at a time and reapplying them as the seasons progress or as vegetables show a need for more, you can avoid many problems. Chemical fertilizers are easily overdone, and subtle bad effects accumulate over a long time. Apply these fertilizers sparingly, and refer to the fertilizer recommendation chart.

One easy way to tell how much fertilizer your garden may need is to have a sample of your soil tested by your Cooperative Extension Service agent. Only a small fee is involved, and the results are accurate. Using a spade or trowel, cut a slice of soil six

One of the healthiest ways to gamble is with a spade and a package of garden seeds.
Dan Bennett

Table 12. **Limestone Needed to Change the Soil pH (pounds per thousand square feet)**

Desired Change in pH	Limestone Required		
	Loam	Silt Loam	Clay Loam
5.0–6.5	115	140	160
5.5–6.5	85	100	115
6.0–6.5	45	55	60

Note: Vegetables differ in their ability to grow in acid soils.

Source: Cooperative Extension Service, United States Department of Agriculture.

inches deep from one part of your garden. Avoid areas where manure or fertilizer has spilled. Place a one-inch section of the slice in a pail, and repeat the procedure for other parts of your yard. Mix the soil thoroughly, then remove about a pint of it, allow it to dry, and place it in a container for testing.

Limestone should not be treated as a fertilizer. It does contain calcium, which is important to vegetables, but it is used mainly to sweeten acid soils. Soils of the Southeast are acidic, generally speaking, because of heavy rainfall (so-called acid rain is something entirely different, however). Acidic soils are bad for plant roots, earthworms, beneficial bacteria, and fertilizers. Lime dissolves slowly and neutralizes acidic soil. It is best not to add it more often than is indicated by a soil test made every three or four years. Table 12 indicates the quantity of lime needed to change the pH of various types of soil.

Weeds in the Garden

Organic mulches can be effective weed killers if they are available inexpensively from a nearby source. Otherwise weeds must be curbed by the ancient tactic of cultivation—pulling, hoeing, and tilling. Some herbicides work wonders, and I know one gardener who uses a dozen Chinese geese to eat the grass in his garlic, basil, and muscadines.

Mulches will go a long way toward shading weed seeds and preventing them from sprouting. The organic materials commonly used include straw, peanut hulls, chopped cornstalks, ground corncobs, grass clippings, leaf mold, compost, newspapers, sawdust, and bark. Synthetic materials can be plastic (polyethylene), wax-coated paper, aluminum foil, and combinations of kraft paper and polyethylene.

Heavy mulches can smother many weeds, but most are effective only when used over a newly prepared or weed-free soil. Mulches perform several other important functions: conserving moisture in the summer, adding fertility and tilth to the soil when they are turned under the following season, keeping the soil cool during hot summers (crucial for plant growth in the Deep South), and improving the garden's appearance.

> What is a weed? A plant whose virtues have not yet been discovered.
>
> *Ralph Waldo Emerson*

The relatively new plastic mulches, especially the black types that prevent light from penetrating, will certainly keep down weeds. In our part of the country, however, plastic causes as many problems as it solves. It doesn't decay, so there is the chore of pulling it up after it tatters in the sun and wind. It is a nonrenewable resource and is therefore not very economical in the long run. Most important, however, plastic mulches will help the soil warm up early in the spring. This feature may be less important in our area than in Florida or south Texas, where the growing season is longer, and may also be more helpful to commercial growers, who appreciate an extra couple of weeks of growing season. But the fact remains that plastic mulches rapidly make the soil too hot for summer vegetable roots, even in the late spring. The only way to combat this problem is to use straw or some other mulch to cover the plastic and shade it from the May and June sun. This measure is neither practical nor particularly effective in most cases.

Shredded paper makes a fine mulch, keeping down weeds and soil temperatures. In addition, it seems to deflect insects, possibly because of its brightness. Unfortunately, after a few good waterings it reaches a pastelike consistency and then becomes hard as plywood. Folded newspapers several sheets thick, like plastic mulches, will perform well as long as slits are made to allow both water and air to penetrate to the vegetable roots. It is generally recommended that only black-and-white paper be used in the garden; the heavy metals found in colored inks should be kept away from growing vegetables. Both plastic and paper mulches should be removed before the soil is reworked.

Chemical weed killers (herbicides) have been used by farmers for several decades now, with good results. Some of them have been proclaimed safe for home garden use. Any of them, to be effective and safe, must be used exactly according to directions on the label. Some new herbicides, beginning with one called glyphosate, are very effective at killing actively growing weeds, particularly hard-to-kill perennials such as nut grass and Bermudagrass. These materials have no residual effect on the soil, making them safe, and they kill weeds completely, roots, nuts, stems, and all. Unfortunately, they must be applied to the foliage of actively growing weeds. If the herbicides accidentally contact the leaves of your garden plants, then these may be stunted or killed, too. For this reason the labels clearly state that you should not use these materials around vegetables.

I dodge the problem by using glyphosate (sold under various brand names) on weeds before I plant my vegetables. When I had a nut grass problem, for example, I prepared my garden beds, let the nut grass emerge, treated the growing leaves with glyphosate, waited a few days to see the results, and then planted my garden.

There are many gadgets on the market for cutting, pulling, and burying weeds. Some are quite effective. Push-pull devices, soil knives, rooters, even the old jupiter wheel hoe—all have their uses. Gardeners with large areas planted in conventional three-foot rows often use power tillers to rip up and bury weeds, but this time- and labor-saving technique often turns up more weed seeds, spreads diseases, and damages delicate vegetable roots.

Sometimes, when I have the time, I water the garden and flower beds and wait an hour or so for the soil and weed roots to soften. Then I hand pull weeds and lay them upside down for the sun to kill. When I have a lot of weeds, I may use an old-fashioned hoe, to which I first apply a flat-bladed file, making the corners and edge knife sharp. I am perfectly aware that most gardeners (and certainly I myself) would rather not be seen doing anything as primitive as hoeing the garden, but while a dull hoe can be a dreary, clumsy tool, a sharp hoe is a lightweight precision instrument.

Seeds or Transplants?

Should you buy transplants, grow your own from seeds, or just wait until the right time and gamble on sowing seeds directly in the ground? The answer depends upon several factors. Some vegetables do not transplant readily (see table 13), and their seeds are best sown directly in the ground. You should also consider whether your local stores carry good varieties for the South—and for your

Table 13. **Vegetables Grouped by Ease of Transplanting**

Easily Transplanted

beets	cauliflower	onion
broccoli	chard	tomatoes
cabbage	lettuce	

Requires Care to Transplant

carrots	eggplant	pepper
celery	okra	spinach

Very Difficult Unless Containers Are Used

beans	cucumber	turnip
cantaloupe	peas	watermelon
corn	squash	

Source: Cooperative Extension Service, United States Department of Agriculture.

particular area—and appear to take care of the plants they stock. Can you depend on the weather and on your abilities to care for seedlings when direct seeding? If you decide to grow your own transplants, will you really give them the light, humidity, and temperature they require for success, or will you end up with leggy, weak plants—a waste of time and money?

I usually buy transplants of common vegetables just to be sure of success, but then I demand that they be strong, stocky, and true to variety. (I have no qualms about going back when I feel I didn't get what I paid for.) Then again, I also check seed racks every season for new varieties which I may want to try.

It is, however, a tremendous pleasure to order from seed catalogs. The vast majority of people who do so are quite satisfied with their purchases. They find the variety greater than that at local stores. Furthermore, the quality is usually good, and stock is reasonably priced. The planting instructions accompanying each order are usually complete. Vegetable seeds top the list of popular items ordered, followed by flower seeds, bulbs, fruit trees and roses, and a wide assortment of tools, ornamental plants, water plants, and even beneficial insects.

Vegetable Varieties

Home-grown vegetables taste better than store-bought ones not just because of the place where they are grown but also because commercially produced vegetables have been bred to withstand long truck rides and still look good on grocery shelves for days on end. How long would the more tender, succulent home varieties hold up under such conditions? Different varieties have been bred for different purposes, and it therefore makes sense to choose the ones that will do what you want them to do under your own growing conditions.

Not all varieties of each vegetable do well in the South. We have some pretty rough garden diseases, and not all varieties of vegetable are resistant to them. Vegetables also need to have heat tolerance. Common varieties of tomatoes, for example, often shed flowers when the temperature soars quickly. Certain varieties have been developed to tolerate even our weather (table 14). The Vates collard, to take one case, will overwinter much better than the older, more popular Georgia collard. By the same token, some varieties of broccoli will produce nice heads more quickly than others. Relative speed is important for spring-planted broccoli and for cauliflower, cabbage, onions, potatoes, English peas, and others, because hot weather ruins them. By planting early-maturing types, you can beat the heat, harvest a top-quality crop, and clear the space for summertime vegetables or flowers. With fall vegetables, the same philosophy holds true—late tomatoes or peppers should be ready to harvest before frost.

The tomato, the South's favorite vegetable, is susceptible to many sorts of problems. If it is planted too early, it may fail to develop an adequate root system, although aboveground growth may appear to be normal for a time. Excess fertilizer can cause blossom drop, as can very windy weather with low humidity; unduly cool weather can make fruit misshapen. Too much shade and excess rain make plants spindly and often promote disease. Leaves curl during hot weather, especially if the plants are pruned heavily.

By selecting VFN hybrid tomatoes you will stand a better chance of avoiding damage from wilt diseases and nematodes, which feed on plant roots, often cause root knots and galls, and prevent plants from getting the moisture and nutrients they need. Fungicide sprays are helpful in controlling foliar diseases and blights. When drought is followed by heavy rain or watering, tomatoes may become cracked or may burst. Blossom end rot, a common ailment, is caused by a lack of calcium in the developing fruit. To prevent it you should add lime (or gypsum if the soil is not acidic) every two or three years. Make sure the plants stay neither too wet nor too dry; either condition can keep roots from absorbing calcium for the fruit.

Table 14. **Recommended Varieties of Popular Vegetables**

Asparagus. Mary Washington.

Bean, snap. Bush: Astro, Highlander, Gator Green, Contender, Slender-white. *Pole:* Kentucky Wonder 191, Blue Lake, Dade.

Bean, lima. Bush: Thorogreen, Thaxter, Henderson Bush, Dixie Butterpea, Nemagreen,[a] Jackson Wonder. *Pole:* Carolina, Florida Speckle, Willow Leaf.

Beet. Detroit Dark Red, Burpee Red Ball, Ruby Queen.[b]

Broccoli. Green Comet,[b] Green Duke, Premium Crop.[b]

Brussels sprouts. Jade Cross.[b]

Cabbage. Early Round Dutch, Red Acre, Red Head,[b] Stonehead,[b] Market Prize, Gourmet, Rio Verde. *Chinese:* Michihli types.

Carrot. Red Core Chantenay, Imperator,[b] Spartan Bonus, Danvers 126.

Cauliflower. Snow Crown,[b] Snow King,[b] White Contessa.

Chard, swiss. Fordhook, Lucullus, Rhubarb.

Collard. Vates, Georgia LS.

Corn, sweet. Funk's Sweet G-90 Merit, Golden Security, Seneca Chief, Silver Queen, Southern Delicious.

Cucumber. Pickling: Carolina, Green Spear, Triple Mech. Liberty. *Slicing:* Ashley, Slice Master, Gemini, Victory,[b] Burpless.

Eggplant. Black Beauty, Florida Market, Dusky.

Kale. Dwarf Siberian, Vates.

Kohlrabi. White Vienna, Grand Duke,[b] Purple Vienna.

Lettuce. Head: Great Lakes.[b] *Leaf:* Grand Rapids, Salad Bowl,[b] Slobolt, Buttercrunch,[b] Black Seeded Simpson.

Muskmelon. Edisto 47, Hales Best No. 36, Ball 1776.

Mustard. Florida Broadleaf, Southern Giant Curled, Tendergreen, Greenwave.

Okra. Clemson Spineless,[b] Emerald, Perkins Spineless.

Onion. Crystal Wax, New Mexico White Grano, Granex.

Parsley. Moss Curled.

Peas. English: Little Marvel, Laxton, Green Arrow, Wando,[a] Creole. *Sugar:* Sugar Snap.[b] *Southern:* Mississippi Silver,[a] Mississippi Purple,[b] Magnolia Blackeye,[a] Mississippi Cream,[a] Pinkeye Purplehull.

Peanut. Florigiant, Florunner, Starr, Comet.

Pepper. Sweet: Bell Boy,[b] Emerald Giant, Keystone Resistant Giant, Yolo Wonder L, Sweet Banana.[b] *Hot:* Long Cayenne, Hungarian Wax, Jalapeno.

Potato. Irish: Red LaSoda, La Chipper, Superior, Norchip. *Sweet:* Centennial, Jewel,[b] Unit 1 Porto Rico, Travis.

Pumpkin. Jack-O-Lantern, Connecticut Field, Spirit,[b] Triple Treat, Cushaw.

Radish. Cherry Belle,[b] Scarlet Globe, White Icicle.

Rutabaga. American Purple Top.

Soybean. Vegetable: Kanrich.

(continued)

Table 14. (continued)

Spinach. Spring: Long Standing Bloomsdale, Melody.[b] *Fall:* Hybrid No. 7, Dixie Market, Chesapeake Hybrid. *Summer:* New Zealand.

Squash. Summer: Early Yellow Summer Crookneck, Early Prolific Straightneck,[b] Goldbar, Patty Pan (scallop), Aristocrat (zucchini).[b] *Winter:* Table Queen (acorn), Waltham Butternut,[b] Early Butternut Hybrid,[b] Sweet Mama.[b]

Tomato. Marion, Floradel, Better Boy,[a] Traveler 76 (pink), Big Seven,[a] Bonus, Spring Giant,[b] Walter, Small Fry.[a,b]

Turnip. Purple Top White Globe, Just Right,[b] Tokyo Cross.[b] *Greens:* Shogoin, Crawford, Seven Top.

Watermelon. Charleston Gray, Jubilee, Crimson Sweet, Sweet Favorite.[b]

[a] Root knot nematode resistant.

[b] All-America Selection.

Source: Cooperative Extension Service, United States Department of Agriculture.

Ask Felder

How can I keep the birds from pecking my tomatoes?

You may want to scream sometimes, but even that won't deter birds in the tomato patch for long. Placing stockings over unripe tomatoes will still allow them to develop. The best way to prevent bird damage, however, is to pull the fruit before it is red. Tomatoes will continue to ripen after being harvested, but you must get them when they first turn pink,—or the birds will beat you to them!

What is eating just the flowers off my tomatoes?

Tomatoes, beans, peppers, and other vegetables will drop their blooms when the temperature soars quickly, or when warm nights are followed by daytime 90s. Too much nitrogen fertilizer also causes poor flower set, as does windy weather with low humidity, extended periods of overcast or cool weather, and insects or diseases. Flowers not staying on the plants? Pick a reason!

When yellow or zucchini squash have lots of flowers but no fruit, a sexual problem may be involved. Likewise, if finger-sized fruit forms but rots before growing, you may need to offer help. Each plant has both male and female flowers, but they are on separate stalks. Sometimes early in the season there may be only male or only female flowers. This situation is usually temporary, however, and often results from overfertilization, overcrowding, or odd weather.

The male flowers form on the ends of simple stalks and have yellow pollen on the anther within. Female flowers, which are the same color and size as the male, form on the ends of what appear to be small fruits (but are actually unfertile). Unless both flower types are present and open at the same time, no fruit will develop. And even if both are present, pollen must be transferred from the male stamen to the sticky pistil within the female flower—a job normally done by bees. If both types of squash flowers are present and open but no bees are on hand, try hand pollination. Simply break off a male flower, stem and all, and pull the yellow petals off to reveal the pollen-covered anther. Use it like a paintbrush to dab a few grains of pollen onto the pistil inside an open female flower. You should have crisp, beautiful squash within three or four days.

You can reduce damage from nematodes by rotating suscep-tible vegetables with nematode-resistant varieties, using lots of or-ganic material in the soil and keeping your garden supplied (but not oversupplied) with fertilizer as well as water. Sheets of plastic spread over infested areas and left to steam in the sun for a few weeks will greatly reduce the nematodes there, at least temporar-ily—and enough to get in a good crop or two before retreatment. Constant tilling will dry the soil in the summer and fall to the point where nematodes cannot survive in great numbers.

Another factor to consider in choosing varieties is production. Some broccoli varieties make fine heads and then peter out, while others, upon having their tops cut off, make a second crop of side shoots which may be even more bountiful than the original. The latter thus give a much better yield for the space than you would get from replanting another vegetable. Likewise, some turnips are grown for their tops, some for their roots, and some for both—and there are specific varieties for each use, some being distinctly better than others. Seed catalogs have a wealth of information about varieties. Another way of finding dependable varieties of vegetables is to ask what the old-timers are planting. If you do so, however, bear in mind that many new varieties have been devel-oped which are essentially the same as the old ones but are more resistant to diseases or easier to harvest.

Once I have found out which varieties of, say, peppers are locally popular, I read up on them. Do they make lots of peppers

Hot weather seems to make my hot peppers too hot. Can I keep this from happening?

There is a lot of difference in the heat of chile peppers. The difference is in the variety, though, and not in the weather. The long, thin cayenne is red-hot and colorful, but hotter yet is the small serrano, only about two inches long and a bit thinner than the medium-heat jalapeno. The mildest chile pepper, the variety found in canned "green" chiles, is a long, tapered big pepper known as Anaheim; they are best for adding to corn, squash, or beans, or stuffed with cheese, battered, and fried as chiles rellenos (I use a hand-held propane torch to char the skin for peeling, and to add a delightful smokey flavor to the meal).

Chile peppers require warm soil and plenty of mulch and water for best production, and may be frozen or dried for storing as edible ornaments and later use.

per plant? Are they big and thick walled? Does the flavor withstand freezing? Will they do well in our summer heat and persist into the fall? Is the plant sturdy, or will it need staking? After all, there are dozens of varieties of sweet peppers from which to choose, so why simply settle for what happens to be most readily available? All the while, I consider other, newer varieties, and only then do I make an informed decision about what to plant. Stick with what you like and try new varieties on a limited scale. If you proceed in this way, you can have a dependable garden and still experiment in the quest for something different.

New varieties are constantly being promoted in seed catalogs and by bedding plant growers. Of the dozen or so worth trying each year, consider the All-America Selections. AAS winners are the cream of the crop, so to speak—varieties which have had extensive trials and are deemed the best. Disease resistance, heavy yields, sturdy plants, unusual color, shape, or use, and other factors are considered when AAS varieties are chosen. Some of the memorable older AAS varieties include Clemson Spineless okra and Ruby Queen beet.

While not all varieties each year are AAS, many are well worth trying on a limited scale. Most are available through seed catalogs. Try them under fair conditions, in good soil, and with the care you would ordinarily give your best vegetables. The new ones may taste better than your old ones. Then, too, the new varieties may mature earlier or may have fewer problems with pests and with the weather.

Planting and Interplanting

Many gardeners set their summer plants and seeds out too early, when the soil is still cold and wet, and their gardens rot or are nipped by late frosts. Without artificial protection, and sometimes even with it, summer vegetables will be stunted and slowed down for the entire season. It is better to wait until the soil itself warms than to try to give your plants a head start just because the daytime air temperature feels good. By the same token, cool-season plants such as lettuce, brussels sprouts, and carrots are often planted late and languish in the heat, going to seed or developing a bitter taste.

By staying within the well-established planting dates (neither too early nor too late), you will have your best chance of enjoying good harvests. Remember that we in the middle South have nearly all year to grow vegetables, so there is no real reason to rush plants into the ground.

Buy the freshest bedding plants available while they are young and actively growing rather than those which have been picked over and neglected at retail stores for several days. When selecting plants, try to choose sturdy ones and not just big ones. Stocky green plants with plenty of roots in relation to their size will nearly always produce more quickly and abundantly than the leggy yellow ones right beside them.

Set out bedding plants late in the day in well-prepared soils and with plenty of water to help them weather the shock of transplant. If the weather is hot or the wind stiff, or if the plants have come from a shaded greenhouse, jam a small board or piece of card-board on the windward or sunniest side for a few days. Cover the seeds in hot weather with moist potting soil. Then lay a board or other shade material over the soil to keep it from crusting and dry-ing. When seedlings first appear, remove the shade immediately so that they can get all the sun they need for a strong start.

Thinning seedlings is both a chore and an emotional trial for most folks. When you plant seeds in the row or broadcast over the soil, make every effort to use the recommended amount. Plants really do not perform well when they are crowded; in fact, some

Ask Felder

Why are my turnip greens so bitter?

When crisp nights arrive in the fall, such cool-season vegetables as turnips, mustard, and collards develop a sweet flavor not found until then; the bitterness of summer-grown greens is lost. Plan your planting in the late summer or fall so that harvest dates fall between the first average frost and the predicted killing freeze for your area. While light frost has little effect on tender greens, other than enhancing flavor, and even freezing weather will not kill spinach, kale, or collards, prolonged hard freezes will often slow or stop their growth. Plan to replant if necessary, since most of these can make another stand during the warm spells we usually get in January and February.

Why do my turnips never make roots?

Over and over, proof is seen that diseases and lack of production are the major results of over-crowded vegetables and flowers. Thinning to the suggested spacing may be hard to do, yet it is critical to the health and performance of your plants.

vegetables actually create a substance in their roots which slows the growth of nearby plants.

Crowded stands of vegetables do not usually produce, so give each individual plant, whether it is a bean, carrot, or turnip, its own space in which to grow (tomatoes, okra, squash, and other large plants need not only individual amounts of sunshine and water but also room to reach full size and still have good air circulation). Overcrowding can also increase plants' susceptibility to disease. Thinning to the recommended spacing may be hard to do, but it is critical to the health and performance of your plants. Beet and lettuce seedlings are delicious in salads, by the way.

It is possible to interplant vegetables, although there is evidence that some inhibit the growth of others. There is a dearth of research showing which plants make the best companions, so read what you can and experiment with the rest. In general, long-season plants should be grouped together for ease of maintenance, and tall plants should not be situated where smaller ones will be shaded. Also consider pest control. Some plants will need to be sprayed from time to time, and you may not want the spray material to contaminate others nearby. Some small, fast-maturing vegetables such as radishes and leafy greens may be interplanted with slower types such as carrots or broccoli and pulled early, before they are shaded or start to compete with the longer-term ones.

Harvest and Storage

Some vegetables mature more quickly or slowly as the weather gets hotter or cooler. Some also have long seasons for harvest, and different varieties of each type may have a longer or shorter number of days to maturity. Vegetables picked at the right time are at their peak of nutrition and quality. Pick them too early or too late, and they may store poorly (or not at all), may be too tough or tender, or may have off flavors.

There is no general rule of thumb concerning when to harvest all vegetables. Many vegetables are prepared differently at various stages of development (tomatoes, for example, are often fried green in the South, long before they are mature—and by harvesting them green you can keep the birds from getting them). Generally speaking, however, harvest when the vegetable is mature, not before, and avoid leaving ripe fruit on the plants, where it may decrease future yields. Try not to damage plants when harvesting; that way potential diseases are less likely to enter the plant. Use a knife for tough stems, and don't let freshly harvested vegetables remain in the heat of the sun, since they will rapidly deteriorate.

By harvesting at the best stage of maturity and cooling the vegetables as soon as possible, you can reduce spoilage considerably, at least for a while. Some vegetables can be stored for many weeks; others are all but impossible to keep for more than a few days. Some vegetables grown in the South are entirely different from those grown out West or in the North and are not as easily stored. Onions, sweet potatoes, and Irish potatoes are difficult to keep without a curing process to prepare them for storage. Leafy greens should be placed in plastic bags before they are refrigerated to prevent them from rapidly losing moisture.

The best rule of thumb, after harvesting fresh vegetables, is to cool the produce as soon as possible to slow down moisture loss and to discourage spoilage until the vegetables are frozen, canned, or dried.

No two gardens are the same. No two days are the same in one garden.

Hugh Johnson

Insects

The most important thing to know about insect control is the importance of identifying the pest responsible for the damage. The many beneficial insects keep at least some problems in check, and so an all-out air strike on the garden with chemical pesticides often does as much harm as good. If you know the culprit, it will be possible to target the attack so that nearby plants and creatures emerge as nearly as possible unscathed.

Sometimes the best control is hand picking the pests, using physical barriers to protect the plants, or rotating crops around the yard or garden to avoid a buildup. These cultural techniques, together with the elimination of weeds and debris which harbor insects and snails, will go a long way toward reducing the problem. In some extreme cases, for example when borers or spider mites attack repeatedly, it may be best to plant another vegetable entirely. Also, by planting within recommended dates, you may avoid many late-season pests, such as corn earworms and fall stinkbugs. Biological and natural controls include predatory insects (ladybugs and so forth) and other bug eaters, such as toads, anoles, skinks, brown worm snakes, and chickens. There are also a number of natural insecticides, including the famous *Bacillus thuringiensis,* or BT, which kills only the larvae of moths and butterflies. BT, available as a spray or dust, has no effect whatever on the health of people, beneficial insects, birds, or plants and is devastating to cabbage loopers, tomato hornworms, and other caterpillars.

Natural materials are not necessarily safe in all cases, however. Nicotine sulfate has long been used to control aphids and other sucking insects. It is a natural product—a derivative of tobacco—but it is also deadly to people. Chemical insect control has come a long way in the past decade or two. Long-term residual poisons are no longer available for home garden use. Instead we now have materials which are designed to break down quickly in the environment and which, if used according to directions and with proper precautions, are no threat to our own health. Insecticides, like herbicides and fungicides, really do lose strength within a few months of being opened. Discard old bottles regardless of how strong they may smell. Buy only as much as you can use this season and early in the next.

There are basically two types of harmful insects, each charac-terized by its own method of damaging plants. Chewing insects (worms, crickets, and beetles) actually eat holes in leaves, roots, stems, and fruit and can be controlled with several types of dusts and sprays. Sucking insects, such as aphids and stinkbugs, on the other hand, must be killed with sprays designed especially for them. What may be effective against one type of feeding insect may not even slow others down. Often you must wait after spray-ing insecticides onto vegetables before you harvest the vegetables, sometimes a couple of weeks or more.

To kill fire ants, for example, I use inexpensive liquid insec-ticides mixed exactly according to directions, and pour enough of the mixture onto each mound, one at a time, to fill the mound completely. I usually need a gallon or so per mound. I do this as if I were pouring syrup over pancakes, without kicking the mound or punching holes in it, late in the afternoon when all the ants are at home. By morning all of the ants are dead.

Disease Prevention

In addition to the diseases caused by pests, we southerners must contend with weather-related problems, such as cracking of fruit, drowned roots, sunscald, wind-whipped leaves, and high humidity. Table 15 describes some common forms of trouble. The very best gardeners know that little can be done about many natural calami-ties. Still, we can do our best to prepare a well-drained soil, use correct amounts of fertilizers and lime, plant at the right season (and space plants properly), avoid heavy watering late in the day, buy top-quality or fungicide-treated seeds, choose disease-resistant varieties whenever possible, and keep disease-spreading insects under control. These practices will greatly reduce the amount of damage that our plants suffer.

Fungicides certainly keep diseases from destroying crops if they are selected according to the specific disease and are used religiously. It is important to know that, while insecticides kill bugs, fungicides do not kill diseases but rather control them. The materials work like protective films on healthy parts of plants and fruit to keep them healthy. It is necessary to begin using fungicides at the very first sign of disease and to continue the treatment on a

Table 15. Common Garden Problems

SYMPTOMS	POSSIBLE CAUSES	CORRECTIVE MEASURES
Plants stunted in growth; sickly, yellow color	lack of soil fertility or soil pH abnormal	use fertilizer and correct pH according to soil test. Use 2 to 3 pounds of complete fertilizer per 100 square feet in absence of soil test
	Plants growing in compacted, poorly drained soil	modify soil with organic matter or coarse sand
	insect or disease damage	use a regular spray or dust program
	iron deficiency	apply iron to soil or foliage
Plants stunted in growth; sickly, purplish color	low temperature	plant at proper time. Don't use light-colored mulch too early in the season
	low available phosphate	apply sufficient phosphate at planting
Holes in leaves; leaves yellowish and drooping, or distorted in shape	damage by insects	use recommended insecticides at regular intervals
Plant leaves with spots; dead, dried areas; or powdery or rusty areas	plant disease	use resistant varieties, remove diseased plants when they are noticed and use a regular spray program
Plants wilt even though sufficient water is present	soluble salts too high or root system damage	have soil tested by county extension agent; use soil insecticides, fungicides and resistant varieties
	poor drainage and aeration	use organic matter or sand in soil
	insect or nematode damages	use recommended varieties and soil insecticides or nematicides
Plants tall, spindly, and unproductive	excessive shade	relocate to sunny area; keep down weeds
	excessive nitrogen	reduce applications of nitrogen
Blossom drop (tomatoes)	hot dry periods	use mulch and water; plant heat tolerant varieties
	minor element deficiencies	use fertilizer containing zinc, iron and manganese
Failure to set fruit (vine crops)	poor pollination	avoid spraying when bees are present
Leathery, dry brown blemish on the blossom end of tomatoes, peppers, and watermelons	blossom end rot	maintain a uniform soil moisture supply; avoid overwatering and excessive nitrogen

Source: Cooperative Extension Service, United States Department of Agriculture.

regular basis (more often during rainy or muggy weather than during dry spells) so that the diseases cannot spread. As with insecticides, often you must wait before you harvest the vegetables.

Fungicides, again like insecticides, work well when a little dish detergent is added to spread the mixture out and to help it adhere better. Fungicides wash off during rains and wear off with time, so it is important to reapply them regularly, or results will be spotty. It is frustrating to know that, since the main benefit of using fungicides is the prevention of diseases, there will be few, if any, visible signs that they are working.

Organic Gardening

Gardeners interested in using only natural materials to fertilize and to control diseases and insects must pay special attention to soil preparation. Organic materials work slowly and should be added at least three weeks before planting. Be sure that organic matter is thoroughly blended with the soil. Undecomposed lumps make it harder to seed evenly and promote nutrient deficiency and problems such as damping-off of seedlings.

Animal manures, because of their low phosphorous content, should be supplemented with rock phosphate or bone meal. Manure used as a sidedressing should be scattered along each row. Other organic substances that provide plants with nutrients include greensand, rock potash, gypsum, cottonseed meal, seaweed, and wood ashes. Substances that will decrease soil acidity include oyster shells, wood ashes, and dolomitic limestone.

It's easier to control insects organically on a small scale than on a large scale, but various garden practices combined will make the job easier. Plant resistant varieties, take seed only from disease-free plants, and avoid transplants with pests. Place cardboard collars around plant stems at ground level to deter cutworms. Till the garden early to give the vegetation time to rot before you plant. Mulch your crops. Clean up crop refuse promptly. Plant as early in the season as possible. Eliminate weeds (they harbor insects and diseases) as well as diseased plants. Pick off larger insects, use natural products such as BT to control moths and hornworms, and encourage natural insect predators. Soap and water, or a dilute mixture of onion, garlic, and marigold, may be sprayed on plants to control some insects; a few droplets of mineral oil applied to corn silk may deter earworms. Repel aphids with aluminum foil mulch. Catch slugs with boards and burlap or by means of beer traps. Water in the morning, and don't touch the plants when they are wet. Don't smoke in the garden. Rotate crops, and mix plants in the row to keep diseases from spreading rapidly. Also try companion planting.

Raised Beds

Since ancient times, people have grown vegetables, flowers, herbs, and fruit in raised beds and containers. The Chinese have known for many hundreds of years that, when soil is fortified and pulled into high beds, gardens warm more quickly in the spring and remain well drained during rainy seasons. Moravian settlers at Winston-Salem, North Carolina, used intensively planted beds to get greatest yield from small spots beside their neat houses and businesses. Today urban homeowners and apartment dwellers are experimenting with variations on this old garden practice, and the trend is even swinging toward larger, permanent containers as attractive additions to the landscape. The popular television series "Victory Garden" has publicized raised beds and wide rows and uses them almost exclusively.

Raised-bed gardens solve such perplexing problems as poor soil, little time for garden maintenance, and lack of garden space. These beds have many advantages over regular garden rows. Since they are usually small and easy to reach from most angles, they can be tended by handicapped gardeners, especially if they are elevated (or if the pathways are sunken). They offer good looks with low maintenance, requiring little time to plant, weed, water, and neaten up. They can be added to patios or decks or built right on top of any type of problem soil, even over old driveways. They can be designed to blend harmoniously with any architecture or landscape. Raised beds drain well, so they can be planted without a fuss, regardless of the weather—a special boon to southern gardeners.

Roses, herbs, peonies, and specimen trees, all of which need perfect drainage during our torrential rains, may be showcased within the confines of oversized planter boxes, which are in essence raised beds. The extra touch of refined building material can attractively interrupt the monotony of level landscapes.

Since weeding, watering, and planting are relatively easy, raised beds are much easier than regular garden beds to manage when they are full of flowering annuals or vegetables. Depending on the amount of sun or shade available, plants set into raised-bed gardens can offer a wide range of choices for height, color, and texture in the landscape. In fact, seed companies nationwide are racing to develop more attractive and productive flowers and vegetables for small spaces, and raised beds make tending these miniature plants a snap. Most experienced gardeners seem to enjoy planting a mixture of plant types, including ornamental plants and ground covers, perennial bulbs and flowers, annuals, herbs, and vegetables all together in close combinations for full-season color and effect.

Redwood and cedar both make long-lasting frames for landscape use, especially when they blend into the existing landscape features. Bricks of all shapes and colors, stone from Arkansas or Georgia, concrete blocks, landscape timbers, treated lumber, posts sunk side by side in the ground, and of course railroad ties are materials often used with great effect in making raised beds long-lasting and attractive in the landscape. Anything will do, as long as it can hold from six to twelve inches of prepared soil in place and provides drainage.

Since creosote and pentachlorophenol vapors may harm some plants, either avoid direct contact between plants and such treated building materials or choose copper-treated wood. The pressure treatment given to this material has been proven safe for vegetables and herbs. Such wood may cost slightly more initially, but it will last for many years (even in the Deep South). Untreated wood may rot in only two seasons.

Butted ends have an inherent strength, but mitered ends look more finished and stay in place better. Treated wood usually swells or shrinks after a few months on the ground. Molding or facing can add an elegant touch. My own beds are simply mitered, nailed, braced from within against stakes, and left to stretch and shape themselves otherwise as they please. Eventually I hope to replace most of them with flagstone or other, heavier material, but for now I find the wood quite satisfactory.

The size of a raised bed is a matter of purely personal preference. Five- and six-foot widths are often recommended, but I have found that narrower gardens (four feet wide or less) are comfortably within the reach of most people. Since most flowers and vegetables really need not have fantastically deep roots, shallow beds will suffice.

Double digging is a lot of work, so I combine digging and raised sides to increase my workable soil area. My beds are generally eight or so inches high, with the native soil dug about a foot deep and amended with enough sand and organic material to fill it almost to the brim with soil mixture. The garden has both the advantages of a raised bed and the added protection of soil depth to protect roots in the winter.

Paths around and between beds should be permanent, enticing, and easily maintained. My first beds were two feet apart, which was fine until the foliage and flowers matured and began spilling over. Three feet or more is not too wide for comfortable walkways, and four or five feet will accommodate two adults walking side by side. Neatly trimmed turf can be soft and soothing to the foot, but the path must be wide enough for mowing, and Bermudagrass should be avoided at all costs. Crushed shells, gravel, stones, flagstone, brick or other paving material, bark, and other mulches may be used to create comfortable low-maintenance paths. I have recently begun using the shaved peelings cast off from the pole-making process. They are wider than sawdust but thinner than bark. The material packs down well, excludes weeds, and, when wet, gives off a rich golden glow. Unfortunately, it may be difficult to locate.

A wide variety of soils will do for raised beds. It will initially be easy to haul in good-quality topsoil, preferably loam, assuming that it can be found and will not turn out to be all clay with noxious weeds, but dirt alone will perform poorly in raised beds or in containers of any sort, for that matter. A blend of soil, coarse sand (sharp, clean builder's grade), and generous amounts of organic material will vastly improve most native soils. Avoid river sand, since it is often contaminated with weeds such as nut grass and may also house microscopic nematodes which have washed out of agricultural fields. Organic matter includes peat, compost, cheap potting soil, finely ground pine bark, peanut hulls, bagasse, or any other biodegradable material. I have found that it is far better to use a combination of different types of organic material for the best long-term effect, since each type has different qualities. The organic material helps most soils to drain excess water better and

When it's too cold for comfort, the sun-filled garden promises that winter will be brief.

Norman Kent Johnson

will also hold moisture longer for plant use. Local nurseries usually have huge piles of ideal potting soil mixes which, when added to existing soils, make a good medium for growing most flowers and vegetables.

If you suspect the final soil mix of being sour (acidic), thoroughly mix in a little limestone as a neutralizer. It is wise to have your soil tested first, however. Generally speaking, a good rule of thumb is to add five pounds of ground limestone (not quicklime, gypsum, or slag) for every hundred square feet of bed surface. A pint is a pound, by the way, or the equivalent of one cup for every ten square feet (two feet by five feet). Lime lasts for three or four years, and the treatment should be repeated only when a soil test indicates that it is needed.

The simple but often overlooked step of having the soil tested can mean the difference between malaise and hardiness in your plants. It can quickly pinpoint easily corrected deficiencies. Fertilizers—especially the strong generic garden types—can easily be overused. Be sure to choose fertilizers that contain micronutrients (boron, copper, zinc, and so forth), or your vegetables may suffer from the "iron-poor sap" syndrome so often seen in potted plants. Mulches on the soil surface help keep soil temperatures from wild fluctuations in both summer and winter, hold down weed problems if they are used thickly enough, and conserve moisture. As a bonus, straw and bark may be added to the soil when the beds are reworked. Like ground covers and attractive stones, mulches can give extra texture and color to the garden. Their advantages outweigh their drawbacks as potential hiding places for snails and crickets.

High-quality vegetables can be grown in pots and other containers as long as enough sunshine is available and careful attention is given to watering. Pot size is not as important (except of course to root crops) as adequate water and well-drained soils. Fertilizers, especially those containing micronutrients, are necessary in small, regular amounts.

Drainage holes are needed for containers, and soil should be porous and easy to keep moist (it should not be soggy). Cover the sides of dark pots, or group them together, to prevent heat buildup. Bags of commercial potting soil, in fact, make fairly good containers in themselves ("pillow gardens") as long as drainage slits, together with water and fertilizer, are provided. Mulches on the soil surface will keep soil cool and moist longer. Try pine needles, bark, or colorful rocks.

Hanging baskets make good gardens, too. Try miniature varieties of vegetables for best results, and don't forget to plant for fall, winter, and early spring—many cool-season vegetables look good outside when everything else is bare, and containers can be brought in during extreme weather. Add a flower or two to spruce up the looks of container gardens.

Raised beds and containers both dry out more quickly than solid-soil gardens and flower beds. Regular attention to irrigation is certainly crucial to plant growth. Here, as elsewhere, slow, deep soakings are much to be preferred over light sprinklings, especially if the soil is allowed to dry between times. Plant roots will grow only where the essentials of life, especially air and water, may be found. Frequent shallow waterings only cause shallow roots. Thorough soakings, on the other hand, send moisture down deep, and air is able to penetrate as the soil surface dries, encouraging strong, deep roots. Mulches will considerably help to moderate the need for water, but the frequency of watering is important, too.

Drip, or trickle, irrigation puts a thin, steady stream at the base of plants, where they need it, rather than diffusing water over the entire beds (weeds, leaves, and all). The advantages of trickle irrigation include the convenience, the low pressure needed, fantastic savings in water bills, and increased plant growth. Basically, trickle irrigation involves a system of specially developed pipes which are designed to hold up for many years under adverse weather and deliver small amounts of water at a time to plants by way of small emitters alongside the plants. A filter and inexpensive pressure regulator complete the setup, and timers are available to run the system when it is not convenient for the gardener to operate it. The moderately high initial cost of a trickle system may be amortized and justified through water savings, steady plant growth, and many years of use.

Vegetables Indoors

Even in the dead of winter you can enjoy growing an easy, nutritious vegetable garden right in your own kitchen. The seeds of all plants are full of the enzymes and vitamins that the future plant will need to start growing, and we can take advantage of them by sprouting them in jars and enjoying them as healthful, tasty additions to meals.

Over two dozen easy-to-sprout seeds can be found at health food stores or can be bought through mail order catalogs. Table 16 lists many tasty possibilities. Some vegetable seeds make sprouts that are poisonous—for example, those of tomatoes and peppers—so don't blindly experiment. Since many garden seeds are treated with fungicides or insecticides, always be sure that the seeds you intend to sprout are clean and untreated.

Sprouts usually take two or three days, five at the most (depending on the type of seed). All you need for equipment is a jar or other container for soaking the seeds (usually just overnight) and a screen or cheesecloth for rinsing. I use (and reuse) a quart canning jar, with a piece of wire screen stuck in the jar ring where the lid would normally go. Some seeds are very tiny and may wash out through the mesh of regular screen material, so cheesecloth may be needed rather than screening. A bowl or pan with two or three small objects (wood blocks will do) can be used as a drain board. You may prefer to cover the sprouting jar with a box or can; seeds grown in the dark do not taste as strong as those grown in the light).

Place two or three tablespoons of seeds in the jar, fill it with water, and let the seeds soak until they swell. Soybeans may need twenty-four hours, while mustard, flax, and cress need no soaking. All the rest generally take about eight hours or just overnight. An extra soaking may prevent some seeds from germinating at all, so don't overdo it.

After soaking, rinse the seeds several times with clean water, using the screen or cheesecloth, and turn the jar upside down on the blocks in the pan to drain. If you wish, cover the jar and pan to keep things dark. Most people like to sprout seeds in the dark the first day or so and then place them in a bright (not sunny) spot the last day to green up.

As the seedlings grow, they must be rinsed so that they can breathe yet remain moist and so that they stay free of molds. Pour a little tap water into the jar through the screen or cheesecloth two or three times a day, and then drain it right back out. One rinsing in the morning and another in the early evening may be fine, but three rinses a day are best. Some seeds do not take rinsing very

Table 16. **Sprouting Characteristics of Twenty-eight Seeds**

VARIETY	SOAKING TIME (HOURS)	RINSE AND DRAIN (TIMES/ DAY)	AV. TIME TO HAR- VEST (DAYS)	SPECIAL HANDLING	SUGGESTED USES
Alfalfa	8	3	3–4	none	salads, sandwiches, juices
Bean, mung	8	3	3–4	boil 3–4 minutes be- fore eating	salads, omelets, soups, Oriental dishes, snacks
Bean, pichl	8	3	3–4	none	salads, soups, omelets, Oriental dishes, snacks
Beets	8	3	3–5	none	salads, juices
Buckwheat	8	3	2–3	remove remaining husks	salads, juices, pancakes
Cabbage, Chinese	8	3	3–4	none	salads, juices
Chia	8	no	3–5	mist	salads, sandwiches, casseroles
Clover, red	8	3	3–5	none	sandwiches, salads, juices
Corn	8	3	2–4	none	tortillas, vegetable casseroles, soups, etc.
Cress	no	no	3–5	mist gently with water 3 times a day or mix with other seeds	salads, sandwiches, breads
Dill	8	3	3–5	none	salads, sandwiches, juices
Fenugreek	8	3	3–5	mist gently with water	salads, snacks
Flax	no	no	3–5	mist gently with water 3 times a day or mix with other seeds	salads, juices
Garbanzo	8	3	3–4	none	vegetable casseroles and soups
Lentil	8	3	2–4	none	salads, juices, vege- table casseroles, soups, etc.

Table 16. (continued)

VARIETY	SOAKING TIME (HOURS)	RINSE AND DRAIN (TIMES/ DAY)	AV. TIME TO HAR- VEST (DAYS)	SPECIAL HANDLING	SUGGESTED USES
Millet	8	3	3–5	none	salads, juices, vegetable casseroles, soups, etc.
Mustard	no	3	3–5	mist gently with water 3 times a day or mix with other seeds	salads, juices
Oats	8	3	2–3	remove remaining husks	breads, granola, snacks
Peas, Alaskan	8	3	3–4	none	salads, soups, omelets, snacks
Peas, porridge	8	3	3–4	none	salads, soups, omelets, Oriental dishes, snacks
Peas, special	8	3	3–4	none	salads, soups, omelets, snacks
Radish	8	3	3–4	none	sandwiches, salads, juices
Rye	8	3	2–3	none	breads, granola, snacks
Sesame	8	3	2–3	none	breads, granola, snacks
Soybean	24	3	3–5	change soaking water every 8 hrs., boil 10–15 minutes before eating	Oriental dishes, salads, casseroles
Sunflower	8	3	3–5 (green 5–7)	remove remaining husks	salads, snacks
Triticale	8	3	1–2	none	breads, snacks, granola, pancakes
Wheat	8	3	2 or wheat grass 5–7	none	breads, snacks, granola, pancakes

Source: Cooperative Extension Service, United States Department of Agriculture.

well and are best mixed with other seeds or simpy misted with
water to keep them moist. Keep the jar upside down over the pan
so that no seeds stay wet.

After the seeds develop well, having stems, roots, and tender
seed leaves, they can be used immediately or can be stored in the
refrigerator for several days in plastic bags. Most are eaten raw, as
flavorful additions to salads or as crunchy fillers in sandwiches.
They can also be used to jazz up soups and vegetable casseroles.
Some make dandy granola, bread, and fillers for omelets; still others add flavor to juices. Soybean and mung sprouts should be par-
boiled before eating.

Several different seeds can sometimes be sprouted together if
they have compatible harvest times. Corn and lentils, for example,
make an interesting combination in casseroles and soups, and both
need about three days to sprout.

Sprouts are simple to grow and enliven meals throughout the
year. Their nutritional value (vitamins and enzymes) is as important as the texture and color they contribute. And their taste is
often unusual and exciting.

Flowers are the sweetest things God ever made and
forgot to put a soul into.

Henry Ward Beecher

6

Annuals and Perennials
Indoors and Out

Is a tulip an annual or a perennial? The answer is probably not
worth the effort, but the point is worth making nonetheless. Annuals are plants which live for one season—a year or less—before
flowering, setting seed, and dying. Annuals have but one goal in
life, namely to further their species by reproduction. Once an annual has set seed, its life is essentially over.

It is nevertheless true that, if one keeps an annual plant from
flowering, or constantly removes faded flowers in order to prevent
seed development, one can prolong the life of the plant almost in-
definitely, particularly if one also manages such environmental
conditions as light, temperature, and moisture. When selecting
bedding plants, it is best to choose those that are young, stocky,
green, and not in bloom. Otherwise, pinch the flowers off to help
the plant bloom vigorously.

Annuals

Annuals contrast with other plants which live two, three, or a hundred years or more, repeatedly flowering and seeding and yet continuing to grow and rejuvenate year after year. Oaks, dandelions,

Bermudagrass, and daffodils are prime examples of perennial plants, which live year after year.

Some plants, though, fall into another category. Outdoors in their native homelands they would live for many years, but they die miserably if they are left outside in, say, Alabama or South Carolina. One example is the tulip, a spring-flowering bulb that is a true perennial but is not well adapted to the southeast United States. Like caladium, gladiolus, tuberose, dahlia, canna, and lily, the tulip rots with disease aggravated by too much water and should therefore be planted only in deep, well-drained soil. Tulips are also subject to stress from intense summer heat (plant deeply and mulch heavily) and may fail to grow properly because there is insufficient cold in the winter (new varieties have overcome this difficulty). Tulips should be fertilized with a balanced bulb food (not just bone meal) in the late fall. If the bulbs are fed too heavily, or if they are fed after they have begun growing in the late winter, they will be more susceptible to diseases. Heavy, wet soils—down deep— will also cause rot.

These woes in combination have caused perennial tulips to be considered one-shot annuals here in the Deep South. The same goes for such tender tropical perennials as Swedish ivy, philodendrons, begonia, hibiscus, and Norfolk Island pine. All these plants and many others are used in pots and hanging baskets and as seasonal annuals. Some plants, in other words, may be perennial in some situations and annual in others. Anything that can't take the weather or must be replanted every year can be called an annual (even plants that reseed themselves, such as periwinkle, moss rose, celosia, and cleome, or spider flower).

Tulips should be used in mass plantings or as temporary accents, like any other annual. Store tulip bulbs in marked bags in the refrigerator for six or eight weeks before planting. Do not refrigerate daffodil bulbs, or their flowers will be early and on very short stalks. Daffodil varieties for the South are confusing to many people (one gardener in Mississippi has over 800 different kinds, but they don't all do well). A good all-around selection of daffodils would include Actea, Carlton, Mount Hood, Ice Follies, Tête-à-tête, Thalia, Cheerfulness, Peeping Tom, and February Gold. The sweet, many-flowered Paperwhites are fine as well. Daffodils need lots of sun, but that can be found under deciduous trees and in between summer perennials such as daylilies and phlox. Low-growing

The Amen! of Nature is always a flower.
Oliver Wendell Holmes

ground covers that accept winter sun, such as Asiatic jasmine, English ivy, and junipers, can be seasonally brightened with daffodils. Consider planting bulbs under pansies, which will hide the browning foliage while being brightened by the intermittent blooms.

Paperwhite and Soleil d'Or are two good daffodils for indoor forcing; hyacinths and tulips may also be enjoyed if they are placed in the refrigerator for four or five weeks first. Six or seven daffodils will usually fill a pot, as will three hyacinths. Anchor the bulbs in gravel, add just enough water to reach the bulbs' bases, and place the pot in a cool, dark spot (a cabinet or closet, even the refrigerator, is fine) for three or four weeks. When sprouts are three to four inches long, put the pot in a sunny window and water as needed. You should have flowers in about two weeks (the whole process takes about six weeks from start to finish).

Dutch iris, often overlooked, make very dependable, hardy perennials in many colors and varieties. They also make long-lasting cut flowers. When they are planted in masses of a dozen or more, their display is spectacular. Plant them about six inches apart and four deep. Daffodils and Dutch iris are both hardy perennials in the South; others include allium, garlic, amaryllis (in most areas), hybrid lilies, iris, peony, and muscari, or grape hyacinth.

Because annuals are used in so many situations, and because so many types are available (tables 17 and 18 show only some of them), it is important to choose carefully, bearing in mind the effect desired. Coleus and impatiens, for example, will burn up in hot sun, and so they should be kept in shady areas. Marigolds and zinnias, on the other hand, need full sun to bloom. Tall annuals such as amaranth or sunflower will overshadow tiny sanvitalia or alyssum. Some annuals do well in containers; some do not.

Marigolds and impatiens, portulaca and verbena, periwinkle, begonia, and other plants are massed in beds, as annuals are most commonly used, but flowers such as ageratum, pansy (winter), sanvitalia, alyssum, and ornamental peppers also appear widely as edging around walks, beds, and borders. The tall sunflowers, hollyhocks, tithonia, foxglove, amaranth, and cleome can be used as high screens or as background plants in a border. Vines can be trained onto trellises or arbors or fences, especially morning glory, moonflower, "tater vine" (*Dioscoria*), cypress vine, and black-eyed susan vine (*Thunbergia*). Zinnia, globe amaranth, snapdragon, cosmos, marigolds, and many more plants are good for

Table 17. **Characteristics of Selected Annual Flowers**

PLANT	HEIGHT (IN.)	BEST USE	REMARKS
Ageratum (*Ageratum houstonianum*)	6–20	edging	tall varieties grown for cut flowers; good rock garden plant; also used for window and patio boxes
Alyssum (*Lobularia maritima*)	2–4	edging	because of its extremely low habit of growth, it is excellent as small area ground cover
Baby's breath (*Gypsophilia elegans*)	12–18	borders	source of cut flowers and plants for drying; filler material in arrangements; sometimes used as background material in rock gardens
Begonia (*Begonia semperflorens*)	8–10	bedding	dig and bring inside for winter pot plants; hybrids more tolerant of sun; excellent for patio planters
Balsam (*Impatiens balsamina*)	12–28	bedding	new dwarf varieties excellent for bedding or border plantings
Candytuft (*Iberis* sp.)	6–12	edging bedding	rock garden plant or filler; select dwarf ones for bedding; ground cover; perennial in S.C.
Celosia (*Celosia argentea*)	6–36	bedding	source of cut flowers and plants for drying; taller types excellent for borders; plumed and crested are the two types of flower heads
Coleus (*Coleus blumeii*)	20–24	edging bedding	grown for decorative foliage; good plant for massing as well as potting for patios and terraces
Cornflower (*Centaurea cyannus*)	12–36	bedding	source of cut flowers; good for rock garden
Cosmos (*Cosmos bipinnatus*)	24–48	borders	source of excellent cut flowers and as background in borders
Dahlia (*Dahlia* sp.)	12–40	bedding edging	source of cut flowers that bloom early; tubers may be kept after first season's growth
Dianthus (*Dianthus chinensis*)	8–15	bedding edging	select heat-tolerant varieties
Dusty miller (*Cineraria maritima*)	8–24	bedding	helps tie together or give unity to a border of mixed colors; good contrast against evergreens

Table 17. (continued)

PLANT	HEIGHT (IN.)	BEST USE	REMARKS
Four-o'clock (*Mirabilis jalapa*)	20–36	borders	mainly used as filler in flower border; flowers open late in day or when cloudy
Gaillardia (*Gaillardia polchella*)	12–30	borders	source of cut flowers and plants for drying; may be treated as a perennial
Geranium (*Pelargonium hortorum*)	6–30	bedding planters	grow indoors as pot plant in winter or outdoors on the patio or terrace in summer; most satisfactory where water doesn't touch foliage
Globe amaranth (*Gomphrena globosa*)	6–24	borders	source of cut flowers and plants for drying; dwarf varieties useful for bedding
Impatiens (*Impatiens sultanii*)	6–15	bedding	good plant for window gardens; deep-shade plant
Hollyhock (*Althaea rosea*)	18–72	screen borders	best used in back of border or as a screen; many varieties will live on as a perennial
Larkspur (*Delphinium ajacis*)	18–48	screen borders	source of cut flowers and plants for drying; make successive sowings for cut flowers
Marigold (*Tagetes* sp.)	6–30	bedding edging	source of cut flowers; good window-garden plant; one of most dependable annuals
Morning Glory (*Ipomoea purpurea*)	vine	screen	a vine that grows 8 to 12 feet tall; must have wire or string for support
Nasturtium (*Tropaeolum* sp.)	12–15	bedding edging	needs well-drained soil; blooms quickly from seed; fertilize sparingly
Petunia (*Petunia hybrida*)	8–24	bedding	good plant for window gardens; long blooming period; may need pruning in midsummer
Phlox (*Phlox drummondi*)	6–15	bedding edging	plant in fall to bloom before summer heat
Poppy (*Eschscholzia californica* and *papaver* sp.)	12–16	borders	source of cut flowers; sow in fall
Portulaca (*Portulaca grandiflora*)	6–9	bedding edging	good plant for rock gardens; likes hot, dry locations in light soils

Table 17. (continued)

PLANT	HEIGHT (IN.)	BEST USE	REMARKS
Rudbeckia (*Rudbeckia birta*)	20–24	borders bedding	source of cut flowers; heat loving; is perennial in S.C.
Irish lace (*Tagetes signata*)	6–9	edging	excellent annual edging for walks or flower borders
Scarlet sage (*Salvia splendens*)	10–36	borders bedding	dwarf varieties bloom early, tall varieties bloom later
Snapdragon (*Antirrhinum majus*)	10–36	bedding borders	source of cut flowers; dwarf types are good for window gardens; select varieties with hot weather tolerance
Strawflower (*Helichrysum* sp.)	12–36	borders	source of cut flowers and plants for drying; considered one of the best everlastings
Sweet pea (*Lathyrus odoratus*)	vine	screen	should be sown from November to March; source of cut flowers; dwarf types are good in borders, beds, or boxes
Verbena (*Verbena hortensis*)	9–18	bedding	good rock garden plants
Vinca (*Vinca rosea*)	10–18	bedding	perennial grown as annual; good plant for window gardens; unlike *Vinca minor*, *rosea* thrives in full sun
Zinnia (*Zinnia* sp.)	6–48	bedding borders	source of cut flowers; endures heat; probably easiest flower to grow except for mildew which gets on foliage

Source: Cooperative Extension Service, United States Department of Agriculture.

cutting. You can save the seed from your marigolds (unless the plants were hybrids, which do not make viable seed); store it in a cool, dry place for use the following spring.

Ornamental peppers, sanvitalia, cosmos, cypress vine, cleome, tithonia, moonflower vine, kochia, amaranthus, luffa gourds, and many other unusual but easy-to-grow plants are impossible to find as bedding plants, so they must be grown from seeds. Shop locally for interesting possibilities, and begin subscribing to several seed catalogs as a way of bringing new and exciting plants into your life.

Good summer bulbs include gladiolus, tuberose, amaryllis, caladium, dahlia, and elephant ears. Buy them at nurseries in January, before they have been picked over. Select good, firm bulbs (they should resemble cooking onions). Store bulbs at room temperature until planting time.

Table 18. **Cultural Information for Selected Annual Flowers**

NAME	LOCATION	SPACING (IN.)	FLOWER COLOR AND OTHER CHARACTERISTICS
Ageratum (*Ageratum houstonianum*)	sun	9–12	blue, pink, and white flowers appear like tiny powder puffs; flowers from July until frost
Alyssum (*Lobularia maritima*)	sun or shade	5–10	rose, white, dark violet, but mainly white; flowers throughout summer in shade
Baby's breath (*Gypsophilia elegans*)	sun	12	has small, airy white, blush, or rose pink flowers; peak flowering period in mid-summer
Begonia (*Begonia semperflorens*)	shade	8–12	white to red in color with glossy green to bronze foliage; colorful from June until frost
Balsam (*Impatiens balsamina*)	shade	8–12	pink, white, red, salmon, and purple; flowers may be either single or double; peak flowering in June
Candytuft (*Iberis* sp.)	sun	8–12	white and lilac; evergreen; flowers in spring
Celosia (*Celosia argentea*)	sun	8–12	flowers are crested or plumed; colors are red, yellow, orange, and rose; good color from July until frost
Coleus (*Coleus blumeii*)	shade	12	foliage varies from tints of green, yellow, and red to all combinations of the three; colorful until frost
Cornflower (*Centaurea cyannus*)	sun or light shade	12–18	blue, pink, white, or rose; foliage gray; peak flowering in May
Cosmos (*Cosmos bipinnatus*)	sun	12–18	red, yellow, orange, pink, and white; flowers from late June until frost
Dahlia (*Dahlia* sp.)	sun	12–24	mixed colors; mostly red and white and many flower types; blooms August until frost
Dianthus (*Dianthus chinensis*)	sun	6–12	mixed colors; mostly red and white and many flower types; blooms August until frost
Dusty miller (*Cineraria maritima*)	sun	8–12	grown for gray or cottony white foliage
Four-o'clock (*Mirabilis jalapa*)	sun	12–18	red, yellow, or white tubular flowers; flowers peak in July
Gaillardia (*Gaillardia polchella*)	sun	9–12	mostly red with yellow-bordered flowers; flowers midsummer until frost

Table 18. (continued)

NAME	LOCATION	SPACING (IN.)	FLOWER COLOR AND OTHER CHARACTERISTICS
Geranium (*Pelargonium hortorum*)	sun	12–15	red, pink, salmon, and white; July through frost is most colorful bloom period
Globe amaranth (*Gomphrena globosa*)	sun	6–12	white, purple, rose, and orange; blooms profusely from July until frost
Impatiens (*Impatiens sultanii*)	shade	8–12	white, red, rose, pink, orange, and yellow; some varieties have variegated blooms; foliage is very attractive; flowers June through frost
Hollyhock (*Althaea rosea*)	sun or part shade	12–18	semidouble and double flowers of red, pink, yellow, white, lavender, and rose; flowers from late June until frost
Larkspur (*Delphinium ajacis*)	sun	12–18	blue, pink, white, and rose flowers; sometimes called annual delphinium; flowers in late spring
Marigold (*Tagetes* sp.)	sun	6–12	yellow, orange, to red flowers of several types; dwarf varieties ideal for edging and borders; colorful until frost
Morning glory (*Ipomoea purpurea*)	sun or part shade		red, rose, pink, white, blue, and purple flowers up to 8″; flowers from July until frost
Nasturtium (*Tropaeoleum* sp.)	sun	9–12	most colors except blue; flowers late spring
Petunia (*Petunia hybrida*)	sun	12–15	wide color range with single and double flowers; flowers from planting until frost; best flowering in June and July
Phlox (*Phlox drummondi*)	sun	6–15	wide color range; blooms in late spring
Poppy (*Eschscholzia californica* and *papaver* sp.)	sun	6–12	Iceland poppies most popular of the annual types; the colors are white and yellow, yellow and pink, yellow and green, orange, pink and rose; flowers are up to 4 inches; blooms in late spring
Portulaca (*Portulaca grandiflora*)	sun	6–12	low, spreading habit of growth; pink, red, white, yellow, salmon, and rose colored; double or single flowers; flowers from late June until frost
Rudbeckia (*Rudbeckia hirta*)	sun	18	yellow flower often dark at base; flowers in July and August

Table 18. *(continued)*

NAME	LOCATION	SPACING (IN.)	FLOWER COLOR AND OTHER CHARACTERISTICS
Irish lace *(Tagetes signata)*	sun	8–12	looks like a heather; grown mainly for foliage; actually a small white-flowered marigold that blooms in early fall
Scarlet sage *(Salvia splendens)*	sun	8–12	noted for its brilliant red flowers; new varieties are purple, rose, and white; flowers from June until frost
Snapdragon *(Antirrhinum majus)*	sun or light shade	10–12	many colors and varieties; flowers spring and early summer
Strawflower *(Helichrysum* sp.*)*	sun	12–18	purple, red, gold, white, yellow, and rose-colored flowers; flowers from July until frost
Sweet pea *(Lathyrus odoratus)*	sun	8–12	wide color range; flowers at same time as pansies
Verbena *(Verbena hortensis)*	sun	8–12	white, pink, rose, red, or blue flowers borne in flat heads; stems are spreading; flowers from July until frost
Vinca *(Vinca rosea)*	sun	8–12	very attractive foliage to complement 5-petaled rose, pink, white, and crimson flowers; flowers July until frost
Zinnia *(Zinnia* sp.*)*	sun	8–15	great diversity in flower color and flower types; colorful until frost if mildew is controlled

Source: Cooperative Extension Service, United States Department of Agriculture.

Remember that caladiums are tropical tubers and will be damaged at temperatures below 50 or 55 degrees. Caladiums should be dug before frost and allowed to dry indoors for a week or more before their dead leaves are gently pulled off. Store them in bags or boxes of peat or vermiculite after dusting with Captan and Sevin to prevent damage from insects and diseases during storage. To get a head start on them before spring, set them in well-drained potting soil in a sunny window where temperatures are about 65–70 degrees. The soil outside will not be warm enough for them until another two months or more have passed, so take care of them in the meantime.

Geraniums can be stored over the winter bone dry. Simply take them out of the soil before frost and shake or wash the dirt from the roots. Air dry them on newspaper in the kitchen or other warm room for a week or so. Hang the plants up or store them in a cool place until spring. Then trim them so that they are five or six inches long and pot them up or stick them right into the ground. They will root and begin blooming in as little as four or five weeks.

For drying there are strawflowers (the best everlastings), gaillardia, celosia, baby's breath, globe amaranth, and larkspur. Marigolds, periwinkle, zinnias, salvia (scarlet sage), four-o'clocks, and snapdragons appear in borders all across the South.

Annuals have the best color of any plant, whether they bloom or not. There are many overlooked tropical foliage plants, such as wandering Jew, spider plant, Swedish ivy, and even small shefflera and philodendron. These can always be propagated and held over from year to year or dug up, potted, and used as house plants. Other foliage annuals include caladium, amaranth, coleus, begonia, asparagus fern, and ornamental kale or cabbage (winter). To keep caladiums leafing out, incidentally, you should snip off, not pull, the odd-looking flowers and give the plants a light feeding and watering. Inspect the plants for flowers every week or so, and remove them as you see them.

They'd lived through all the heat and noise and stench of summertime, and now each widely opened flower was like a triumphant cry, "We will, we will make a seed before we die."

Harriette Arnow

Apartment dwellers, lacking space for shrubs and trees, can nevertheless garden with annuals. Handicapped or elderly persons and even people with little time for gardening will find the easy-to-grow flowering and foliage annuals perfectly suited to their needs. There are upright or hanging plants, varieties perfect for the hot sun (periwinkle, peppers, moss rose, portulaca, and verbena), and plenty for the shaded porch (fern, coleus, begonia, caladium, and, best of all, impatiens).

Annuals also light up the landscape in the winter. Some vegetables, such as Red Sails lettuce, make superb winter borders and edging plants; ornamental kale will tolerate quite a bit of heavy frost—in fact, a light frost brings out its best color. Pansies, especially the hybrids, will endure the worst weather possible and will bloom until they are replaced in the spring. Bundles of pansies are not as good for setting out as are those grown in the plastic market packs, which are well rooted and less likely to suffer serious transplant shock. The hybrids are best of all, however (I plant Universal), and are usually sold in peat pots.

Pansies have long been planted for spring bloom in the South, and they often bloom as early as December only to be knocked down by freezing weather in January. Swiss Giants are noted for their very large flowers, but the new hybrids far surpass them in number of blooms, intensity of color, and tolerance of both heat and severe freezes. In fact, my Universal hybrids are often in bloom by Thanksgiving and continue, through the most severe weather, even under snow and ice, until I take them out in late May or early June to make room for summer flowers. What the hybrid pansies lack in size they more than make up for in number, with rich colors that last from fall until summer.

Always pinch or prune the tips from salvia, periwinkle, marigolds, impatiens, and other summer flowers to get them started faster in the landscape. Fertilize them with liquid plant food once in May, and mulch to help the soil stay moist, weed free, and not too hot. A good root system established in the spring will pay off handsomely in July and August.

Set out caladiums, geraniums, begonias, and coleus in the shade garden for summer color. Sun lovers are too plentiful to mention in detail here but include salvia, ageratum, zinnia, cosmos, celosia, alyssum, periwinkle, and petunia. Ornamental peppers are increasingly being used as low-maintenance bedding plants, especially planted in masses that show off their flower and fruit color to good effect.

Perennials and flowering shrubs look ragged by midsummer, and annuals certainly help them along. The careful selection and placement of annuals can help restore heat-faded colors until the perennials get their second wind.

Southerners are beginning to appreciate vegetables as edible ornaments suitable for use in flower beds and containers. Tomatoes, which were long regarded as poisonous, were nevertheless grown for their attractive yellow flowers and big red berries. Squash plants make fast, bold statements in the early summer border (until the vine borers find them), having huge orange blossoms. The new Blondy okra is a compact plant with attractive,

---

I am growing some ornamental peppers along my flower bed. Are they good to eat?

Ask Felder

Certainly they are—but some are hotter than the hinges of Hades! They make excellent pepper sauce as well as interesting dried wreaths.

hibiscuslike flowers and edible pods—and it requires hot, hot sun. Sweet potato vines are lush ground covers. Container-grown lettuce and carrots fill a void on patios when winter weather forces the ferns indoors. Vegetables make interesting, inexpensive annuals for show.

The South has weather that is a problem for gardeners in some respects. Our sun is hotter, so we can't grow most geraniums and begonias on the sidewalks as they do in Seattle and Niagara Falls. Annuals here need more roots to supply the plants with cooling moisture where even the shade is hot, so soil preparation is more critical. Add fertilizer and some organic material such as peat, compost, or cheap potting soil. Watering becomes of prime importance to annuals, even for pansies, which may dry out in winter winds during warm dry spells. A slow, deep soaking once every week is much preferable to several light sprinklings in that it enables annuals to develop sturdy, deep root systems. Our soils are acidic, and lime must be added every three or four years.

The joy of being able to cut flowers freely, lavishly, to decorate the house and to give to friends is an end that justifies a lot of gardening effort.

T. H. Everett

A well-balanced granular fertilizer (8-8-8, 13-13-13, 5-10-10, and so on) worked into the soil before planting or scattered on the soil surface will be less expensive than the sort that must be mixed with water if it is used lightly, but the latter are much faster and milder for established plants. Use the water-soluble kind as a pick-me-up every month or six weeks, carefully following instructions on the label regarding strength. Use the liquids at less than recommended strength in preference to no fertilizer or heavier doses of the granular ones.

Since our nights are so warm, plants tend to get leggier and need occasional light pruning to keep them in bounds. More water means a greater need to replace leached-out nutrients, and so light fertilizations are needed every month or so to keep annuals looking good. By midsummer the heat may cause some annuals, especially petunias, salvia, verbena, and alyssum, to look peaked, and moderate pruning will be needed to rejuvenate them.

Mulches keep roots cool in the summer and warm in the winter and go a long way toward curbing weeds. Pine straw, coarse bark, peanut or pecan hulls, wood shavings, and sawdust are used and are much better for annuals than plastic mulches (which sometimes prevent air and water from reaching roots and may become extremely hot in the summer if not covered). There are also herbicides which, if used properly, control weeds under flowers safely.

Crickets keep eating my marigolds. I thought they were immune to bugs. What can I use to get rid of them?

Marigolds are resistant to soil nematodes, nothing else. Crickets and their close relatives, roaches, will do a great deal of damage to young seedlings. Use a liquid insecticide as recommended by your nurseryman—if the label says it will kill crickets. (Pesticides change from year to year, so I won't waste space on specific materials.) I prefer the liquids over granules because I want good coverage on the plants, where it can do some good, rather than on the ground. Since crickets are night feeders, spray the plants late in the day so the material will be full-strength at night.

Major pests of annuals include insects which cut the plants, chew on foliage, or suck sap and damage flowers. General sprays are effective. Roaches and crickets eat a lot of leaves and young plants, as do beetles and grubs (root feeders). Crickets feed at night, so spray your plants late in the day for best results. Toads, skinks, anoles, and brown worm snakes are all helpful in curbing insects.

Snails and slugs are serious pests which damage and destroy many plants. Commercially available baits containing metaldehyde and mesurol work if they are used regularly. Beer traps have been somewhat effective in catching slugs. To make one, cut a hole in the plastic top of a coffee can or soft butter tub, sink the container into the soil so that the lid is flush with the surface, and pour beer into the trap as a lure.

Moles and armadillos are the largest scourges of the landscape if we can ignore squirrels. Nothing has been proven effective against armadillos. Chewing gum and carbide balls are sometimes inserted into mole holes with the desired effect, but the only tried and true mole control is a plunger-type trap. If cats are a problem in your garden, try scattering mothballs or, after preparing the soil for bedding plants, spread chicken wire over the ground. You can then set seeds or plants through the mesh and mulch over the area to make it neat.

Key cultural practices that help keep annuals blooming include the removal of spent flowers, to keep them from going to seed (and so from completing their life cycle), and light pruning to stimulate new growth and flowering. To thrive, however, annuals need well-prepared soil that has been worked up with peat, compost, or other organic material before planting. Otherwise the plants may live, but they will remain stunted and unsatisfactory. Lime should be thoroughly blended into the soil. Mulches, regular deep soakings, and light feedings every four or five weeks will all promote vigorous, healthy plants. Give plants plenty of room to spread. Too often we allow reseeded annuals to grow up so thick that they cannot do well. Thin when necessary, the earlier the better.

To keep plants growing in the South, the control of insects and diseases is crucially important. Our seasons are long, our winters are mild, and our nights are muggy, so insects and diseases have a field day nearly year round. The ideal defense, once you have selected the best varieties, is to keep the plants strong and healthy. Marigolds and verbena, however, regularly suffer from spider mite attacks by midsummer. Zinnias suffer from powdery mildew. If you grow these plants, anticipate recurring problems. Spray at the first sign of trouble.

Perennials

Perennials blend with existing shrubs and ground covers, offering subliminally perceived cues for human and animal moods and activities. They weave a colorful seasonal tapestry in the landscape. One day they bloom; a week or two later they are gone, leaving just a trace of greenery, sometimes striking, to remind us that they will return next year.

Too many landscapes are needlessly boring, with the usual shrubs, a few trees perhaps, and a row of flowers set out for the summer. The most popular flowering shrubs in most yards (usually azaleas and roses) often go unnoticed, appearing as they do with monotonous regularity in every yard. Established landscapes often have empty pockets which, if filled with just the right perennial flower, could be transformed into appealing displays of depth and color.

I wouldn't dream of telling a grown person how to arrange flowers in a vase!
Ruth Stout

Anyone who knows how to tend a lawn can grow ferns easily, as well as yarrow, asparagus, summer phlox, and a large number of other appealing plants. The list of wonderful perennials is long even when it is restricted to those adapted to the South. Many are considered weeds because they literally take over the roadsides with no human care whatsoever. Wild grasses, goldenrod, woodland ferns, violets, trillium, and cattails are but a few examples of

---

What are some flowers I can plant to attract hummingbirds?

In general, anything with pink or red flowers will be preferred by hummingbirds. A favorite is monarda (beebalm, *M. didyma,* is red; bergamot, *M. fistulosa,* is pink), and also hibiscus, pineapple sage, and four o'clocks. Consider also complementing your perennials with both the annual red salvia and the shrub called abelia.

---

native perennials. They are often overlooked because they are so common, but they can add just the right touch to a landscape.

There are perennials for everyone, whether we have sun or shade, large estates or small balconies. Perennials are suitable for naturalizing into wooded lots and help you eliminate the need to mow difficult areas such as steep banks or low, wet spots. In shade, for example, you might use hosta, ferns, Lenten rose, butterfly (ginger) lily, wood hyacinth (endymion), violets, and the native foamflower (tiarella). Alstroemeria is an unusual shade lover that blooms in the summer. If your shade is deciduous (you have sun in the winter), try naturalizing the daffodil Ice Follies or the unusual native mayapple. Many types of liriope, together with the evergreen holly fern, will also do very well in the shade.

Some perennials thrive in containers or rock gardens, while others need plenty of room to display their full splendor. The list in table 19 is far from complete. Possible uses for these plants are too varied to detail here. Perennials are valued as cutting flowers, for striking foliage, for fragrance, to attract butterflies and hummingbirds, or just to provide visual relief among shrubs and ground covers. There are perennial bulbs, ferns, succulents, grasses, herbs, and ground covers and even temporary shrubs. Since they are visible only part of the year, they may be planted under deciduous shrubs and even under other perennials. In nearly all cases the pleasure that they give outweighs the effort it takes to get them started.

Temperature, rainfall, soil type, and even altitude all have enormous impact on the performance or success of perennials, particularly here in the Deep South. Perhaps our single greatest environmental hazard is the suddenness and frequency of changes in temperature and moisture. Warm days in the winter abruptly yield to cold snaps, crushing heat, and drought in the summer, inter-

Table 19. **Cultural Information for Selected Perennial Flowers**

NAME	BLOOMS	EXPOSURE
Alaska daisy (*Chrysanthemum maximum*)	late spring	sun
Allium giganteum (ornamental onion group)	spring, summer	sun
Amaryllis	summer	sun, light shade
Amsonia (blue star)	spring	sun
Armeria	spring	sun, light shade
Arum italicum	winter foliage	shade
Asclepias (butterfly weed)	spring	sun
Asparagus	summer foliage	sun
Asters (many)	summer, fall	sun
Astilbe	spring, summer	light shade
Atamasco lily (*Zephyranthes*)	spring	light shade, sun
Baby's breath (*Gypsophila*)	summer	sun, light shade
Banana (*Musa*)	foliage	sun, light shade
Baptisia (wild indigo), *B. alba*, white flowers with dark stem	summer	sun, light shade
Beard-tongue, (*Penstemon*)	spring, summer	sun
Begonia grandis	foliage and flowers	shade
Blackberry lily (*Belamcanda*)	summer	sun
Bleeding heart (*Dicentra exima*)	spring	shade
Bluets (*Houstonia*)	spring	sun, light shade
Blue fescue	foliage	sun
Blue-eyed grass (*Sisyrinchium*)	spring	sun
Blue plumbago (*Cerastostigma*)	summer	light shade
Butterfly lily (ginger lily, *Hedychium*)	late summer, fall	shade
Calla lily	summer	sun near water
Camassia	spring	shade
Candytuft (*Iberis*)	spring	sun, light shade
Canna	summer	sun, light shade
Cardinal flower (*Lobelia cardinalis*)	spring, summer	sun, light shade

Table 19. (continued)

NAME	BLOOMS	EXPOSURE
Carolina bush pea (*Thermopsis*)	late spring	sun
Carex	foliage	sun, shade
Castor bean	summer foliage	sun
Cattails	summer, fall	sun
Chicory	summer	sun
Chionodoxa (glory-of-the-snow)	early spring	sun, light shade
Chrysanthemum (many sizes and types)	spring, summer, fall	sun
Clematis	spring, summer	sun, light shade
Clover (red, not crimson)	spring	sun, light shade
Columbine (*Aquilegea*)	late spring, summer	shade
Comfrey (*Symphytum*)	spring	light shade
Coral bells (alum root, *Heuchera*)	late spring	sun
Coreopsis (native, Goldfink, or Sunray double)	summer	sun
Coneflower (purple echinacea)	summer	sun, light shade
Crinum lily	summer	sun, light shade
Crocus seiberi (*C. zonatus* in October)	late winter	winter sun
Cyclamen coum	spring	shade
Curcuma (hidden lily)	summer	light shade
Cyperus (umbrella sedge)	foliage	light shade
Daffodils (large group includes jonquil, tazetta, many cultivars)	spring	sun, light shade
Dayflower (*Commelina*)	spring, summer	sun, light shade
Dandelion	spring	sun
Daylily (many very good cultivars)	summer	sun
Dianthus plumaris (cottage pinks)	spring, early summer	sun
Echinops (Blue thistle flower)	summer	sun
Elephant ears (*Colocasia*)	foliage	sun, light shade
Endymion (wood hyacinth)	summer	shade

Table 19. (continued)

NAME	BLOOMS	EXPOSURE
Ferns (many kinds)	summer foliage, evergreen	shade, part sun
Feverfew *(Chrysanthemum parthenium)*	summer	sun, light shade
Foamflower *(Tiarella)*	spring	shade
Four-o'clocks	summer	sun
Foxglove *(Digitalis mertonensis)*	spring	shade
Gaillardia	summer	sun
Galanthus (snowdrop)	winter, fall variety	sun, light shade
Geranium maculatum	spring, summer	light shade, sun
Gerbera (Transvaal daisy)	summer	sun, light shade
Gladiolus carneus	spring	sun, light shade
Goldenrod (esp. *Solidago rugosa*)	fall	sun
Grape hyacinth *(Muscari botryoides)*	spring	sun, light shade
Grasses (many ornamental kinds)	summer effect, flowers	sun
Green-and-gold *(Chrysogonum)*	spring, summer	sun
Green dragon *(Arisaema)*	spring foliage	shade
Helianthus angustifolius (perennial sunflower)	fall	sun
Heliopsis (ox-eye)	summer	sun
Helleborus *(H. orientalis,* Lenten rose; niger, Christmas rose)	winter, early spring	shade
Herbs		
Artemisia	spring, summer, fall	sun, light shade
Garlic chives	spring, summer, fall	sun, light shade
Germander	spring, summer, fall	sun, light shade
Mints	spring, summer, fall	sun, light shade
Oregano	spring, summer, fall	sun, light shade

Table 19. (continued)

NAME	BLOOMS	EXPOSURE
Rosemary	spring, summer, fall	sun, light shade
Sage	spring, summer, fall	sun, light shade
Thymes	spring, summer, fall	sun, light shade
Hibiscus coccineus (rosemallow), moscheutos	summer	sun, light shade
Hollyhocks	summer	sun
Hosta (plantain lily)	summer, foliage	shade
Hymenocallis (white swamp spider lily)	spring	sun, shade
Hypericum (St. John's wort)	summer	light shade
Indian pink (spigelia)	spring, summer	sun
Iris (many types)		
Bearded	spring	sun, light shade
Crested	spring	shade
Dutch	spring	sun
Japanese	late spring	sun
Louisiana	spring	sun
Pallida (variegated)	spring, summer foliage	sun
Siberian	spring	light shade, sun
Tectorum (roof iris)	spring	sun
Jack-in-the-pulpit (*Arisaema*)	spring	shade
Joe Pye weed	late summer	sun
Kudzu *Pueraria,* rampant vine)	summer	sun
Lamb's-ear (stachys)	late spring, foliage	sun, light shade
Lamium (ground cover)	foliage	light shade
Larkspur	spring, summer	sun
Leucojum (snowflake: *L. vernum,* spring; *L. autumnale,* fall)	spring, late summer	sun
Liatris (gayfeather)	summer	sun, light shade
Lily (turk's cap, royal, tiger, madonna, others)	spring, summer	sun
Lily-of-the-valley	spring	shade
Liriope muscari (border grass), and *L. spicata* (lily turf)	summer flowers	sun, shade

Table 19. (continued)

NAME	BLOOMS	EXPOSURE
Lycoris squamigera (mystery lily, resurrection lily)	late summer	winter sun
L. radiata (red spider lily)	fall	winter sun
Lysimachia (Japanese loosestrife)	summer	sun
Lythrum (loosestrife)	summer	sun
Marguerite *(Anthemis)*	summer	sun
Mayapple	spring	shade
Michaelmas daisy (fall aster)	fall	sun, light shade
Mist flower (hardy ageratum, *Eupatorium coelestinum)*	spring, summer, fall	sun
Monarda didyma (beebalm, red), and fistulosa (pink bergamot)	summer	sun, light shade
Muscari (grape hyacinth)	spring	sun
Obedient plant *(Physostegia)*	summer	sun, light shade
Orchids (several)	summer	sun, shade
Oxalis	spring, summer	sun, light shade
Ox-blood lily *(Habranthus;* may be listed otherwise)	early fall	sun
Ox-eye daisy *(Chrysanthemum leucanthemom)*	fall	sun
Peony (early-blooming varieties)	spring	light shade
Peruvian lily *(Alstroemeria)*	summer	shade
Phlox divaricata (wild blue phlox)	spring	sun
Phlox paniculata (summer phlox)	summer	sun, light shade
Phlox stolonifera (creeping phlox)	spring	sun
Phlox subulata (moss pink, thrift)	spring	sun
Pineapple sage (red) *(Salvia elegans)*	summer, fall	sun
Platycodon (balloon flower)	spring, summer	sun, light shade
Pokeweed *(Phytolacca)*	summer	sun
Pyrethrum *(Chrysanthemum coccineum)*	spring	sun

Table 19. (continued)

NAME	BLOOMS	EXPOSURE
Queen Anne's lace (reseeding biennial)	summer, fall	sun
Rain lily *(Cooperia, Zephyranthes)*	summer	sun
Tritoma, knifhofia)	summer	sun
Rohdea	winter berries	shade
Rudbeckia hirta (black-eyed susan, Goldsturm)	summer	sun
Salvia farinacea Blue Bedder	spring, summer	sun
Scabiosa	summer	sun
Scilla (squill)	late winter, spring	sun
Sedum (stonecrop; several types, esp. *S. spectabile*)	fall, foliage	sun
Sempervivum (hens and chicks)	summer, foliage	sun, light shade
Shasta daisy *(Chrysanthemum maximum)*	spring, summer	sun
Sneezeweed *(Helenium)*	summer	sun
Solomon seal	spring	shade
Spiderwort *(Tradescantia)*	spring, summer	sun, shade
Star of Bethlehem *(Ornithogalum)*	spring	sun
Sternbergia (fall daffodil)	late summer	sun
Stokesia	summer	sun
Sweet potato vine *(Dioscoria)*	summer vine	sun, light shade
Tuberose	summer	sun, light shade
Trillium	spring	shade
Verbena (venosa, bonariensis)	summer	sun
Veronica spicata (speedwell)	summer	sun
Viola	spring	shade
Virginia bluebells *(Mertensia)*	spring	cool shade
Woolly mullein (biennial)	summer	sun
Yarrow (several)	spring, summer	sun
Zephyr lilies	summer	sun

rupted by torrential gully washers. On the other hand, the South offers gardeners a great asset: there are no clearly defined seasons, and we can garden year round, with planning. We enjoy a long growing season, during which a seemingly endless succession of perennials can be grown.

Temperature changes are perhaps the hardest environmental blows for many plants to deal with. Some cool-natured plants may be grown in light shade, which will take some of the direct heat off foliage. Mulches will certainly moderate the soil temperature, summer and winter, and will offset sudden changes in it. By avoiding winter hot spots (southern exposures against brick walls, which warm up easily during sunny winter days), you can help cold lovers such as peonies stay dormant long enough so that they will bloom the following year.

Flowers are words which even a baby may understand.
Arthur C. Coxe

While many perennials will tolerate heat or drought, some obviously will not. And some absolutely must not stay wet during downpours that last for days. A well-drained soil is a must to keep many of these plants from drowning or rotting during our rainy winters and springs. The addition of generous amounts of organic material (peat, compost, old manure, or potting soil) will loosen heavy clays and will enrich sandy soils. When the soil is very clayey, it's best to use peat moss and finely ground bark mulch with the manure (add five pounds of lime per 100 square feet of bed when preparing the soil to neutralize the acids in the organic matter). It would also be good to add clean, coarse masonry sand and perhaps some perlite. Watering during dry spells, especially for the first couple of years, will get most perennials off to a good start and will help them to multiply and perform well for many years. Some perennials prefer an alkaline soil, while others like to be grown in acidic conditions. As with annuals and other plants, soil preparation is of utmost importance.

Generally speaking, you should divide spring bloomers in the fall and divide summer or fall bloomers in the spring. Other times of the year are fine for many plants, but in general the rule holds. The amount of time that should elapse varies with the plant. Some hybrid daylilies in good soil, if they are well tended, may need dividing every three years. Others may go five years or more with no real problems. Consider how thick the plants are and how well they perform. When they start to look too crowded or begin to have small flowers, then divide them and replant them in well-prepared soil. Other, equally general rules are: never divide anything unless you have already prepared the soil to receive it, and allow bulbs at least six weeks (longer is better) after flowering before lifting them or removing foliage. All-purpose foods for bulbs should be used sparingly in the fall (bulb roots grow all winter, when they can use fertilizer); spring feedings promote diseases.

Take a few minutes each week to remove all spent flowers. By keeping the plants from setting seed, you can often force them to put out new growth from secondary buds on which additional flowers will form. Also consider planting some of the hybrid varieties to prolong the blooming season.

Peonies will abort their flowers if they are given too much water, but the foliage will remain nice. Give the plants a thorough, deep soaking as needed, usually once every week or so, rather than on a fixed schedule. Watering more often may cause root rot or ungainly rank growth. Less may lead to permanent root damage. Water early to prevent unnecessary exposure to diseases (most leafspot and flower diseases need several hours of continuous moisture to develop). Water early enough in the day to allow the plants to dry before dark.

When I first planted perennials I did not realize how quickly and thickly some would grow months before the transplant season. It is better to get to know new plants' habits first, from soil needs to heat and sun tolerance. Look over the available possibilities, ask people in your area who love flowers, and see what they grow and how. By starting out with only a handful of good peren-

---

There are so many wildflowers along the roadside, and I know I'm not supposed to dig any, but wouldn't it be all right to take the seeds from some of them?

Ask Felder

This depends. Most states now have laws protecting wildflowers, yet even laws aren't effective in keeping people from decimating certain flowers. Do this: through your county agent, contact the state university's botany department, and there will be a member of your state's native plant society to put you in touch with whatever plant you want. (I have spent as little as 50 cents before on wonderful native plants through the native plant society, and now have all I can use and more.) Consider, too, enjoying wildflowers as they appear in nature, instead of having to own every one you see.

nials, you can easily add a few more each season, even just one or two, until you have quite a collection. Before long you will be able to share or swap divisions of your own plants for new varieties. If you are interested in acquiring native wildflowers, ask your county agent to put you in touch with the local university's botany department, where a member of your state's native plant society can tell you how to find whatever plant you want.

When you buy perennials, select individual plants by variety, not color. There are some very good common plants in the trade, and you will find many more available from your friends which will do well in the landscape. There are also new and old cultivars developed for better performance. As many as 20,000 plants may be bred for a period of ten years to produce just 25 good enough to market.

Although seeds are sometimes available for perennials, by far the best way to get started is to purchase or order healthy plants. If you are determined to try seeds, try Blue Bedder salvia and monarda. Many herbs can be started from seed as well. Seeds are best started in high humidity, so consider building a simple frame and covering it with plastic. You can then sow seeds in moist, sterile starter mixes, but don't let the sun heat the frame too much; open it in the daytime.

As previously noted, watering, especially during the first couple of years, is crucial for establishment. Mulches will keep down weeds, at least to some extent, as well as helping to cool the soil in the summer and to prevent sudden changes in the winter. Materi-

---

Ask Felder

How can I get rid of Bermudagrass in my flower beds?

If you can hold off planting in the spring until three or four weeks after the Bermuda (and coco weed, or nutgrass) comes out, you can use glyphosate to kill it. Glyphosate, sold under several brand names, will kill only those plants that are actively growing and are indirectly sprayed or brushed with the material. It has no lingering effects on the soil, so you can plant in the area after a week or so—the time it takes to kill perennial weeds.

There is a new chemical available which kills only grasses. It has no effect on marigolds, monkey grass, lilies, or other broadleaf plants, even when sprayed directly on them. Check with your nurseryman for details.

als such as pine straw, composted leaves, old hay, bark, and other organic materials should be preferred to plastic. Heavy mulch around the crown, or base, of some plants will make them more susceptible to disease. Available herbicides will control some weeds around some plants but can be tricky for most gardeners to use.

Insect control on perennials is not a major concern, since most will usually tolerate insecticide sprays (but do not use such sprays on herbs). Chewing and sucking insects, a few borers, and thrips in flowers can all cause extensive damage in a matter of days, but it is still important to identify the pest positively before undertaking an air strike. Beneficial insects (praying mantids, ladybugs, and lacewings) as well as lizards and spiders and wasps will usually be found in heavy numbers around perennials, since the plants provide long-lasting shelter as well as food.

Diseases are best prevented through good culture (proper soil preparation and drainage, watering early in the day, and the removal of old leaves and flower stalks in the winter). Some virus diseases cause streaks in leaves of iris, daylily, and other plants. Insects spread them, so you should eliminate infected plants and spray for insects. To minimize your chances of buying diseases along with new acquisitions, accept only sturdy-looking newcomers, or settle for cuttings or seeds. Mail order nurseries sometimes sell inferior plants and diseased ones, so shop with reputable dealers who guarantee that their plants are healthy.

Powdery mildew will constantly be a problem on phlox, monarda, and asters primarily because of high humidity. Water your plants early enough so that their foliage can dry out before dark. Avoid crowding plants, which will impede air circulation. Fungicides for use on roses will usually be safe on other ornamental plants, but remember that they are preventive only and must be used regularly for good results (be sure not to use fungicides on nearby herbs).

Perennials usually need fertilizer once or twice a year in very moderate amounts. Granular fertilizers harm tender plants with which they come into direct contact, so work them in lightly beneath the foliage mass, and water the soil to prevent burn. Liquid fertilizers are good for temporary effects but can also damage plants if they are used too strongly. Most foliage perennials (ornamental grass, fern, and elephant ear) need a balanced food (all numbers in the analysis should be nearly the same), but flowering plants (lilies, monarda, and tritoma) use a little more phosphorous (the middle number on the label). Phosphorous tends to build up in the soil, so don't overuse bone meal or other high-phosphorous material; be sure to choose a balanced fertilizer.

Keep in mind that simple masses of colors seem spacious and are more effective (and easier to care for) than a kaleidoscope of colors and textures. Few home gardeners really want to be curators of horticultural zoos with one or two of everything. Instead use masses of plants repeated for effect, and keep beds and borders simple. Heights are important, too. Your own sense of what is pleasant will guide you better than anything else can.

Perennials interplanted with other shrubs and ground covers can inject seasonal color or texture into the landscape. Daffodils in ivy beds, clematis vines in ligustrum, ferns near trees—these are good combinations. Perennials can also be used to fill the bare spot where other perennials are dormant. Try placing daffodils between hosta and Siberian iris with daylilies. Unusual contrasts of color and foliage can provide a never-ending source of wonder.

Such warm colors as reds, oranges, and pinks tend to harmonize well. Cool blues and violets do well when juxtaposed with warm colors. You may highlight any color by surrounding it with lighter shades of the same color, and white flowers or silvery foliage will set off just about anything. Major colors may also be repeated, one at a time if they are intense, down the border to lead the eye and create depth.

Some perennials are weedy and may get out of bounds; others are difficult to keep under average conditions and require careful watering and soil preparation. Pay careful attention, too, to the amount of sun these plants will receive year round. Some do not

---

Ask Felder

My coreopsis stops blooming too soon. How can I keep the flowers blooming?

Take a few minutes each week to remove all spent flowers. By keeping the plants from setting seed, you can often force them to put out new growth from secondary buds on which additional flowers will form. Also consider planting some of the hybrid varieties to prolong the blooming season.

---

tolerate the heat of our summers. Also make sure that your soil drains well during rainy seasons.

***Aster** (Aster)*   Asters grow one to five feet tall, depending on variety, and bloom in late summer and fall. In the garden they make good bridge plants that will last until the hot summer is over. They come in many colors. Michaelmas daisy is common and easy to grow. I pinch mine in June to cause branching and keep the plants more compact. Asters like sun and soil that is somewhat dry. Mildew is a problem.

***Astilbe** (Astilbe)*   Astilbe has clumps of fernlike foliage up to two feet high, with taller spikes of feathery flowers that are white, pink, and red. It likes shade, filtered sun, and moist, woodsy soil.

***Balloon Flower** (Platycodon)*   Blue or white balloon flowers resemble two-inch balloons before the blossoms open. These plants make a good companion for daylily. Balloon flowers grow knee high in sun or very light shade.

***Beebalm, Bergamot** (Monarda)*   Red beebalm (*Monarda didyma*) and pink bergamot (*M. fistulosa*), both nearly four feet tall, flower heavily from June or July onward. They need staking and are attractive to bees, butterflies, and hummingbirds. Monarda is easy to start from seed and is slowly invasive. Divide plants in late winter. Give monarda full sun and moist soil. Mildew is a problem.

***Black-eyed Susan** (Rudbeckia)*   This classic perennial is one of the very easiest wildflowers to grow, but cultivated varieties, especially Goldsturm (a stiff, branching plant that reaches three feet in height with many three-inch flowers) are infinitely superior. Blooms have gold petals surrounding a brown cone. Others have yellow, orange, or brown. A double-flowering type is also available. Black-eyed susans like full sun and ordinary soil. Mildew is a problem.

***Canna** (Canna)*   Canna is hardy through most of the Deep South. It is an excellent foliage plant (if you can keep the leaf-eating worms out) even when it is not in bloom. Dwarf types (up to three feet high) are available; my favorite is a plant of my greatgrandmother's which is five feet tall with maroon foliage and even taller spikes of red flowers. It had not bloomed for twenty years until I set some rhizomes in a sunny bed. Canna likes medium rich soil kept slightly moist. It produces summer foliage in shade and flowers in sun.

To see a world in a grain of sand
And heaven in a wild flower,
Hold infinity in the palm of your hand
And eternity in an hour.
William Blake

Cattail (*Typha*)   Cattails are great for low, wet areas. The tall thin foliage and conspicuous flower spikes add interest to a landscape. This plant is too good not to be used, though it is invasive.

Christmas Rose (*Helleborus*)   *Helleborus niger* is low growing, reaching a height of twelve inches. It has interesting foliage all winter, with white or pink flowers in December and January. Lenten rose (*H. orientalis*) flowers in late January to March and has purplish flowers with white shadings. It is a must for its winter foliage and has good-sized flowers at an unusual time of the year. It does not transplant well. Lenten rose likes shade and well-drained, moist soil.

By plucking her petals, you do not gather the beauty of the flower.

Rabindranath Tagore

Chrysanthemum (*Chrysanthemum*)   Several selections of Shasta daisies (May Queen, Alaska, and other varieties) bloom into the summer with clumpy foliage and flowers nearly three feet high. Painted daisy does well. My favorites are the common cushion mums for fall (there are many very good varieties; the available colors include red, rust, gold, yellow, white, pink, and mixed). Mums should be pinched a couple of times from spring to early July (do not prune after mid-July, or the flowers may freeze). Give chrysanthemums sun. Divide them in the spring every three years or so and give them away.

Coneflower (*Echinacea*)   The pretty Latin name is commonly used. This very attractive plant reaches four or five feet in height and is very easy to grow. It has a dark, nearly black cone with recurved purple petals. It attracts butterflies and is excellent in cutting gardens. Coneflower likes sun and poor soil. Mildew is a problem. Grow it with fennel for a striking combination.

Coreopsis (*Coreopsis*)   Coreopsis is undeniably one of the easiest perennials to grow and enjoy. It blooms yellow in the spring and lasts through summer if it is deadheaded (that is, if the spent flowers are promptly removed). It usually grows two or three feet high. Native species are fine, but Goldfink and Sunray are excellent hybrids (my wife likes the double-flowered Sunray more than I do). A summer roadside favorite is three-foot-high, many-branched *C. tinctoria* (one plant in the perennial border is enough). Coreopsis does well in sun and dry, poor soil.

Daffodil (*Narcissus*)   Some daffodils bloom as early as Thanksgiving; the rest hit from January until late March or later, depending on the weather. There are many varieties, shapes, and shades. King Alfred is one of the worst (not dependable; some bulb companies reportedly dump inferior bulbs together and call them all King Alfred). Good choices for a simple collection include Carlton (big yellow), Mt. Hood (big white), Tête-à-tête (miniature yellow), Thalia (miniature white), Ice Follies (yellow petals with off-white cup), Minnow (very tiny miniature yellow), and Poeticus (tall white with yellow cup ringed with red). Daffodils like sun but will do fine under deciduous trees if the soil is prepared well. Fertilize in fall, water in spring, and leave foliage alone (don't braid or mow) for at least six weeks after bloom fades. Divide every four or five years for continued blooming.

Daylily *(Hemerocallis)*   One of the showiest, easiest perennials, daylilies produce foliage up to two and one-half feet tall, with flower stalks (scapes) up to four feet high. Miniatures are available, both for plants and for flowers. Diploid varieties have normal growth and color. Tetraploids have more color, more flowers, and more scapes. Consider planting some of both. Hyperion is a good old yellow; Stella de Oro is a yellow tet that blooms from May until Thanksgiving. Lilies come in all colors except true blue, and there are many variations and flower types. They like sun, light shade, and well-prepared soil that is moist but on the dry side. Divide in winter, spring, and fall. Lilies may be transplanted (but not divided) into moist soil even when they are in bloom (if you work fast).

Elephant Ear *(Colocasia)*   These gaudy plants come in giant kinds and small ones and include dark variegated. Elephant ears are bolder than anything and very easy to grow. They like sun or light shade and prefer moist soil.

Fern   There are several very good types for shade (maidenhair, Christmas, ostrich, royal, and others) and some for part sun. Evergreen holly fern forms clumps and must have shade. It is very hardy, like aspidistra. Ferns prefer moist soil, not wet. Most are unusually invasive over time (but not holly or maidenhair). Ferns have an alluring, mysterious air about them and have a place in all shady gardens.

Four-o'clock *(Mirabilis)*   Four-o'clocks, waist-high plants, are very likely to invade even the worst soils. Their yellow or red tubular flowers open in late afternoon, fill the air with fragrance, and attract hummingbirds. Grown from seed they form a large tuber in the ground and become perennial. They are easy to transplant and easy to grow. They do well with full sun and plenty of neglect on poor soils. Four-o'clocks help keep yarrow upright in my garden and may need staking in rich soils.

Gayfeather *(Liatris)*   Gayfeather produces five- or six-foot spikes of pink or lavender. It is heat tolerant and excellent for backs of borders and behind smaller plants. A native plant, it prefers full sun. Gayfeather is easy to start.

Goldenrod *(Solidago)*   Hybrids are best, but all are welcome in the hot, late summer. Goldenrod has yellow flowers and grows up to four feet tall (some varieties reach only two feet). It should be contained in a bottomed-out bucket sunk into the ground. Goldenrod likes sun and poor soil (fertilizer makes it grow tall and flower less).

Grass   The grasses include several excellent ornamentals. Pampas has been overused; also worth considering are fountain grass, bamboos (these come in several sizes with various growth habits; some are badly invasive), and variegated giant. They are excellent for borders as a winter effect and are also useful in dried flower arrangements.

Iris   Irises offer good foliage effects even when they are not in bloom. Irises grow from two to four feet. Bearded iris blooms in April and May on tall plants, with many colors of blossoms; it produces the best flowers in full sun and is very showy. Siberian iris and Japanese iris tolerate light shade, have fewer colors (the Japanese are mostly blues and purples). Mine are planted shallow and are not mulched, to prevent rot. Divide iris in fall or early spring; sever rhizomes with sharp knife. I have so far had good success with the bulb-type Dutch iris, which gives interesting flowers on short plants. *I. Cristala* is a tiny native, very sweet. Louisiana iris does well in moist conditions. Pallida has variegated foliage worth considering.

Kudzu *(Pueraria)*   Kudzu, a conspicuously invasive plant, has its place as a fast vine (it can grow a foot a day) if it is controlled (it must be killed when it is out of bounds). It produces heavy-scented purple flowers in late summer. Kudzu needs little care but burns badly at the first touch of frost.

Lamb's-ear *(Stachys)*   Lamb's-ear is excellent for silver gray foliage and grows to two feet. It tolerates sun or light shade and sets off other plants. Lamb's-ear needs dividing every couple of years to correct center dieback.

Lavender Cotton *(Santolina)*   There are two types of santolina, one silver gray and one bright green. Both produce two-foot mounds of foliage and yellow button flowers. Full sun is required; well-drained soil is also a must.

Lily (*Lilium*)   The lilies are too many to mention. All are easy to grow in well-drained rich soil. They often need staking. Lilies grow three or four feet tall (some taller) and bloom between May and August. There are many unusual colors, from the white Easter lily (it blooms in May if grown outdoors) to turk's cap and tiger lily. These plants are a must for tall, showy effects. They like sun or light shade and moist, well-drained soil.

Loosestrife (*Lythrum*)   Loosestrife is similar in effect to liatris. An invasive plant, it reaches six feet in height and produces spikes of pink, red, or purple flowers in midsummer. It will tolerate light shade and wet soils.

Monkey Grass (*Liriope*)   The different types of monkey grass have different uses. *L. spicata* (lily turf) spreads rapidly and has spikes of blue flowers in late June and July. *L. muscari* forms slow-spreading clumps and has many types, including variegated. The flowers are purple and blue, white, and even pink. *L. muscari* can be set directly on top of well-prepared soil and will root standing up to give height to the plant. Don't be too quick to discount the various liriopes even as small shrubs (they reach two feet in height and maybe more). Some have incredible flower stalks and berries. Liriope grows well in sun, part shade, and dense shade. A smaller relative called mondo grass, or ophiopogon, makes an excellent dense ground cover in heavy shade and can even be mowed for a turf effect in shade. I use it to supply winter greenery where ferns, Solomon seal, and astilbe grow and in between hosta.

Peony (*Paeonia*)   The American Peony Society says that peonies don't grow in the Deep South, but many southerners enjoy them anyway. The blooms are very showy in spring, with white, pink, red, and maroon flowers. Established plants produce many four-inch flowers and foliage to two feet. Peonies must have well-drained soil, must be protected from hot sun, and must have plenty of cold in winter (no mulch). Early-blooming varieties are least likely to suffer heat and rain damage (heavy moisture will abort flowers, but the foliage will still be nice). It may take two or three years for a division to begin flowering. Give peonies morning sun, afternoon shade, and rich soil.

Peruvian Lily (*Alstroemeria*)   The Peruvian lily's spreading, not quite invasive, low-growing foliage seldom gets taller than a foot and sends up three-foot stalks topped with flaring, trumpetlike blossoms of red and yellow that are three inches long. The plant is a very good choice for cut flowers (they keep over a week), but it is old-fashioned and hard to find in catalogs. Peruvian lily prefers heavy to medium shade and rich soil.

Phlox *(Phlox)*   Phlox comes in several distinct kinds, all good (and all old-fashioned). *P. subulata* (moss phlox, or thrift) is a common traditional ground cover for rock walls, with pink-magenta the most common color. Phlox tolerates drought and heat and is low growing and cascading. *M. divaricata* (wild blue phlox) grows up to two feet tall, blooms even in shade (rare for a blue flower), and is loose and open in shade but compact in sun. *P. paniculata* (summer, or garden, phlox) is upright and branching and reaches a height of four feet. It comes in many colors that bloom from June onward and is very showy like crape myrtle. It is excellent for strong color on medium-sized plants. Mildew is a problem. Phlox does best in sun with good soil. Seedlings revert to common pinkish purple.

Plantain Lily *(Hosta)*   Hosta is underused. Its luxuriant summer foliage forms a rosette and reaches bushel-basket size (some species are small; others have larger or rounder leaves). The leaves come in many shades of green, bluish, yellow, and cream; variegated foliage is also available. Hosta produces flowers on stalks to four feet in May and June. Some are very showy. It may be used as border, for accent, or in a mass. It is easy to divide in spring as foliage begins to emerge, and it rapidly becomes established. Hosta likes shade and moist woodsy soil.

Pokeweed *(Phytolacca)*   Pokeweed's poisonous berries look attractive hanging in loose clusters from the tall, multibranched plants with red stems. They create a nice weeping effect. Poor soil and full sun are all that is needed.

Salvia *(Salvia)*   *S. farinacea* is an upright, vase-shaped plant that grows to three feet or a little more in height and is constantly covered from spring to fall with spikes of blue flowers suitable for cutting. It is good for bees, and the cool blue color is hard to beat in the summer. *S. farinacea* grows easily from seed and comes back vigorously every year. *S. superba* is similar, with intense, purple-blue spikes. *S. elegans* (pineapple sage) is a four- or five-foot late bloomer, probably the best red plant for hummingbirds. *S. leucantha* (Mexican sage) is tall and bushy, late blooming, and purple.

Sedum *(Sedum)*   The sedums include some classic perennials. The upright, bushel-basket-sized *S. spectabile* is a widely grown, extremely hardy multistemmed plant up to two feet tall and nearly as broad across. It has fleshy light green leaves and produces showy heads of flowers from late summer until frost (even the seed heads are interesting). "Indian Chief" is a common name. The varieties Brilliant and Autumn Joy bloom pink and maroon, respectively. Sedum is very easily propagated from cuttings (incredibly easy to root) or by division. Sun is needed for flowers, shade for foliage alone. Other sedums are ground covers and evergreen.

Snowflake *(Leucojum)* Snowflake is the perfect complement for other spring bulbs. Up to two feet in height, this clump-forming plant makes nice winter foliage (like monkey grass) and has stalks of nodding, bell-shaped white flowers with a green spot on each petal. It is hard to beat for hardiness. An autumn-flowering variety is available and one with yellow spots.

To create a little flower is the labour of ages.
William Blake

Spider and Resurrection Lilies *(Lycoris)* Lycoris supplies foliage in winter for a seasonal clump effect and flowers on leafless scapes in August and September. Spider lily has red flowers on stalks up to two feet tall with winter foliage like liriope. The resurrection lily has two-foot scapes with several pink trumpets and broad, light green winter foliage up to two feet tall. It is very striking to see these two spring up from nowhere in the late summer. The foliage makes a good seasonal border or accent. Lycoris needs winter sun and well-drained soil.

Spiderwort *(Tradescantia)* Spiderwort, a native, is excellent for blue flowers (white and pink are available) on ends of stalks that reach one and one-half or two feet. The leaves and stems are succulent. The three-petaled flowers measure up to an inch across. Spiderwort is easy to grow from cuttings or division. It is tolerant of moist or dry soil, sun or shade (it grows dense and short in sun, leggy in shade). Spring and summer flowers fade by noon.

Stokesia *(Stokesia)* Stokes' aster is easy to grow. Foliage in a one-and-one-half-inch rosette produces stalks with one- or two-inch light blue flowers (a white cultivar is available) suitable for cutting. Stokesia is a good companion for daylilies. It is heat and drought resistant and flowers best in full sun.

Tuberose *(Polianthes)* Tuberoses are clumpy plants up to one foot high, with three-foot spires of extremely fragrant white flowers in early July to mid-July. There are single and double forms. Tuberoses make good cut flowers to sweeten up the barn.

Verbena *(Aloysia)* Verbena has intense purple-blue flowers from May until fall on thickly spreading ground cover. In cultivation it gets rank and lean and may even stop flowering. It is very invasive, spreads by underground stolons, and needs the worst possible soil, hot sun, and no care whatsoever.

***Violet* (*Viola*)**   These low-growing winter plants have purple, pink, or white flowers and like shade.

***Woolly Mullein* (*Verbascum*)**   Mullein, a biennial (it reseeds every two years), has wide, thick, hairy gray leaves on a single gray stalk. It sends the flowering stem up to seven feet or more, with dozens of yellow flowers. It should be replanted from seedlings every year. Mullein favors sun and dry soil.

***Yarrow* (*Achillea*)**   Yarrow has ferny leaves and grows three to four feet tall (it needs small stakes). Flat heads of white, pink, red, yellow, or gold flowers appear from spring to late summer and are good for drying. I grow yarrow among four-o'clocks for support, to add interesting contrast, and to have both plants out of the way. Yarrow prefers mostly sun and will tolerate moist or dry soil. It may become invasive.

***Yucca* (*Yucca*)**   Yucca comes in several types, some clump forming (not tall and likely to fall over). My favorite is *Y. fila-mentosa*, which gets only two or three feet tall but wider (it is never out of control). Distinctive, threadlike filaments hang off the edges of the leaves. A tall stalk with many white flowers appears in the spring. Yuccas are excellent for anchoring the perennial border during winter when little else is green.

Herbs

The culinary, ornamental, and medicinal herbs are among the most interesting plants you can grow. Different plants have different requirements where light, moisture, space, and soil pH are concerned. For most of them, however, well-drained soil, water, and cooling mulch in the summer are critically important.

Most herbs may be started quite readily from seeds, from transplants, or from divisions and cuttings taken from established plants (see table 20). Some hard-to-find herbs, such as French tarragon, are not available from seeds and must be grown from cuttings; the tarragon found on seed racks is not French but an inferior selection. Cuttings often root readily in water or in a well-drained potting soil (a peat and perlite mixture with perhaps some sand

Table 20. **Herbs for the Home Garden**

HERB	BOTANICAL NAME	PLANTING TIME	PROPAGATION	HEIGHT[a]
		Perennials		
Balm	*Melissa officinalis* Linn.	spring	seed, divisions, cuttings	medium
Catnip	*Nepeta cataria* Linn.	fall, early spring	seed, root divisions	tall
Chives	*Allium schonoprasum* Linn.	early spring	bulbs, seed	medium
Costmary	*Chrysanthemum balsamita* var. *tenacetoides* Linn.	spring	seed, root divisions	medium
Garlic	*Allium sativum* Linn.	fall	bulbs	medium
Fragrant geraniums (apple, lemon, peppermint, rose, cold tender; treat as an annual)	*Geranium* spp.	spring	rooted cuttings, divisions	medium
Horehound	*Marrubium vulgare* Linn.	early spring	seed, root division	tall
Hyssop	*Hyssopus officinalis* Linn.	spring	seed, rooted cuttings, root divisions	medium
Lavender	*Lavendula vera* D.C.	fall spring	rooted cuttings (seeds best in cold frame)	medium
Mint (apple, orange, peppermint, spearmint)	*Mentha* spp.	spring	cuttings, stolons	tall
Sweet marjoram	*Origanum majorana* Linn.	spring	from seed started inside, cuttings, crown divisions	medium
Parsley (biennial)	*Petroselinum hortense* Hoffm.	early spring	from seed indoors	medium
Pennyroyal	*Mentha pulegium* Linn.	spring	divisions	low
Rosemary	*Rosmarinus officinalis* Linn.	spring	seed indoors, cuttings, divisions	medium
Sage	*Salvia officinalis* Linn.	spring	seeds, cuttings, layerage, divisions	medium
Tansy	*Tanacetum vulgare* Linn.	spring	seed, divisions	tall
Tarragon	*Artemisia dracunculus* Linn.	fall spring	seed indoors, cuttings, root divisions	medium
Bush thyme	*Thymus vulgaris* Linn.	spring	seed indoors, divisions, cuttings	medium
Winter savory	*Satureia montana* Linn.	spring	seed	low
		Annuals		
Anise	*Pimpinella anisum* Linn.	early spring	seed directly in garden	medium
Basil	*Ocimum basilicum* Linn.	early spring	seed	medium

Table 20. (continued)

HERB	BOTANICAL NAME	PLANTING TIME	PROPAGATION	HEIGHT[a]
		Annuals		
Borage	*Borago officinalis* Linn.	early spring	seed, resows itself	tall
Dill	*Anthemum graveolens* Linn.	spring	seed, resows itself	tall
Fennel	*Foeniculum vulgare* Hill.	late fall, early spring	seed, resows itself	tall
Sesame	*Sesamum indicum* Linn.	spring	seed	tall
Summer savory	*Satureia hortensis* Linn.	spring	seed	medium

[a]Height: low = one to twelve inches; medium = twelve to eighteen inches; tall = eighteen or more inches.

Source: Cooperative Extension Service, United States Department of Agriculture.

added). Avoid setting plants outdoors too early in the season, when the soil is still cool, and prune mildewed plants severely to force healthy new growth.

Do not use pesticides, even so-called natural ones, on herbs that will be added to food or tea. None of the pesticides now available has been cleared for use on herbs. Insects and diseases are sometimes problems in southern herb gardens, but the best controls are cultural techniques. Buy only plants of good quality, or raise your own; provide well-drained soil; and avoid watering late in the day (plants should be dry before dark). Weed and water regularly. Remove diseased plants as soon as you spot them so that problems do not spread. Insects are best controlled by hand picking the large ones. Lizards and praying mantids will consume large quantities of insects each day.

Some of the perennial herbs are hardy enough to do well outdoors through the winter. Others may not stand our rainy season or the heat of the summer. Some are borderline and may do well one year and not the next or may vary from town to town (and may even perform better or worse in different soils or beds in the same yard).

My garden has oregano mixed in with liriope so that it stays out of the way (and I love the way the flowers rise above the lavender spikes of the monkey grass). My attempts to grow cumin have thus far failed miserably, however. Last time, when it finally did begin to flower and make seeds, it began to disappear, and I discovered by flashlight that snails and slugs preferred it to everything else I had planted.

Parsley is exceptionally aromatic and lush when it is harvested fresh from your own herb garden. Even though it must be replanted every year, it is usually easy to grow if it is kept watered in the summer. Basil is also prolific from seed or transplant. Strongly scented and tasty, it comes in several shapes, sizes, and even colors. The common sweet basil grows to knee high or taller, and dark opal basil is nearly as big, with purple leaves (very attractive in a flower bed). Pinch off the flower spikes to keep the plants bushy and leafy. A small, compact, little-leaf basil called Spicy Globe has done well for me all summer as a foot-tall mounded border. Its tiny flowers are a delicate frosting. Lemon basil and cinnamon basil are other variations on the theme. The different types have distinct flavors and may be preserved in oil or vinegar for salad dressing. Mixed with a little oil, garlic, and pine nuts or walnuts, basil makes a fine pesto sauce for pasta, tomatoes, and even eggs.

Sages, thymes, and mints come in a wild array of flavors and sizes. They (and other herbs) lose quality toward the end of the day and are best gathered as soon as the morning dew has evaporated. Most of the volatile oils which give herbs their flavors and aromas are produced in great amounts just before and during the flowering stage of plant growth. Fresh herbs have the best flavor, but they lose their freshness after several days even when they are refrigerated. If a recipe calls for dry herbs or doesn't specify, use twice the amount of fresh.

Parsley, marjoram, chives, thyme, and basil are some of the herbs that do well as house plants in pots. One of the major advantages of herbs is their adaptability to pot culture. Even in the ground, herbs do best in raised beds (which are simply large containers of well-amended soil). In fact, some herbs really ought to be grown in pots, for they won't overwinter outside. Try basil, sage, parsley, thyme, mint, chives, rosemary, and lemon verbena. Herbs grown in containers or in areas that get heavy rainfall should have very light feedings once or twice a year but never during the flowering stage, when volatile oils are being produced at their peak. Too much fertilizer (even a little too much) can cause rapid, weak growth that is low in the oils responsible for the herb's flavor.

Dry herbs by placing them between paper towels and setting

There is one thing that you will find practically impossible to carry into your own greenhouse, and that is tension.

Charles Potter

them in a microwave oven for a minute. Check them for dryness after they cool, then microwave them for a few more seconds until they are crumbly. Store them in dark jars (light causes them to lose flavor). This method is suitable for use with basil, sage, mint, and oregano. Air drying may work for some herbs, but southern humidity increases the amount of time needed, and some herbs darken when they are air dried. Try spreading them on paper in a warm oven (temperature of 150 degrees or less) with the doors ajar for several hours.

Freeze fresh herbs after rinsing off dust and patting away the moisture. Then place them in freezer bags and freeze immediately. Snip off pieces and mince them while the herbs are still frozen. Mint, tarragon, parsley, chives, and marjoram freeze well. You can also wash fresh herbs, chop them, and freeze them in ice cube trays filled with water. When cubes have formed, store them in plastic bags and pop them frozen into soups, stews, and sauces.

Herb vinegars and oils are a snap to create and make nice gifts. Gather fresh herbs (dill, basil, tarragon, mint, oregano, and rosemary, singly or in combination), rinse off the dust, and pat them completely dry (any remaining moisture will cloud vinegar). Pack clean jars or bottles nearly full with leaves, some of which have been lightly crushed. Fill with olive oil or with hot (but not boiling) vinegar. Cover and steep for three or four weeks at room temperature. Strain and bottle before use.

House Plants

Holiday plants, such as poinsettia and Christmas cactus, have peculiar needs, especially coming as they do from warm, humid greenhouses into a relatively dry home. Winter is a difficult season for house plants, since they aren't growing as vigorously as in warmer days. Then, too, we run our heaters and dry out the air. Plants' problems are compounded by overcast weather, low humidity, lack of light, overwatering, and drafts. Move plants away from windows at night if the window is leaky or if the weather is severe. Watch for insects, particularly spider mites and mealybugs, and treat as soon as you spot a problem. Remember, too, that plants may die if they get either too much or too little water. Give plants a thorough soaking in a sink or tub (soak thoroughly until water drains from the bottom of the pot). Then wait until the soil gets dry again. Don't judge dryness just by looking at the soil; you can usually tell by simply lifting the pot to gauge its weight. In the case of large pots, probe the soil deeply with your finger.

Poinsettias should be pruned back by the very last day of August so that they will have plenty of time to bush out and produce a concentrated display. They require lots of tender care, but they can be made to bloom at any time of the year as long as they are given good growing conditions during the day and thirteen or fourteen hours of total darkness every night without fail for a month or so. Since it is their new growth which turns red (or white, depending upon the cultivar), the plants must be kept growing actively during the day. In other words, they need bright light (perhaps a little sun), plenty of water (the soil should be neither too wet nor too dry), and light fertilization (follow the directions on the label). You may move the plants into a dark room every afternoon and bring them back out the next morning, or you may cover them with boxes at night. Pinching or light pruning can force poinsettias to branch out and be bushier, with more flower bracts later. Pinch them no later than September 1 for Christmas blooms; begin giving them long nights in early October.

Christmas cactus can be made to bloom almost any time of year by tricking nature. You must provide cool nights, dry soil, and short days. Withhold water (but not to the point of letting the plant wither), and at the same time bring the pot indoors at night into a very cool room (you may prefer to leave it out in the fall except when frost is predicted). At the same time keep it in a dark room for thirteen or fourteen hours every night (but provide light during the day as usual). Buds should start forming within a few weeks. When they do, you can stop the special treatment, begin watering again, and give the plant a very light application of a balanced fertilizer made for house plants.

When spring comes, house plants may be moved outdoors, but do not set them directly in the sun after they have been in a dark house. If you do, they will show signs of sunburn within weeks. Place them initially in a shaded area outdoors for a spring cleanup. Inspect them for mites on the undersides of leaves, repot as necessary, trim away scraggly, leggy winter branches to promote denser and more vigorous stems and growth, and fertilize lightly. While

No plant is a "house" plant. All are invited guests. Choose adaptable types that will "accept" your invitation.

Neil Sperry

the plants are outside they will need protection from strong spring winds and drying, since they will lose moisture more quickly in warmer weather and brighter light than they did indoors. Ferns and airplane or spider plants may be divided at this time. Cuttings taken from many plants will root quickly during the next couple of months.

Ideal containers for growing herbs and other potted plants in summer and fall include baskets, lined wooden crates, barrels, old watering cans, and all sorts of construction pipes and flues. We have all seen old tires painted white and filled with iris and moss rose, but daylilies and periwinkle also look nice planted in them.

Clay pots dry out more quickly than plastic pots but can be sunk into the ground and mulched with sawdust to slow down evaporation. Sawdust also deters snails. Containers dry quickly in the heat of July, especially clay pots and small containers with large plants. Be sure to water thoroughly (I prefer to water everything twice around, so that the second watering really soaks in). Some plants may do best in the full sun, but they will sometimes need watering sometimes every day or two. Mulches on the surface of potting soil, even pebbles, can slow the rate of evaporation. Hanging baskets in particular can dry out and will either become permanently susceptible to wilt or will suffer root damage from being allowed to stay dry even once. Light fertilization with a balanced, water-soluble plant food in July can give potted plants and baskets just the right pick-me-up so that they will keep looking good in the fall.

In October you should examine indoor plants for problems, rinse them off with tepid water, and begin withholding fertilizers, which won't be needed as much in the winter. Before bringing plants indoors for the winter, give them a few days (and if possible a couple of weeks) in an interim location, so that they can gradually adjust to less light and lower humidity. In response to reduced light and humidity many plants naturally lose a few leaves (quite a few in some cases) when they are brought indoors. They will normally begin to put forth new ones within a few weeks, however. Avoid the temptation to overwater or fertilize to compensate.

Before moving the pots indoors, check carefully for insects and mites. Wash the leaves, top and bottom, with mild, soapy water to remove dust and insect eggs. Soak the soil at least once with copious amounts of water to flush out ants, roaches, centipedes, and

I think the reason most of us do like houseplants is simply that they are alive.

Jerry Baker

pillbugs. Mild liquid insecticides can be used as drenches, but be very careful to water the soil several hours or more beforehand to avoid root burn. Do not use Malathion on jade plants or ferns. Read the label for other restrictions.

New plants purchased during the winter should be placed out of drafts and away from cold windowpanes but in spots where they can get lots of light. Water them only as necessary (lift the pot). Fertilizers are generally not needed during the winter months, since low light and low humidity keep most plants growing slowly. You can raise the humidity by grouping plants together.

To everything there is a season, and a time to every
purpose under the heaven.

Ecclesiastes

Felder's Magnolia Almanac
Southern Gardening
Month by Month

JANUARY

Things to See Now   "There are those that bloom in the winter" reads the inscription at the foot of gnarled camellia shrubs in
Mynelle Gardens in Jackson, Mississippi. Camellias are at their
peak in January—red, pink, white, and variegated, they may have
had some damage from severe freezing winds, but will usually continue to bloom out the rest of this month and into the next. Also
enjoy the promise of spring in newly-emerging daffodil foliage, interesting new birds, bare branches, berries, ice crystals on the car
window, the neighbor's hybrid pansies (still in bloom in spite of it
all), wood smoke, funny winter hats, and little tufts of wild garlic
bringing seasonal attention to the lawns.

Vegetables   Cold, rainy weather makes a great time to plan the
year's activities and study seed catalogs. Be sure to check the All-
America Selections. When you choose varieties, look for disease
resistance. Order large enough quantities for continuous planting,
and leave space in the garden each year for experimentation.

Sow seeds in a coldframe for transplanting to the garden in

179

Save Those Ashes   Wood ashes are very alkaline and can be used in the garden and on the lawn if not piled on too heavily in any one spot. Ashes from the fireplace have many valuable micronutrients as well as generous amounts of potash, so they can enrich the flower beds as well. The problems with ashes are two-fold: they are strong, and so must be used sparingly, and they are highly water-soluble, which means they wash away quickly and should be replaced every couple of months or so. Do not use ashes or other liming material around such acid-loving plants as azalea, dogwood, camellia, Irish potato, blueberry, or centipede grass.

March. You can start broccoli, cabbage, leeks, and cauliflower now. Meanwhile, till the vegetable garden at the first opportunity so as to incorporate compost and other organic materials.

This is also a good time to have your soil tested if you haven't done so for three years or more and are worried about excess fertilizers or acidity. Weather permitting, you could also put out onion sets or transplants for spring bulbs. If a really cold spell comes, though, your onions may bolt before they have made bulbs.

Remove weeds from the asparagus bed, and fertilize by broadcasting half a pound of a general garden fertilizer per 100 square feet. Add a layer of fresh mulch to discourage late winter and summer weeds. If you buy Irish potato seed potatoes now, you can cut them into egg-sized pieces and air dry them indoors for two or three weeks before setting them out. Your foresight this month will prevent the potatoes from rotting later on. Allow ten pounds of seed potatoes per 100 feet of row.

Fruit Plants   Watch for a pretty day and prune the muscadine vine—or prepare the soil to set out one or two vines. Muscadines should be pruned heavily every winter, or they will become an unproductive, tangled mass.

You can plant peaches, apples, pears, and plums right now or as soon as they arrive at your local nursery. Be sure that you don't let the roots dry out, even for a few minutes, or the plants may be permanently stunted. Have the nurseryman place the trees in bags packed with moist sawdust. Prune the trees when setting them out. Mulch and water figs heavily to prevent winter injury from freezing or wind drying.

Ornamentals   When weather permits, cut back ornamental grasses, now completely dormant, to less than a foot from the ground. Add the trimmings to the compost heap or use them as mulch.

Bring spring indoors by cutting limbs from budding forsythia, jasmine, pussy willow, and honeysuckle. Simply remove branches with a broad, angular cut and set them in lukewarm water. Replace the water and recut the stems weekly until flowering subsides. Look around the landscape for healthy, pencil-thin shoots from last year's growth to collect next month for hardwood cuttings.

Select summer bulbs such as gladiolus, tuberose, amaryllis, caladium, dahlia, and elephant ears at your local nursery this month before they have been picked over. Good bulbs should be firm and unblemished, like cooking onions. Store bulbs at room temperature until planting time. Remember that caladiums, which are tropical tubers, will be injured by temperatures below 50 or 55 degrees. Pot them up and set them in a sunny window where the temperature is 65–70 degrees.

Winter damage to landscape plants in January often appears as browning out in July. Cover roots with a four- or five-inch layer of mulch so that they do not dry out. Avoid transplanting shrubs, trees, or flowers this month; wait until late February or March.

House Plants House plants grow less vigorously this month than they will in warmer weather. Watch for insects, particularly spider mites and mealybugs, and take appropriate measures promptly.

Water plants by giving them a thorough soaking in a sink or tub, then withhold water until the soil becomes dry again. Too much water kills just as surely as too little. Protect your house plants as much as possible from the winter hazards of low humidity, lack of light, dearth or excess of water, and drafts.

Lawn This is not the time to fertilize, but you may want to apply a preemergence chemical for summer weeds. Before you buy, make sure the weed killer is safe for use on your particular type of lawn, and wait a few weeks afterward before sowing grass seeds. Many pesky weeds, such as dandelions, garlic, and wild onions, are small and can be treated very effectively with postemergence herbicides. If you do a thorough job now, you'll have none of these weeds for the rest of the winter and spring.

Reminder Don't forget to feed the birds! They need not only food but also water. Bird food is not cheap, but it is better to get the best rather than use cheap "wild bird" mixes which may have large amounts of inedible bulk. Sunflower seeds are the best all-around bird food, but mixing them with thistle and bread crumbs and other foods will attract a greater variety of birds. Scatter some

The most noteworthy thing about gardeners is that they are always optimistic, always enterprising, and never satisfied. They always look forward to doing better than they have ever done before.
Vita Sackville-West

on the ground for shy birds, and good luck with the squirrels. Look for pine siskins, cedar waxwings, and golden finches (not golden yet). And don't forget birds need fresh water!

FEBRUARY

Things to See Now   American narcissism at its best! Daffodils have been peeking about for a while, but February's show is too satisfying for description. Entire hillsides are covered with naturalized varieties, and scattered, neat rows of yellow and white nodding blossoms show where old homesteads once stood. There are surprise clumps where no one remembered daffodils had ever been tempting many to gather flowers from the neighborhood. Heleboris (Lenten rose) is at its best, although a little of the foliage burned by winter winds may be removed for better display of the flowers (more leaves will grow later). Snowflakes (Leucojum), violets, early spirea, and forsythia are almost always the first signs of spring, even in this month of dreary rains and frosts dashing enthusiasm bred by days of summer-like sunshine. This month shows off the dark cedars and bright white sycamore bark, and early plums will quite predictably have their rosy-pink flowers caught by frost.

Birds are more frantic now than before, and berries from nandina and holly begin to disappear in alarming numbers. The squirrels somehow know when bird food is put out. And here's hoping the groundhog up north didn't see his shadow!

Vegetables   Use the few days of good weather to turn leaves and compost under and prepare rows for spring. In the process you will uncover overwintering insects and prevent the late winter weeds from getting too large later. If a soil test showed that you need lime, now is the time to add it—or you can have your soil tested this month if you aren't sure.

The Irish potatoes you prepared last month can be set outside in a protected place for a few days before planting to allow them to cool off from being indoors. Don't plant potatoes too deeply, or they will rot. They can be mulched heavily and will still make a fine crop in the mulch.

You can set out onions, English peas, turnips, swiss chard, beets, carrots, and transplants of broccoli, cabbage, and cauliflower this month, but be prepared to cover tender seedlings with

Probably more pests can be controlled in an armchair in front of a February fire with a garden notebook and a seed catalog than can ever be knocked out in hand-to-hand combat in the garden.

Neely Turner

One snake in the compost is all I care for, although there are a couple others I would tolerate. I have no qualms whatsoever about the little brown "worm" snakes that live in the mulch; they eat slugs and spiders, crickets and roaches. And they are too small even to be scary, except perhaps when first encountered (is snake fear genetic or learned?)— rarely do they get over eight or ten inches long, remaining gray-brown and gentle when disturbed. Their cousin the Dekay snake is not much bigger but has a pretty pattern.

All in all, everyone should be kinder to the garden reptiles and amphibians. Toad, anole, skink, brown snake—it's their world, too, and all we do is plant things to attract food for them. Just be sure to check the potted plants before bringing them in for the off season—many a houseplant has suddenly sprouted baby reptiles in mid-winter, as the warmth indoors incubates eggs.

Just One Snake

plastic or hay during sudden freezing winds. Tubers of Jerusalem artichokes can be planted, but don't forget that they spread wildly.

Take the tiller and other power equipment into the shop for a tuneup. Change the sparkplug, oil, and air filter. Sharpen blades and tines. Have wheels and cables greased, too.

Fruit Plants   Plant new trees, vines, and bushes now if the selection at the garden center isn't too poor. Never allow roots to dry out before planting, and don't forget to prune new plants when you set them in the ground.

Spray trees with dormant oil to control overwintering scale insects, but don't spray if a freeze is predicted within two or three days.

Ornamentals   To commemorate Arbor Day, the Soil Conservation Service, Forestry Commission, or Cooperative Extension Service may be offering free tree seedlings in your area. This month is fine for setting out bare-root or container trees if the soil is well prepared (no easy task in February) and if the plants are watered when they are set out.

George Washington's Birthday is the traditional day for pruning roses in the South except for the spring-blooming climbers. Cut back last year's growth and remove dead canes, clutter, and blackened, diseased plant parts. This is the ideal time to replace or plant roses, since nurseries have stock and the worst of the winter is over.

Prune landscape shrubs now, especially junipers, cedars, arborvitae, and hemlock. Wait until after flowering to prune spring bloomers such as azalea, kerria, quince, and weigela. Boxwoods can be pruned, too, although they take longer to put forth new growth.

Hardwood cuttings may be taken now of rose, althea, crape myrtle, forsythia, spirea, and other deciduous shrubs. Insert ten-inch cuttings of last summer's growth into well-drained soil so that only two or three inches protrude from the ground. As the cuttings leaf out in the spring, roots will begin to grow. Water and mulch during the summer, and transplant to permanent locations in the fall.

Fertilize trees and shrubs by broadcasting a light application of a balanced plant food under the branches (not on the trunks) and watering it in. Use a scant handful of fertilizer (about half a cup per square yard) for small shrubs, established older shrubs, and even trees.

Mondo grass and liriope can be neatened for the year by cutting off the old, winter-damaged foliage from last year. Use very sharp shears or a keen knife to remove the old leaves. Also remove the dead foliage of iris, daylilies, chrysanthemums, phlox, peonies, and other dormant perennials. Mulch pansies and other tender plants to protect them from hard freezes.

Pull ice off bent tree limbs, and prune out broken branches or storm-damaged plants. Prune branches flush with the trunk; stubs do not heal properly and invite decay.

This is one of the best months for transplanting trees and shrubs. Smaller transplants, especially trees between knee and waist high, will nearly always outgrow larger ones, since more of their roots are saved in proportion to their tops. Remember that side roots are usually more important than deep roots.

Attack winter weeds with postemergence herbicides, and use preemergence material to anticipate summer weeds. *Do not* fertilize your lawn this month or next unless you have winter rye as an overseeded winter lawn, in which case a light feeding is appropriate.

Reminder   Birds need food and water now more than ever! Purple martins will need clean houses by the end of the month, and the most popular all-purpose bird food will include sunflower seeds with a little millet. Suet will be rewarding for woodpeckers and other hard-to-attract birds. Water will be very important for birds when the weather is dry, windy, or freezing.

MARCH

Things to See Now Odd weather to give gardeners fits—balmy days followed by screaming winter storms and winds, hail destroying the daffodils the night before a show. Color is everywhere, both in the field and on the vine, and the subtle shades of green give trees and shrubs their distinctive spring mantle. Colors: buttercups across the fields, yellow jessamine and wisteria, white iris "flags" around older homes, tulips, the first hummingbirds, dogwood, the gaudy redbud, and, if you are fortunate enough to have one, the star magnolia, mole hills, more and more daffodils of all kinds, rampant lawn "weeds" (garlic and onions, henbit and chickweed) spicing up the brown plain of the neighborhood, wild pears and other fruit trees in bloom, bedding plants at local garden centers, garlic flower heads, oak catkins, and pine candles.

As neighborhoods come alive with azaleas (even normally-dreary homes take on a gay atmosphere with these traditionally over-used shrubs), kites begin to flutter in the skies as warm breezes stir fuzzy new leaflets in treetops. Fisherwomen are out on the river bank (sitting on their bait buckets, since the soil is still cold).

Moss-pink cascades from rock walls and around country mailboxes, and the first pink oxalis blossoms appear atop the old-fashioned clover clumps. Bees begin buzzing in earnest over the hollies as the anticipated "surprise" frost nips early deutzia and other spring bloomers. Nondescript clumps in perennial borders and beds begin their spring push into the sun.

Vegetables Ask your county agent to tell you the average frost-free date for your area, and use the information as a tool for planning without regarding it as a hard and fast rule. Don't be tempted by the occasional unseasonably warm days this month; bypass the warm-season vegetables for now (instead, start them in a coldframe, keep the roots warm, and provide lots of sunshine to promote strong stems). Outdoors, plant seeds of lettuce (try the newer, more colorful varieties, such as Red Sails, for ornamental as well as nutritional value), radish, salad onions, sweet corn, beets,

> You fight dandelions all weekend, and late Monday afternoon there they are, pert as all get out, in full and gorgeous bloom, pretty as can be, thriving as only dandelions can in the face of adversity.
>
> *Hal Borland*

Chufas

Used to be, folks would plant some chufas in the spring for harvest the following fall (one fellow related to me a story about the worst whipping he ever got, when as a boy he ate all the chufa in the house, so there was none to plant in the spring). According to Euell Gibbons, ancient Egyptians ate chufas, even put them in tombs of Pharoahs (who apparently "wouldn't be caught dead without a supply"). Although there was already a native chufa here, a strain from Africa was introduced to the South as a potential money crop in the mid-1800s, but the harvest labor was too great and folks who bought groceries apparently weren't interested enough.

Chufa is a nutsedge, like coco grass, but one with tubers that are perfectly edible. It is not quite crunchy, but full of sweet white "milk" with a flavor that is unusual but not disagreeable, something like coconut and almond. It is good fresh, can be roasted until brown and ground into a coffee substitute (without the caffeine), or dried in a very slow oven and ground into flour (usually mixed half and half with wheat flour).

Get chufa tubers where game food is sold; nowadays, only turkey hunters plant the things (a fellow gave me a bagful from his supply). A current popular seed catalog offers chufa for sale. It would be worth a try in a friable, moist soil.

---

spinach, and turnips. Coldframes can get very hot in March, so be prepared to open and close them as necessary.

Black plastic, row covers, hot caps, and other devices for warming the soil, however temporary, can help your summer garden get off to an early start, particularly in the case of eggplants, tomatoes, squash, and peppers. With these plants you should avoid using organic mulches, which will actually prevent the soil from warming up.

Irish potatoes blackened by frost this month will usually put forth new growth and produce well. They and other late winter vegetables will need an additional light sidedressing with fertilizer to promote fast growth and maturity. Provide plenty of water during warm spells, and keep weeds pulled from between onions and other closely spaced root crops.

Fruit Plants Strawberries can be set out now in garden rows or wider beds. Soil must be prepared well, with the addition of plenty of organic material and a little fertilizer. Give the plants plenty of space to run this summer, and remove flowers to promote vigorous new growth (most folks would rather have the first few strawberries, but if these are allowed to form, the plants may be weak and unproductive later). If rots have been a problem in the past, ask your Cooperative Extension Service for a spray guide; most diseases must be anticipated with a preventive measure rather than attacked with a cure.

Spray fruit trees with a combination of insecticide and fungicide from bud break until harvest if you had problems last year. Most garden centers sell these combination sprays premixed. Be sure to read and follow label instructions. If young trees are bearing no fruit, there is no real need to spray them regularly. Spray early; once insects and diseases attack, you have no good way of regaining control. Don't use insecticides while bees are working your flowers. If you kill the bees, you'll have no fruit set. Wait until most of the flower petals have dropped and bees are no longer present.

Bees sometimes spread the bacterium that causes fire blight on apples, pears, quince, and crabapple. You can spray with streptomycin, available at your local garden center, during blossom time to prevent the bacteria from infecting your trees. The spray doesn't hurt bees and must be applied as they work the flowers. This is the only time of year when streptomycin sprays are effective. Don't worry about spraying peaches and plums.

Fertilize fruit trees by broadcasting a light amount under the outer spread of branches and watering it in. Most mature plants need about a pound or two per year of age (the exception is blueberries, which do fine with little or none).

This may be the last call for setting out bare-root vines and trees, since they will be too shocked if they are set out after they bud or leaf out. Be sure to water newly set fruits thoroughly during the first summer (once a week is about right if the soakings are slow and deep and the plants have been mulched to prevent excessive drying).

Ornamentals   The most important factor in success with landscape plants, other than choosing a good plant properly to begin with, is soil preparation. Be sure your plants have well-drained soil and adequate water; nursery stock in small containers will dry out quickly if it is not planted in soil that roots can readily penetrate.

Fertilize existing shrubs and trees with all-purpose plant foods this month or next, using a quart (two pounds) for every hundred square feet. Mulches should be at least three inches deep; add more mulch as the old layer settles. Prune spring-blooming shrubs as soon as the flowers are gone. Avoid a flat-topped effect by cutting at different angles.

Examine shrubs and small trees for split bark caused by winter damage.

Lawn   Rake last fall's leaves now, or mow them into mulch, so that the sun's rays reach your lawn as it starts to green up. Mowing will also kill many winter weeds before they go to seed.

Winter weeds now at their peak include dandelion, henbit, garlic, onion, chickweed, and buttercups. Control them with sprays, but avoid combination weed killers and fertilizers; fertilizers now are useless to your lawn and may promote weed growth. Two or three applications of postemergence sprays may be needed to eliminate existing weeds, but preemergence weed killers applied now can defeat crabgrass, dallisgrass, and other summer villains before they get started.

Cut old leaves from mondo grass without damaging the tender new ones. Be prepared to use insecticides at the first sign of pests. Pick off diseased flowers from azaleas to prevent problems next year. House plants may need repotting or dividing now. The best selection of summer bulbs—caladiums, lilies, freesias, gladiolus, and so forth—is available right now.

Reminder   Take a drive around the town and into the country to see what you'd like to have next year in your own landscape. Pick a flower or two, and smile at other gardeners. Cut old leaves from monkey grass without damaging the tender new growth. Birds are in their spring transition and need water and food. Soil temperatures are still cold, and summer flowers and vegetables will rot or become stunted if made to get outside too early. Watch for insects on plants, and control them at first signs to prevent heavier infestations later or to keep diseases from being spread. Pick off diseased flowers from azaleas to prevent next year's problems. Houseplants may need repotting or dividing now, at the beginning of the season. The best selection of summer bulbs (caladiums, lilies, freesias, gladiolus) is to be had right now, before the "Good Friday rush."

APRIL

Things to See Now: People are out, waiting for ball games and Good Friday, stretching unused parts of their bodies and crowding the garden centers as if spring is the only time of the year for planting. Lawns begin greening up, spotted with Star-of-Bethlehem and bordered with fresh foliage of liriope and sedum, and iris of all types everywhere—the showiest flower of the month. Tulips and nearly the last of the daffodils are soon followed by some very early daylilies and canna. Spiderwort and bleeding heart begin their show along with fiddleheads of summer ferns and yarrow. Columbine, sweet William, coral-bells, lunaria, blue phlox, trillium, and scattered coreopsis compete with the shrubs and trees of the landscape. Red buckeye in the shade, fringe-tree, fothergilla, banana shrub, pomegranate, rhododendron, Vanhoutte spirea, lilac (for those who can grow them), viburnum, weigela, climbing rose, and more dogwood than one can stand at once.

Vegetables   If you planted the right crops a couple of months ago, you are starting to enjoy harvests of onions, beets, lettuce, turnips, carrots, English peas, and perhaps a cabbage or two. Gardeners who set out beans, okra, and tomatoes are now able to replant at the right time into soil warm enough to discourage root rot and other problems. When you buy transplants, look for young and vigorous plants rather than old and tough ones. Give them a boost by using a starter solution.

Bed sweet potatoes to produce fast sprouts for setting out next month. With bed temperatures near 80 degrees, it will take about a month or so for strong growth. Sweet potato vines make a fine ground cover beneath other long-season vegetables such as okra and peppers or in between rows to help curb weeds.

Weed control is important this month, as new seedlings will grow quickly and can become harder to eradicate later. A flat-bladed file can become your best friend in the garden if it is used to keep a hoe sharp.

Blackberry Winter

Blackberry Winter is the period around or after Good Friday, when spring seems to have sprung. The birds are all chirping, shorts are seen on young boys and men alike; the early tomatoes are planted, the beans are "stuck" and blackberries are in full bloom. The weatherman's warnings are for nought, for everyone knows that old man winter has left for good.

Then along comes a "blue norther" that rains sleet and frost and a few swirls of snow onto the land, and everyone acts as if it doesn't happen every year.

Sidedress vegetables with nitrogen fertilizer (usually one teaspoon of ammonium nitrate per plant, away from the stem, or one pint jar full for 100 feet of row). This fertilizer will keep vegetables growing and producing without forcing too much top growth. Southern peas, sweet potatoes, and peanuts do not need additional fertilizer; it will make them go all to vine.

For worms on cabbage and other cole crops, ask for sprays that include *Bacillus thuringiensis,* or BT. Where other insects, such as aphids and cucumber beetles, are concerned, keep in mind that spray-on insecticides work better than dusts, since they are easier to apply beneath leaves. Check the label to see how long to wait between applications and before harvest.

Check your storeroom now and discard all old pesticides. Fertilizers do not lose strength, but insecticides and fungicides do so even if they are kept tightly capped. You can ruin a garden by using material of the wrong potency.

Break off garlic flower heads, or the plants will produce no bulbs. Onions that have gone to flower will not produce bulbs either but can be used as salad onions.

Fruit Plants   Ordinary insecticide sprays will control many young crawling insect larvae. Continue to spray if a late frost did not kill the fruit buds, and be sure to cover the fruit. Pecans are leafing out now, and if knots and galls were a problem last June, now is the time to spray if it can be done safely and economically with home spray equipment. The tiny insects responsible for the galls do all their damage during the first two or three weeks of leaf and twig growth.

When there's new growth bursting out all over, everything fresh, green, and flourishing, the plants are little rockets of success going off every time you look at them.
Jacqueline Heriteau

Blueberries and blackberries are still blooming, and muscadines are just about to start. Be sure not to spray where bees are working.

Container plants may still be set out this month and next, providing that the soil is well prepared. Be careful not to drown newly planted trees and vines with water for the next few weeks. Mulches will help keep down weeds.

Water is essential to strawberries during fruiting. A slow soaking every week is better than frequent light sprinklings. Netting may help you protect the crop from the birds.

Ornamentals   Set out annuals and perennials this month from seed or transplants. For best results, work the soil deeply, blend in organic material, and water as necessary. Add two or three peren-

I still use a dipper my greatgrandmother Pearl made out of a gourd several decades ago. The dipper gourds and martin house gourds are not grown as much as they used to be, so curing them has gone somewhat by the wayside. Besides, who needs them when plastic martin houses are so popular, right?

Grow Your Own Birdhouse

Just to pass on the tradition, let me stress how easy it is to grow and cure gourds. Simply press the seeds into a warm, moist soil in a sunny spot, and they'll be up in a few days, no more than a week. As the vines grow, water them early in day, to prevent mildew and rot from killing the vines and ruining the fruit.

When the vines die (usually killed by frost), pick up the gourds, store them off the ground to prevent rot until they are cured (brown color). To make a martin house use a circular saw to cut a two-inch hole (larger for dipper) in the side, punch three holes in the bottom for drainage, and hang a wire through two more holes punched in the neck.

---

nials to a bed or border each year, and use only the best cultivars for your area. Swap plants with your neighbors for a large, varied, inexpensive collection.

This is a good time of year for dividing chrysanthemums, daylilies, yarrow, rudbeckia, monarda, hosta, herbs, canna, four-o'clocks, coreopsis, and elephant ears. Do not dig, move, or mow the foliage of daffodils until at least six weeks after they have finished blooming (even plaiting the leaves can cut down on next year's flower).

Some annuals are impossible to find as bedding plants and must be grown from seed. They include ornamental peppers, sanvitalia, cosmos, cypress vine, cleome, tithonia, moonflower vine, kochia, amaranthus, luffa gourds, and many other unusual but easy-to-grow plants. Subscribe to seed catalogs so that you will hear about new and exciting vines and plants coming on the market.

Annuals need good soil preparation, regular watering, and freedom from the competition presented by weeds. Organic matter and fertilizer worked into the soil will give them energy at the outset, but be prepared to feed them again later to keep them going strong. Plants must have room to spread. Thin when necessary, the earlier the better.

Prune shrubs if necessary rather than waiting until they have wasted energy on growth that you intend to remove. Even summer bloomers such as crape myrtles, altheas, hibiscus, and abelia may be shaped now without jeopardizing the flowers later. Fertilize heavily, and prune shrubs during bud break to help them heal and sprout quickly.

House Plants   Introduce house plants to the outdoors gradually, starting them off in a shaded area where you can give them a spring cleanup. Check for mites, repot as necessary, trim scraggly growth, and fertilize lightly. Plan to protect them from strong spring winds; they will lose moisture more quickly outdoors in the warm weather and bright light than they did indoors. Ferns and airplane (or spider) plants may be divided this month.

Clay pots will dry more quickly than plastic ones during the next few months, but they can be sunk into the ground and mulched with sawdust to slow down evaporation. Snails do not like to crawl over sawdust.

Lawn   Now that the lawn is greening up, avoid using weed killers for the next month or two. Don't dethatch or rake the lawn hard, either, or you may interfere with the lawn's efforts to root quickly for summer strength. Mowing will control most winter weeds (but not dandelion). Generic garden fertilizers (13-13-13, 6-8-8, and so forth) have too much phosphorous and too little nitrogen (the nitrogen in them is often too strong as well) to give the lawn lasting benefits. Buy only top-quality lawn food from a nursery for your grass, and wait to apply it until the lawn has been mowed two or three times; the grass cannot use the fertilizer until a new root system has been established during the greenup period.

Set your mower blade to the proper height for your particular type of turfgrass. A sharp mower blade will give your lawn the neatest, freshest, cleanest appearance. Have a spare blade to use while the regular one is being sharpened.

Check your hoses, soakers, and trickle irrigation setups this month to make sure there are no kinks, leaks, or other malfunctions.

Reminder   Birds are attracted to dripping and splashing water, and to elevated pools and baths. Clay saucers make good splash pools when a few pebbles are added, and especially if a slowly-dripping jug of water is suspended above the saucer for noise and sight to attract the birds.

Take any unusual diseases (azalea leaves, lawn spots) or insect damage to your nursery or county agent for identification before treating with chemicals. Your extension office can send samples and specimen to the university for quick and accurate diagnosis.

MAY

Things to See Now   Daylilies and roses have begun in profusion, along with early blossoms of the bull bay Southern magnolia and red trumpet honeysuckle. Young boys, fresh out of school, are seen, lugging lawn mowers up the street, and there are plenty of neat vegetable gardens still tended and weed-free, some in shade where winter sun has been banished by neighboring trees. Mimosa and catalpa are in bloom, along with yucca, astilbe, and roadside Queen Anne's lace, coreopsis, field daisies, and early black-eyed Susans. Peaches are at the market stands, plus new potatoes and squash. Peonies are at their best in May, especially the early varieties (later ones tend to "blast" in heat and rains). Alaska daisies introduce their cousin Shasta, and the billowy fennel becomes a dark contrast to the lacy ferns of yarrow. Perennial blue spires of Blue Bedder salvia (*Salvia farinacea,* or mealycup sage) begin their summer-long show in the sunny border, adding just the right touch of coolness to daylilies. Butterfly weed dots the roadsides with intense orange, less so when forced to grow in the richer soil of the garden; like the brilliant blue-purple verbena carpeting roadsides, butterfly weed is showier in the wild. Amaryllis, garlic, allium, and both Madonna and Royal lilies add tall exotic emphasis to the border. Other perennials in bloom now include hollyhock, golden marguerite, asters, larkspur, digitalis, gaillardia, Oriental poppy, evening primrose, torch-lily (tritoma or Kniphofia), iris, gerbera daisy, and scabiosa.

Abelia begins its draw on hummingbirds about the time sweetshrub and banana shrub (*Magnolia fascata,* now known as Michelia figo) bloom with their wonderful fragrance. Smoke-tree (*cotinus*), roses, and star jasmine are in bloom on my street, along with a few late azaleas. And the pile of prunings grows along the curb.

Vegetables   Herbs can be planted now in raised beds or along the edge of garden rows where they won't interfere with other garden activities. Basils, dill, coriander, summer savory, parsley, and borage are grown as annuals, but the perennial thyme, rosemary, oregano, mints, sage, tarragon, and sorrel should have their own permanent beds or containers. Herbs need full sun and well-drained soils.

Stake tomatoes, but don't prune any suckers from them until

the first flowers have formed. You might stake peppers, too, not because of heavy yields but to keep summer showers and stiff winds from knocking them over and destroying their root systems. Beans, peas, okra, melons, and other summer vegetables can be planted now for very fast growth.

Insects and diseases are becoming conspicuous problems. Be sure you have identified the trouble before you choose a chemical treatment.

Set out sweet potato slips this month, keeping in mind that roots develop rapidly in warm, moist soil. Some gardeners will be able to harvest Irish potatoes, but don't leave freshly dug potatoes in the sun, or parts of the potatoes' interiors will turn green and poisonous. Cure Irish potatoes in warm, dry shade for a couple of days before storing them in a cool, dark place.

Water thoroughly about once a week, wetting the soil deeply but trying to keep leaves of vegetables dry. Water in the morning, and invest now in soaker hoses or trickle irrigation for the weeks ahead. Thin young plants to give them room to grow. Harvest maturing vegetables while they are tender, before heat ruins them or forces them to form flower heads or seeds. Sidedress the garden. As you harvest, fill empty spots in the rows with fresh plants or seeds.

Squash plants often have an imbalance of male and female flowers early in the season. Thinning and watering will help them past this difficulty. If your plants don't have both flower types at once, give them time. In the absence of bees, you may eventually need to hand pollinate the female flowers, an easy job indeed.

Fruit Plants   Keep spraying tree fruit for insects and diseases, especially peaches and plums. Prune out deadwood on figs before wasps, bumblebees, and yellow jackets have the chance to build nests there. Fresh mulch will keep fig roots cool all summer. Eliminate some of the young fruit from trees so that the plants will be more vigorous producers later. Also snip all berries off first-year blueberries. They will become sturdier, with stronger root systems, and will produce a heavier crop next year.

Rusty spots on apple and crabapple trees are signs of cedar-apple rust, an infection that has spread from nearby cedar trees. The rust starts as gelatinous growths on cedars in April and will cause infected apples and crabapples to drop leaves; treat next spring by spraying the cedars.

Horticulturally, the month of May is opening night, Homecoming, and Graduation Day all rolled into one.

Tam Mossman

Ornamentals   Buy only top-quality bedding transplants at nurseries, and try to pick plants that are not yet in bloom. Salvia, periwinkle, marigolds, impatiens, and other summer flowers will start faster in the landscape if you pinch or prune their tips. Fertilize with liquid plant food once this month, and mulch to help the soil stay moist, weed free, and not too hot. A good root system now will pay off handsomely in July and August.

Caladiums, geraniums, begonias, and coleus are good in the shade garden for summer color. Sun lovers are many: salvia, ageratum, zinnia, cosmos, celosia, alyssum, periwinkle, petunia, and more. Ornamental peppers make great low-maintenance bedding plants, especially when they are massed for both flower and fruit color. Tall flowering plants such as four-o'clock, dahlia, tuberose, gladiolus, lily, hollyhock, and yarrow should be staked now to provide support for their stalks later without damaging roots. Special cages are available for some of these and also for peonies, or you can use branches or bamboo stakes, tying the plants to them with doubled twine, twisted cloth, or other soft material that will not cut tender scapes.

It is now safe to mow the foliage of daffodils and Dutch iris. You may also move them or dig and store them. Cuttings of phlox, chrysanthemum, and sedum root readily this month. Take the tips of new growth, set them in potting soil or moist sand, and water regularly so that the soil cannot dry out.

Sprays combining insecticide and fungicide will help you con-

---

Cold-blooded Buddy

Of all my cold-blooded buddies in the garden, I think I like the toad the best. He (or she) is as normal as can be, always spending the day in the same exact pile of mulch beneath a sedum, making its way to the second step from the top on my backporch every night the light is left on. Such a territorial creature, too—my mother and dad and I caught a boxful in their rambling yard (they knew just where each one was, and insisted that there were plenty to spare). All but a couple hopped away the first week in their new home, and the single brown one, the only one I could recognize, was one that stayed.

The toads can live for many years, happy to be left alone (by themselves, with no competition) eating crickets, flies, snails, slugs, and other generally destructive creatures. The beneficial insects and lizards are mostly too fast for the toad, and the toad is too big to be worried about it.

trol thrips, aphids, and black spot on roses. Attack slugs, snail, and roly-poly pill bugs by baiting them. Don't give up until all the adults have been killed and all eggs have hatched. Don't use baits for these pests around strawberries, herbs, or vegetables, however, and be sure to follow the package directions carefully.

Lawn Fertilize this month with a good-quality material formulated for turfgrass. Light application of appropriate *slow-release* fertilizer will promote a thick, well-rooted turf—by far the best protection against weeds and other damage later. Too heavy an application can cause excessive top growth (necessitating extra mowing and producing more thatch, disease problems, and hiding places for insects) and even a reduction in root growth. Don't mow at fixed, predetermined intervals; mow only when the grass needs it.

This is a good month to start a new lawn, whether from seeds, sod, plugs, or sprigs. Start with well-prepared soil. Water lightly and frequently at first on new lawns, gradually coaxing roots down deep with more thorough and less frequent soakings. To penetrate properly, roots will need both moisture and air. Too much water will force them to stay shallow where they can breathe.

Reminder Young and especially new shrubs, flowers, perennials, and lawns need water, but not to excess. No rule of thumb for frequency is better than "slow and deep, then let it almost get dry before repeating." Potted plants are getting dry quicker than before, and are more active and need water, fertilizer, and pest control.

Mother's Day is around the corner, and there is a gardening doo-dad or hanging basket to give or perhaps a chore to be done for Mom.

Old, standard flowering plants such as cleome, four o'clocks, cosmos, and others can give just the right lift to a landscape. Peruse seed racks for the more interesting flowers, both annual and perennial.

JUNE

Things to See Now This is the primary month for southern magnolia blossoms, although they have been lending fragrance and lifting spirits for a couple of weeks or more. Cape jasmine is the southern shrub of the month in my book, with its sickly-sweet blossoms ranging in color from pure white to faded brown on the same bush at the same time. But June holds other flowers dear to the heart as well: water lotus and cattail in bloom above the lake, sumac beginning to show its horns just across ditches filled with hemlock and early elderberries, crape myrtle in tentative bloom, lilac chaste-tree (Vitex) covered with purple spikes shimmering with bees, redbud seed pods, the very exotic and insufferably sweet maypop blossom, dahlias, oakleaf hydrangeas in the woods, oregano florets, tiger lilies, summer phlox, spider flower (cleome), and "milk-and-honey" lilies (crinum).

Daylilies and cannas are at their peak, both old-fashioned ones and the gaudiest of the tetraploids. Chinese hibiscus have flattened, plate-size blossoms, and ornamental grasses are at their full summer fluffiness. Signs to berry farms dot the countryside, and cicadas begin their sing-song cadence in the trees.

An overlooked perennial beauty for the shade, Peruvian lily (*Alstroemeria*), makes excellent cut flowers on two-foot stalks, blooming beside hostas and liriope. Cool foliage of aucuba and variegated liriope brighten shaded gardens. Look for an unusual perennial with spikes of red flowers, the coral-bean (*Erythrina*), and notice that the rhododendrons seem to wilt from heat in June almost as soon as they finish blooming—as if they would rather be in higher elevations, where they originate.

Trump creep glows this month. St. John's wort, lamb's ear (stachys), and obedient plant (physostegia) are in bloom, along with summer phlox, monarda (both the red beebalm and pinkish wild bergamot), loosestrife, mallows, continued daisies and butterfly weed, and the first of the gladioli. Annuals are beginning to get their second wind, with renewed sprouts after initial small shows of flowers.

Vegetables If part of the garden failed for some reason or other, just plant again or wait until later this summer to replant for fall harvest. The Irish potato harvest is ending now. Be sure and save some potatoes for fall planting. Corn silks are turning brown as they mature; squash, tomatoes, and cucumber are blooming and setting fruit. Okra and eggplant, like southern peas, will need more heat to begin setting fruit.

Garlic, now completely brown, should be dug, cleaned, and air dried in a warm place out of the rain for a few weeks if it is to be stored for fall and winter use. Dig onions now, too, and store them

Even the most beautiful weather will not allay the gardener's notion (well-founded, actually) that he is somehow too late, too soon, or that he has too much stuff going on or not enough. For the garden is the stage on which the gardener exults and agonizes out every crest and chasm of the heart.

Henry Mitchell

Bibbon's the Better Boy

The first American tomato eater was a daring soul. His name, Robert Bibbon; his age, 49; his hometown, Salem, New Jersey; the date, 1820. The tomato, at the time, was called the Jerusalem apple and believed to be deadly poison. It was known to be in the same family as the deadly nightshade (*Solanacea*). The local physician, Dr. James VanMeeter, stated that "[if] the Colonel eats this fruit, he will froth at the mouth and double over with appendicitis!" Bibbon ate two; since there were no ill effects, the crowd gave him a rousing cheer. Hip-hip-hooray.

Now for the two-bit question: Is the tomato a fruit, as the good doctor stated, or is it a vegetable? The answer is three-fold—legally, it is a vegetable; morphologically, it is the seed-bearing fruit of a vine; botanically, it is a berry.

---

in a cool, well-ventilated spot with an inch or so of the stems attached.

Plant Halloween pumpkins now (Connecticut Field is one popular variety for eating and carving). Thin pumpkin plants to two per hill, and water them well throughout the summer. This is also a good time to plant other winter storage (hard rind) squash, such as acorn, butternut, and hubbard.

Lightly cover plastic mulches with organic materials to prevent roots from being damaged by extreme heat. Keep your tomatoes off the ground to minimize fruit diseases. Blossom end rot or a leathery spot on tomatoes may indicate a calcium deficiency. You can supply calcium by applying lime or spraying liquid calcium chloride on leaves. Avoid leafspot diseases by keeping leaves dry while you water. Suckers from tomatoes root readily this month for planting in late July. They will be ready to transplant or fertilize after they have been set in moist peat and sand and have put forth new growth.

Fruit Plants   Prune current season's blueberry growth to promote fall buds and next year's fruit. Mulch blueberries heavily, and soak them every two weeks or so (but not more often than once a week for mature or established plants).

Blackberries make fruit next year on canes that grow this summer. Remove canes that bore fruit this year (they will only become brambles if you don't), and cut the remaining new ones back to knee height. Blackberries don't need mulches, but water will help them grow after pruning. Treat raspberries as you would blackberries.

When tips of apple and pear branches turn black, suspect fire blight as the cause. No spray will cure the condition. Instead you must prune out the infected twigs as best you can, repeatedly disinfecting your clippers. Next year you can use a spray during full bloom to prevent a recurrence of the infection, which is spread by bees.

Water strawberries, and keep weeds under control so that you will have healthy plants to move this fall. Some gardeners like to thin old plants in June, leaving a six-inch space for new ones to fill during the summer and fall. Apply fertilizer lightly after the plants finish bearing.

Ornamentals   Prune roses after blooming for more vigorous new stems and blossoms and to keep the plants compact. Cut to just above a leaf with five leaflets (the lower you prune, the longer it will take for the new break to emerge, but the stronger the stem will be). Continue to spray for black spot, and add an insecticide from time to time to control aphids and thrips if you have them in great numbers. Pick bagworms off needle leaf plants or spray with an appropriate insecticide.

Pinch the tips off chrysanthemums to make them bush out and produce more flowers this fall. Pinching will also keep the plants compact. Spent flowers on perennials and annuals keep the plants from growing and putting forth new blooms. In the case of annuals, you're trying to keep seeds from forming. Don't forget to pinch the flowers off the basils in your herb garden, either, or your plants will get leggy.

There's still plenty of time to plant gladiolus corms, cannas, dahlias, and caladiums if they are in good condition. Stake the glads and dahlias at planting time so that they will stay upright later.

Avoid bumping or nicking the trunks of young trees. Use commercial tree trunk wrapping material or mulch near the trunks to keep down the grass and weeds until the trees are several years old and have thicker bark.

This year's tender young branches of azalea, ligustrum, holly,

---

Mothballs are the cure for just about everything—from getting rid of fleas and moles to keeping dogs and squirrels out of flower beds. Although they may be more a placebo than anything else, they do have some deterrent effect. Keep in mind that they need to be replaced from time to time to remain malodorous.

Try Mothballs

euonymus, Asiatic jasmine, ivy, and forsythia have hardened a little now and will root readily if you take cuttings. Gather them in the mornings while they are still firm and fresh, strip away most of the leaves, and stick them into a moist mixture of peat, sand, and perlite in equal amounts. Rooting powders are helpful. Be sure to keep the cuttings moist and in a bright but shaded area for five or six weeks, or until they root.

Lawn   Use weed killers sparingly, and avoid watering late in the day. Concentrate on making the grass thick and healthy, then worry about weeds. This is a good time to dethatch if your thatch is two knuckles deep. You might also consider aerating now.

Reminder   Heat is coming, as is drought, and plants will need fighting for. Summer flowers are not an accident; pinching faded flowers, watering, light fertilization, and weeding are all important for success with flowers and vegetables.

Father's Day is this month, and many a deserving man can use a lift.

Hummingbirds are easily attracted by pinkish or red flowers, such as monarda, salvia, cuphea, cypress vine, and abilia shrubs. Feeders should be kept full and in plain view so you can enjoy the feisty behaviour of those summer visitors.

JULY

Things to See Now   Pawpaws—those sweet, creamy tree fruits the size of eggs—are ripening, as are garden vegetables galore. The wailing of cicadas in the trees is now background noise, taken granted by all but visitors to Dixie. Lantana and bougainvillea are hotly contesting one another for the most blooms in the sunniest part of the landscape, not to be outdone by crape myrtle, black-eyed Susan, and purple coneflower. Confederate jasmine fills the air with fragrance as the last of the main flush of magnolia blossoms fall, revealing brown seed pods the size of my fist. Annuals such as the tall spiderflower or cleome and cosmos are not as common these days as mass-produced periwinkle, salvia, and marigold, but more folks are using impatiens (including the tougher New Guinea hybrids) for shady spots than before. Ferns are mysterious and somber, and hosta lilies still add a cool touch to the shade garden.

The blackberry lily (*Belamcanda*) and tuberoses are blooming now, along with hibiscus (and althea, or Rose of Sharon) and some of the ornamental grasses. If you have been removing spent flowers, you still can enjoy the balloon flower (*Platycodon*), black-eyed Susan, monarda, daisies, and coneflower. Blue salvia is still going strong. Clerodendron (glory bower) is striking at this time, as is the foliage of castor bean and elephant ears. The sedum called "Indian Chief" (S. spectabile) is now bushel basket-size and, if located in a sunny spot, is beginning to form flower clusters. What a unique plant! And four o'clocks just keep on pushing taller and broader, with more fragrant red or yellow flowers than ever.

Vegetables   Harvest promptly to keep plants productive. Okra, squash, cucumbers, eggplants, and pole beans stop flowering if even a hint of mature fruit remains on them. Keep spraying for insects and diseases. Hot temperatures alone will cause the flowers to shed from peppers, tomatoes, and beans, but these vegetables will recover when the weather moderates later—if they aren't allowed to dry up and aren't overtaken by weeds and pests. Provide a slow, deep soaking once a week, and avoid wetting plant foliage. Organic mulches pay off this month by reducing soil temperatures, moisture loss, and weeds. Hoeing this month will help, but be sure to keep the hoe sharp. Work and harvest in the mornings, when the vegetables are fresh and the temperature is still cool.

Harvest squash and cucumbers when they are small. Eggplants should still be firm and glossy. Pick tomatoes before they are in full color, and let them ripen inside; that way the birds won't get them. Muskmelons (cantaloupes) are ripe when they slip from the vine. Honeydews should be slightly soft at the blossom end and will slosh when shaken. Ripe watermelons show a creamy spot where the melon has lain on the ground. Pick corn when a thin, milky juice comes from a punctured kernel. If the juice is clear, the corn is immature; if the juice is thick and white, it's overripe.

You can still plant Halloween pumpkins early this month if you haven't already done so. Set out fall tomatoes, too. Many late summer vegetables can be planted to fill out empty rows. Rutabagas, which take a long time to mature, should be planted from seed in late July. Basil, mint, oregano, and lemon balm may be cut back severely and refertilized for a new flush of growth; dry or freeze the trimmings for use in the kitchen.

Most Southerners need an introduction to their gardens in summer. I think they would be pleased with them if they could once break with the tradition of abandoning the borders to weeds when the flare of spring has passed. We can have bloom in the summer if we want it, but we must plan for it and work for it . . .

Elizabeth Lawrence

Fruit Plants Figs are ready for harvest now, and you will be racing the birds for them. Netting is practical on small or young bushes but not on big ones. Give the bushes extra water and mulch to protect the shallow roots. Pawpaws are also ripe, as are mulberries and some sorts of bunch grapes, usually the tart ones that are suitable for jellies.

Apples and pears may need additional pruning now because of fire blight. Tip prune blueberries lightly one more time; otherwise avoid pruning in the heat. Trim muscadine vines now only enough to keep them away from the lawn mower. Concentrate on providing all plants with adequate water.

Ornamentals You can still set out chrysanthemums, especially cushion mums, watering and pinching to make plants that will be compact with a profusion of blooms in September and October. Do not pinch mums after mid-July or so, or the buds may be killed by frost come fall. Light fertilization and weekly soakings will also help.

Roses almost stop blooming in July and August but will do well in September if you fertilize and water them and prune them back about one-third this month. Keep spraying for diseases and insects.

Insects and mites often cause a black film to develop on the leaves of crape myrtles, gardenias, hollies, pecans, and other shrubs and trees. To control this sooty mold, spray for the insects, adding a little liquid dish detergent to help the spray stick and loosen the film.

Summer Brown Out

Mid-summer brings dozens of calls from over-wrought landscape gardeners whose shrubs have suddenly "browned out," a limb or entire plant at a time. In most cases (if lawn-mower or string-trimmer damage can be ruled out) this is caused by winter damage many months before. I recommend simply checking the lower limbs and trunks for split or "busted bark," and scratching the bark with a knife or thumbnail to test for green tissue underneath. If the inner bark is not bright green, or if the bark is split, then the damage is old. Why does this happen in mid-summer? Simply because, although the plant was severely damaged, the damage was not enough to kill it outright, but only enough to impair the flow of water to leaves. As the summer progressed, the heat and dry weather put ever-increasing strains on the damaged plant, and a point was reached in the middle of a heat wave where the plant simply could no longer provide itself with cooling water through damaged trunks and limb.

You still have plenty of time to plant seeds and transplants of summer annuals for fall color. Fast-growing zinnias, marigolds, cosmos, and nasturtiums will perform well in the cool of late August and September and until frost. The bedding plants you see at nurseries will perform well if you set them in amended soil, pinch them back, fertilize lightly, mulch, and water them.

Keep pruning hedges and other sheared shrubs this month if you need to do so.

Container Plants   Containers dry quickly in the heat of July, especially clay pots and small containers holding large plants. Ideally, you should water everything twice around; the second watering really soaks in. Mulches on the surface, even pebbles, will slow the rate of evaporation. Hanging baskets in particular are likely to dry out and to wilt or sustain root damage as a result. Light fertilization with a balanced, water-soluble plant food can give potted plants and baskets just the pick-me-up they need to keep them looking good into the fall.

Lawn   Raise the mower height a notch or so for the next two months to help your turf cope with the heat and to keep roots cool. The extra height will also reduce water loss. Avoid removing more than one-third of the grass blade at a time. Water early in the day unless the wind and heat together are serious. Iron, now available in most commercial lawn fertilizer formulations, will help centipedegrass and St. Augustinegrass green up in the summer. Avoid fertilizing heavily now; roots are more important than heavy top growth.

Yellow or dying areas in full, hot sun are the main symptoms of chinch bugs, which are ant-sized members of the stinkbug family. These creatures inject poison into the grass while they feed. Liquid or granular insecticides will control them. A repeat treatment will be necessary a week later to kill newly hatched adults and diehards.

Reminder   Birds are attracted to the summer garden by water, especially fresh water that is dripping from a jug into a saucer or raised bird bath. When going on vacation, water everything thoroughly once; then water it all again to make it really soak in. Put potted plants in the shade, and ask neighbors to water and harvest the garden for you.

Work in the garden during the early morning to avoid heat stress, and wear a hat and loose clothes. Vegetables harvested early

in the day will have less "field heat" and retain freshness longer
than those pulled during the heat of the day.

AUGUST

Things to See Now   If it is gaudy color you need, set out the
pink flamingoes and hang out the flag. A scarcity of new flowers in
August makes subtle differences in texture and shades more obvious. The brightness of green arborvitae contrasts with rusty cypress trees (mite infestation causes this). Spanish moss against the
dark trunks of post oaks offers a cool contrast to the moss rose siz-
zling in the sun (usually in black iron kettles). Purple basil, pale
ginkgo, lush ferns, torrid copper plants, weeping willows, brilliant
nandinas, variegated liriope and hosta (both in bloom still), coarse
palms and palmetto and yucca, tropical banana and fatsia and aucuba, golden euonymus and colorful caladiums—there is much to
notice in the landscape of August, in spite of lack of new flowers.

But then, there are wild sunflowers and goldenrod just beginning their shows, along with Joe Pye weed and trumpet creeper.
The blue along the roadside usually means verbena, pokeberry, or
elderberry. A second flowering of wisteria generally makes an August show, just in time to cool off the very common crape myrtles
and altheas (so many varieties, from purest white through pinks,
lavender, and red). The new miniature crape myrtles, developed
in Louisiana, are giving summer phlox a run for its money! Cannas
are still blooming, mostly reds and oranges with a few yellows
scattered about. Lantana is nearly unsurpassable in sunny beds, as
are the unusual opuntia (prickly pear cactus) with its purple fruit.
Junipers have developed the bright blueberries so prized as flavor-
ing for gin.

One particularly fun perennial for the August heat is *Lycoris,*
actually several cultivars. Both the red spider lily of late August
and September, as well as the knee-high scapes of pink trumpets
(L. squamigera) are here, sun or shade (provided their clumps of
leaves are under open, deciduous trees where the winter sun can
energize the flowers). Some folks call the L. squamigera either
"surprise" lily, "Resurrection" lily, or even "naked ladies."

I particularly enjoy riding around town and country, across the
states this time of the year, noticing fences and garden accessories.

Southerners are not as shy about displaying statuary and bottle trees and windmills and hanging baskets. The most soothing sight now, however, is a lawn seen through the mist of an early morning sprinkler system. And, to top it all off, a true southern gardener's choice of summer hats.

Vegetables   Unless you have abandoned the garden to weeds and pests, watering has become your most important chore. Provide slow, deep soakings once a week (perhaps a little more often if the weather is both hot and windy). Use trickle irrigation and soaker hoses if possible, and don't forget the mulch.

When you use insecticides against the army of pests, be sure to follow the instructions on the label about waiting periods between applications or between application and harvest. Remember that newly seeded vegetables are very susceptible to pests left over from old plants.

Pull weeds or hoe them out before setting seeds for next year. Even an abandoned garden should be tilled under and replanted with fall vegetables or prepared for next month's sowing of a cover crop such as rye, vetch, clover, or alfalfa. Repeated tilling at this time of year can also reduce problems with nematodes, which require moisture to survive.

Prepare the garden and plan late summer vegetables, such as southern peas, limas, broccoli, beets, carrots, Irish potatoes (if you saved some last spring), and leafy green vegetables. Protect new transplants and tiny seedling by covering the rows with boards or cardboard so that the soil does not crust or overheat until the plants are stronger.

Winter Onions

Multiplying onions, sometimes called "nesting" onions, are planted in August or September, eaten from all winter (as side dishes, in hushpuppies or omelettes), and allowed to die down in the heat of April or May. Then they should be dug and dried on a support above the ground, so air can circulate, where the bulbs are pulled off the leaves and stored in a cool, well-ventilated place until time to replant.

Try this recipe for green onions passed on by a friend. Briefly mix together chopped fresh green onions with eggs (one to one ratio). Mix in just enough self-rising meal to absorb the egg and make a thick paste. Add pepper to taste. Scramble.

Fruit Plants   Figs have been ravaged by birds and now need chiefly water. Apples, pears, and crabapples are beginning to mature. You'll need to taste test for ripeness because some varieties don't develop much color in our heat.

Both the light- and the dark-colored muscadines begin ripening in mid to late August, as does the Chinese jujube. Elderberries are ripening slowly but can be gathered soon for home wine production.

Ornamentals   Cut back bedding plants to force healthy, vigorous, new growth. Feed them with a balanced fertilizer (one of the kinds that are mixed with water and poured around and over plants). Don't pinch or prune mums, or the new buds may not be ready to flower before the frost kills them. Don't prune landscape plants heavily at this time, or you'll run the risk of winter damage later. Azaleas form their flower buds for next spring during August and September, and thorough soakings with water are crucial for proper root development.

Most roses have now stopped blooming but will start again later when the temperature is more moderate. Keep spraying for pests and diseases, and water thoroughly. Soakings once a week should be enough if the roses are well mulched.

The shade garden should be at its best if you are watering it and fertilizing it lightly. Impatiens, coleus, caladiums, and ferns all contribute seasonal color; you may also be enjoying hosta, aspidistra, fatsia, aucuba, and mahonia.

If heat permits, this is a good time to divide iris, daylily, and daisies and to start new plants from the old. Dig and separate clumps into smaller pieces, each having stem, root, and a cluster of leaves. Immediately replant the pieces in rich, previously prepared soil. Water thoroughly. Seeds of sweet william, yarrow, foxglove, hollyhock, and baby's breath planted now will get a head start on the fall and next spring.

House Plants   Prune back poinsettias by the last day of August so that they will have plenty of time to bush out and prepare a concerted display. Keep watering and fertilizing them as you normally would. Poinsettias require bright light, if not direct sunshine, and lots of care, but you must provide long periods of complete darkness at night before they will produce seasonal color.

Lawn   Your lawn should be in good shape now if you've been watering it regularly, but you'll want to have insecticides handy in

> By August the heat—so welcome in June and early summer—becomes an annoyance, and by the middle of the month generally oppressive.
>
> *John Mitchell*

The well-meaning folks up in Pennsylvania who publish magazines and books for organic gardeners need to visit with me for a day, so I can show them what stinkbugs are. They have sucked my sunflowers dry, put white puncture knots under the skin of my tomatoes, cat-faced the peaches, and caused the pecans to shed. I wish someone would tell those people that the Deep South is different, that we can't plant soybeans in between sweet corn to shade out chinch bugs—the soybeans have more insect and disease problems of their own.

Stinkbugs?

I have no quarrel with organic or natural gardeners, mind you. I use praying mantids and yellow garden spiders, lady bugs from California, along with careful attention to weed control and irrigation (early in the day, to prevent diseases). I supplement the organic matter in my raised beds with manure, bone meal, and cottonseed meal. I compost my coffee grounds and use disease-resistant varieties of everything I can.

But what about those stinkbugs? Has anyone from up north ever seen the size of these stout bugs? Am I supposed to take the "hand-pick" method of control seriously?

case of trouble with chinch bugs and armyworms. Raise the mower setting a notch or two, and keep the lawn supplied with water.

Fertilize now unless you can't move hoses or have already fertilized centipede for the year. Remember that lawn foods of good quality are vastly superior to generic garden fertilizers when it comes to feeding turf. Try to water early in the day so that the grass has plenty of time to dry before dark.

Reminder   Dog days are no fun, but you can note many good ideas for sprucing up yards after only a brief jaunt through town. Order seed catalogues, and use this time of few new flowers to see what else is going on in southern gardens. Add a little variety into the garden, yard, or container garden on the porch.

SEPTEMBER

Things to See Now   Roadside flowers include goldenrod and sunflowers, mist flower (*Eupatorium*) and sumac. Joe Pye weed towers over asters, while mallows fill the ditchbanks. Tumbling over nearly everyone's fence or ligustrum hedge is a white mantle of fall Japanese clematis (*C. paniculata*), and the leaves of beautyberry are as yellow as those of buckeye, falling early in the season to reveal their respective fruits. (Buckeye is as poisonous, by the way, as the magenta beautyberry is gaudy.) Bittersweet vine is full of berries and birds, and the baccharis (salt-bush) are showing the world which one is male (the green one without flowers) and female (those with fuzzy white, thistle-like seed heads).

In the border, the crowns of bushel-basket sized "showy sedums" (S. spectabile) are turning rusty red (Autumn Joy, or Indian Chief) or deep pink (Brilliant), and these flowers will in time remain as maroon seedheads, as coarsely attractive in October as the flowers are now. Butterfly lily (*Hedychium*) is chest high and topped with sweetly fragrant, pure white blossoms, filling a niche in the shade garden that has remained dark and empty till now.

The showiest perennials around the town are chrysanthemums, particularly the hardy cushion mums. Beneath the rare blue of the incredibly still-blooming mealycup sage (Salvia farincacea), my mother's mums have been bright spots in an otherwise hot, dry time of the year. Reds and bronzes, mauve and rust, brilliant yellows, bold pinks, and just about every shade and hue between, make mums the first real link between summer and fall, giving a boost to late daylilies on their second show and to the salvias, and sedum.

Vegetables   This is a good time to set out transplants of broccoli, cauliflower, cabbage, brussels sprouts, and collards. Select only the smaller, more tender, actively growing plants, since they will continue to grow and will mature on time. Hard, woody, leggy transplants often fail to mature properly. Once these plants stop growing (whether because of drought or age or for some other reason), they rarely start up again. At the first sign of white butterflies (cabbage loopers), control the green wormlike larvae with liquid sprays containing *Bacillus thuringiensis.* Liquid dish detergent (one teaspoonful per gallon of mix) will help the mixture adhere better. Reapply BT weekly until harvest.

September is also a good month for planting seeds of spinach, turnips, beets, carrots, and swiss chard. Other leafy vegetables may be planted, but all seeds should be temporarily covered with a board or mulch to prevent the soil from drying, cracking, or crusting. Remove the covers as soon as seedlings begin to emerge. Thin rutabaga seedlings until they are between nine and twelve inches apart, or roots will not form. The thinnings are both delicious and nutritious.

Fire ants are burning the south! Every year, these imported devils infest more counties and parishes, and the only thing that seems to stop them is cold weather—making them a truly southern pest. And a serious one at that.

They were accidentally imported into Mobile, Alabama, around the end of World War I, on a freighter from South America. Since they were so fast to colonize and spread, and there was no natural predator or disease, they went from shocking to bad to worse—and, no end is in sight, in spite of the concerted efforts of many researchers and workers.

Funny thing is, fire ants are easy to kill. Take a hill full, and pour boiling water on, and many ants will die instantly. Use gasoline, or insecticides, and the ants are killed on contact. But if you aren't absolutely thorough, it seems that only a few ants can escape and start two or three new mounds within a day or so. And there is the rub.

If you can kill every single ant in a mound, you will be on the right track for getting rid of all the mounds on your property. Kill just a few, however, and your problems will be compounded. Baits, fumigants, juvenile hormones, granules, sprays, citrus peels, mixing two nests together to get them stirred up against one another, and brick bats are all good for abating the ant population—but they don't always wipe out the entire nest, and the problem will return (sometimes with a vengeance).

Here, then, is my approach. Keep in mind that I have fire ants, have had them for years, have had them eat every single pea seed in the garden and have seen where they cleaned out a nestful of baby bluebirds. I've been stung between my toes and fingers, and had them crawl up my britches. I get infected little sores and horrible itching and some swelling. I hate fire ants.

Also keep in mind that I have access to any control method I can imagine. I choose, however, a simple and straightforward approach: I use inexpensive liquid insecticides, mixed exactly according to directions. Pour enough of the mixture onto each mound to completely fill the entire mound. I usually need a gallon or so of the mixture per mound to make a soupy mess. I do not kick the mound first, or punch holes, or anything like that; I simply pour the mixture slowly around the perimeter and over the mound, just like pouring syrup over pancakes, until the mound is flooded from the bottom up, and all through the tunnels. And I am thorough with each mound before moving on to another.

And I do this late in the afternoon, when all the ants are at home rather than out foraging. By morning, my twenty cents' worth of insecticide has killed them, queen and all, and has become inert—with no harm to pets, lawn, vegetables, or my own health. My secret is no secret; it is a determination to rid my yard of fire ants.

Leaf lettuce and the semiheading varieties do better in the South than head lettuces. Consider the smooth-leaf Buttercrunch, Oak Leaf, Salad Bowl, and the newer red-leaf varieties, such as Red Sails. All may be harvested a little at a time for continuous production.

Squash, tomatoes, eggplants, peppers, and beans will have begun to produce again. Sweet potatoes may also be ready. Check a few hills, and remember that, although the potatoes will grow larger, the longer they are left in the ground, the greater the danger that sudden heavy rains will cause them to crack and spoil. Stay on the lookout for problems with insects and diseases, and apply controls promptly.

Herbs should be ready for drying now. Try basil, sage, oregano, summer savory, and tarragon. Since rosemary is not always hardy in some gardens, you may want to root six-inch cuttings of rosemary in moist potting soil or water (change the water every few days) for replanting next year. Divisions of oregano, thyme, and mint if potted up now and kept outside until they are well established will make welcome indoor reminders of the garden this winter.

Fruit Plants   Muscadines are fully ripe or have just gone by. Homemade wines will develop poorly if temperatures aren't stable, so cover fermentation bottles during the day or keep them in air-conditioned quarters. Try a muscadine hull pie.

The leaves of fruit trees are now sending carbohydrates to the roots for fall growth, so this is not the time to prune. Watch for borers on the trunks of peach and plum trees, and apply trunk sprays this month to prevent damage. The adult borer is a red and black, clear-winged moth that resembles a wasp. If you rake up and destroy mummified fruits beneath trees and pick off those still clinging to branches, you will be removing much of the source of next year's diseases.

Ornamentals   It is too early to plant spring bulbs, but the best selection is now available for purchase. Daffodils, hyacinths, crocuses, Dutch irises, and tulips are dependable for just about everyone. Select bulbs that are firm, big, and free of cuts and defects. Begin preparing the soil where they will be so that they will have the much-needed drainage and adequate fertilizer when they are planted.

Tulips are annuals in the Deep South because we cannot give them enough chilling hours outdoors. Store tulip bulbs in marked bags in the refrigerator for six or eight weeks before planting.

Don't refrigerate daffodil bulbs, on the other hand, or their flowers will be early and will have very short stalks.

Annuals to be planted now for fall and winter color include nasturtium, sweet peas, snapdragon, calendula, and sweet alyssum. If you nick the seeds of sweet peas with a knife so that you can see the creamy inside, they will germinate faster. Pansy seeds may also be planted now, although transplants or bedding plants will perform far better and shouldn't go into the ground until next month.

Divide ground covers and perennials now, including ajuga, mondo grass and liriope, pachysandra, daylilies, coreopsis, phlox, coneflowers, black-eyed susan, iris, stokesia, Shasta daisies, and peonies (if they need it). Seedlings of Lenten rose, columbine, foxgloves, and hollyhocks may be transplanted now into prepared soil in other spots. Seeds of perennial hollyhocks, candytuft, phlox, gaillardia, and daisies may also be planted now.

> The wildflower and the violet, they perished long ago,
> But on the hill the goldenrod and the aster in the wood,
> And the yellow sunflower by the brook, in Autumn beauty stood.
> *William Cullen Bryant*

Shear hedges one more time, but do not prune other landscape shrubs heavily until after a killing frost. New growth resulting from pruning if it is to survive must have a couple of months or more to harden off before the dead of winter.

Roses have started blooming again and may be made to bloom even more next month with light pruning (to just above the first leaf having five leaflets) followed by feeding with a fast-acting liquid plant food. Keep spraying for insects, diseases, and mites.

Lawn Southern lawns of St. Augustinegrass, Bermuda, zoysia, and centipede will benefit from a feeding in late summer or very early fall. This feeding will help them to withstand winter and to green up in the spring. This feeding, however, must be administered before the first average frost. Later feeding will prevent the grasses from hardening off properly and will thus undermine their frost and freeze resistance. Unless you have already done so this summer, apply a winterizer or other lawn food containing potash soon, and be done with it until after spring greenup.

Leaves that turn brown or display fall colors are showing signs of summer drought. Water shrubs and trees now to help them store food for the winter and for next spring's flush of growth.

Reminder Leaves are turning brown or showing fall colors, not because it is Autumn, but because of summer drouth. Water shrubs and trees now, to help them store food for the winter and next spring's flush of growth.

Continue to feed hummingbirds. This practice will not make them stay around too late to migrate; it will help them add fat for the long flight across the Gulf of Mexico. Providing fresh water for all birds will pay off handsomely for them and you, too.

OCTOBER

Things to See Now   John Elsley, horticulture director at the famous Wayside Gardens company, once remarked, "While we can't really escape spring color, no fall color too often means that the gardener has simply failed to take advantage of the exciting plants available."

October in the Deep South is one of extremes, when shirt-sleeve days shorten and cool nights make us think of first frosts. Gardeners really scramble to cover the tomatoes and periwinkle, and wish they had already set out pansies and broccoli. School band practice is in the afternoon air, woodpiles are getting thick and tall, and brown leaves have already been raked at least once by conscientious gardeners.

The birds have finished off the purple berries of pokeweed, and the leaves of the medium-size French mulberry shrub (beauty berry, an American native) have dropped to reveal thick clusters along arching stems of lavendar-magenta berries (which are edible, but not palatable). Dull blue berries adorn junipers along the way, and those of pyracantha are maturing from yellow to orange to crimson red. Nandinas and hollies, too, (at least the females) are berrying up for winter, waiting only for the cedar waxwings to sweep into town. Magnolia pods are brimming with red fruit, just with the dogwoods, and both are ready for harvest and planting (rub the seeds out of the red-fleshed drupe first, or germination will be diminished).

Pyrethrum and Korean hybrid chrysanthemums are splendid now, embellishing the later-blooming cushion mums. A favorite chrysanthemum for the South is the lavender-blue Country Girl, noted for its profusion of cool blossoms and vigorous, sprawling plants. Asters, beginning to fade now, are more noticeable for some reason than when first showing. Foliage of spider lilies is peeking into view, only to get mown down when too close to the lawn, while caladiums are disappearing. Pine straw, a good investment, appears as if by magic in bags along roadsides.

The best blooming shrub of this month and next, without peer, is the camellia known as sasanqua. Single and double flowers of white and red are available on this medium-to-large, glossy shrub, but shades of rose and pink seem to be favored across older landscapes.

Vegetables Be prepared to protect late summer vegetables this month with plastic sheets and mulch. Light frosts can be kept from harming tomatoes, peppers, and eggplants for a night or two, but you should finish harvesting them and concentrate instead on your winter garden. Cut pumpkins and winter squash with a short piece of stem attached when they are firm, true to color for their variety, and hard beneath your thumbnail. Store them in a cool, dry place. Gourds may be left on the vine until after a frost, but edible squashes should be brought indoors.

Sweet potato vines may be killed by a light frost without damage to the potatoes. Dig the roots immediately afterward and bring them indoors to cure before storage. Any frosted roots should be discarded. Some varieties of broccoli will produce extra sideheads until they are killed next month by a hard freeze, but cauliflower produces only one head. Pull the upper leaves over cauliflower heads and fasten with a clothespin to prevent sunburn discoloration. Thinnings from lettuce, beets, turnips, and swiss chard are very tender and nutritious as salad greens. Collards, turnips, kale, and other greens actually improve in flavor after a frost. Wait to harvest the Irish potatoes you planted in August until the plants have been killed by frost.

Plant more mustard, spinach, turnips, and leaf lettuce this month; a small salad garden will be refreshing later in the fall. Onions planted now may not form bulbs in the spring because of fluctuating weather; it's better to plant them in January and February. You may plant garlic now, though, bearing in mind that the

---

Tomatoes All Winter

Tomatoes about to be caught by frosts in October and November can be pulled green and brought indoors for a slow ripening. Those with pink color will ripen quickly and should be left out in the open. If the fruits are large and mature enough to have formed a hard ring around the stem and have a whitish green cast, they can be wrapped in paper and stored indoors for a slow ripening. By doing this, you can have ripe tomatoes for New Year's Day.

bulbs won't be ready to harvest until next May or June. Plant the individual cloves twice as deep as they are tall, in a place where they won't interfere with spring planting.

Discard unused vegetable seeds if they have been subjected to heat or humidity this past summer. Store what you want to save in the refrigerator (not the freezer) or in some other cool, dry place. Make notes on your good and bad experiences this year, and plan to order more of the successful varieties. Save only the best seeds; seed packets are one of the least of your garden expenses.

Your compost pile can use all the leaves, spent flowers, weeds, kitchen debris (but no meat or bones), and grass clippings you can give it. Don't add diseased plants pulled from your garden or border, since diseases only grow stronger in compost. Add a touch of lime, some nitrogen fertilizer (including pea and sweet potato vines), and turn the pile to mix it up. Moisture will help the process, so leave a slight well uncovered at the center of the heap. Turning the compost from time to time will be your main chore for the rest of the winter.

Good winter cover crops that may be sown now include clover and ryegrass, but I have always preferred hairy vetch and wild winter peas for their bulkiness and nitrogen-forming habits. Both need to be mowed before being turned under in the spring so that they will not choke the tiller. Use a pound of seed or more per 1,000 square feet; even raised beds can benefit from this wholesome method of fortifying the soil, since the plants' roots absorb nutrients and break up clods while controlling erosion. Turn the plants under in the spring.

Fruit Plants   Oriental persimmons are ripe and attractive this month. Some varieties can be eaten green right from the tree. Muscadine vines and blueberry bushes, both handsome at this time of year, should not be pruned, or winter damage may result.

Pecans may be shedding leaves early because of summer and early fall mites, diseases, and insects. This leaf drop will certainly reduce next year's crop, since autumn leaves generate hormones for spring flowers. You can't do much about it except make notes that will help you prevent the problem next year.

Give strawberries one more shot of fertilizer and a good deep soaking. Pull weeds (they shelter insects and diseases), and thin plants to reduce competition next spring. Strawberry plants are superhardy and don't need mulches.

> To take a spade or spading fork on a crisp fall day and without undue haste or back-breaking effort to turn over slice after slice of sweet-smelling earth can bring rich rewards to the gardener who fully understands just what he is accomplishing.
>
> *T. H. Everett*

Kites fly in March and April, so why not in October when the winds are as strong or stronger? It is because the southerly spring breezes are generally of warm air rising, which lifts upwards, while autumnal breezes are from the north-northwest and are of cooler, descending air which presses downward.

Go Fly a Kite

Ornamentals The past couple of months have been hot and dry, and the wind has picked up considerably. Many shrubs will need a deep soaking to prevent undue winter damage (most of it stems from drying winds and drought, not from actual freezing, except in unusual cases of sudden, severe cold fronts). Roots of plants, which do most of their year's growth in the fall, need moisture.

Mulches conserve moisture and keep the soil warm longer into the winter, helping roots stay active and vigorous. Spread five or six inches over the soil, and keep it moist. Water the root zone, not just the mulch.

Prepare the soil for spring bulbs now, but wait another few weeks before planting them, or they will bloom prematurely. You may set out a few pansies to begin rooting in the season's warm days; bulbs can simply be inserted in between the plants later. Ornamental kale, or flowering cabbage, as it is sometimes called, is another fine winter annual. It eventually becomes an upright, knee-high, colorful plant that is excellent in masses or as an accent. The color intensifies after a frost or two, and the plants will remain attractive through all but the worst freezes if there is no warm weather beforehand. Mulches and watering will be important, and an underplanting of tulips is a good backup plan in case the kale is frozen beyond recovery.

If you haven't yet divided perennials, do so right away or wait until late winter. Otherwise, roots of some of them may not have time to establish themselves before the worst weather comes, and you may lose plants. Wait until spring to divide the chrysanthemums that are now nearing the end of their blooming period. Plant seeds for winter growth of sweet peas (scratch the seed coats), phlox, larkspur, calendula, bachelor's buttons, and sweet william as well as candytuft, foxglove, and daisies.

Shrubs and ground covers may be planted now with great results next year. Roots will grow well into the fall in warm, moist soil, and the plants will have a head start over spring-planted ones.

Water and mulch are essential, but fertilizer is not recommended at this time.

Dig caladiums before frost, and allow them to dry indoors for a week or more before gently pulling off dead leaves. Store them in bags or boxes of peat or vermiculite after dusting with Captan and Sevin to prevent damage from insects and diseases.

House Plants   Examine indoor plants for problems, rinse them off with tepid water, and begin withholding fertilizers, which won't be needed as much in the winter. Give plants a few days in an interim spot to adjust to reduced light and humidity before they come indoors. If they lose a few leaves, don't attempt to compensate with water or fertilizer. Check carefully for insects and mites, and wash leaves with mild soapy water. Flush the soil with copious amounts of plain water to eliminate ants, roaches, and similar pests.

Geraniums can be dug or lifted from pots and stored dry over the winter. Shake or wash the soil from the roots, dry the plants indoors, and store in a cool, dry room until spring.

Christmas cactus will bloom better after being left outside where the nights are cooling; withhold water and fertilizer. Give poinsettias bright light during the day and total darkness for thirteen hours at night if you want them to flower for Christmas.

Lawn   Do not fertilize the lawn! Your grass will remain too tender for too long if you feed it with nitrogen this month or next, and you'll be increasing the chances of winter damage from freezes and drying winds. Also, you don't want to feed the winter weeds that are now beginning to grow. Mow the lawn at the usual height until it goes dormant unless you have centipedegrass, which should be mowed lower the last time you cut it for the winter. Overseed Bermuda with ryegrass this month if you want winter green and don't mind mowing and watering it.

If your lawn or garden needs lime, this is a good time to apply it for next year because it takes several months to begin working.

Reminder   Lime or sulfur put around hydrangeas now will also have time to influence next year's flowers (lime causes pink flower color, sulfur causes blue). Do not lime blueberries, azaleas, camellias, or centipede lawns without a soil test indicating a need for it.

Continue to feed hummingbirds until they leave for South

America. They will need to store up extra fat (which will be lost during the migratory flight). Only a few sickly birds will remain behind when the migratory call beckons.

NOVEMBER

Things to See Now   What tree holds more anticipation in the fall than ginkgo, with its rush of intense yellow leaves that litter the ground beneath within three or four days of turning? Autumn in the Deep South does have its colors, though not in such as vivid display as seen from the Smokies on up into the nether reaches of the Northeast. Chartreuse of hackberry, brilliant scarlet of sumac and poison ivy and blueberry, reds of dogwood and black gum, and orange of walnut and crape myrtle these are common examples of gorgeous fall colors. Many plants go through dramatic changes, such as sweetgum and Chinese tallow ("popcorn" tree), while others just tan out (pampas and zoysiagrass, asparagus, and a host of garden and flower bed species). Deeper colors of azalea, andromeda, and abelia foliage surprise many, as do the unusual pinks and purples of some groundcover junipers. Wild pears, no match for the cultivated ornamental ones (Bradford, for one) when it comes to spring flowers, are equally unmatched by the gorgeous fall foliage.

Two notable blooming shrubs are the unbeatable sasanqua, with pinks, reds, and white blossoms, and eleagnus, with hundreds of silvery-white, highly-fragrant flowers hidden within its massive canes.

Small evergreen shrubs and groundcovers take on new importance as the backbone of the perennial border and the rest of the winter landscape. Boxwoods are suddenly the design rather than the hedge, and yucca, that unduly despised plant, pointedly becomes the sentinel over the lawn. Unusual evergreens planted for winter effect include butcher broom (Ruscus), clump-forming yucca (*Y. filamentosa*), dwarf nandina and barberry, yellow-and-green euonymus, liriope, aspidistra, junipers, and the foliage of spider lily and other perennials.

The red autumnal leaves of Boston ivy fall to reveal intricate patterns of brown against walls and fences, and the poisonous seedpods of wisteria hang menacingly close to curious young hands. Carolina snailseed (Cocculus) is suddenly everywhere, in hedges and up lightpole guy wires, covered with bunches of bright red berries.

Yew, holly, viburnum, nandina, and on the list goes of berried shrubs which come into their own long before we notice them in Autumn. Tallow trees have clusters of waxy, white berries, earning them the nickname of "popcorn trees." This is the time to *do something* about our landscapes, to plant those beauties we are seeing all around us.

Vegetables   Row up an edge of garden for planting onions, potatoes, and English peas in January. Your labor will pay off later; after all, our gardens are usually wet from December until May. In fact, this may be the best time of all to deep plow or till in subsoil, burying diseases and insects and improving the drainage in the process. A soil test will tell you whether you need extra lime after the subsoil and topsoil have been mixed.

You still have time to plant hairy vetch or rye as cover, but don't expect the crop to grow very tall before the cold weather hits.

Remove dead tomato and bean plants and weeds that harbor insects, and compost all but those with obvious diseases. Clean tools of rust and dirt by jamming them several times into pails of oily sand. Before throwing a tarp over the tiller, drain the gas tank and replace the oil. If you take these simple precautions, the tiller will start on the first pull next spring.

Harvest tomatoes that haven't been frosted. If they are mature enough to have begun forming seeds, they will ripen indoors over a period of several weeks; just wrap them individually in paper. Carrots will be easier to pull if you water the soil first. Cut off the leaves immediately, or the carrots will quickly lose moisture and become spongy. You should also harvest any Irish potatoes and turnips that are still in the ground, but you may leave the Jerusalem artichokes, parsnips, and salsify outside until you need them.

Order seed catalogs!

Fruit Plants   Pecans are falling now and should be gathered as soon as possible and air dried indoors on paper to reduce internal moisture-related fungus. Store bags of shelled pecans in the refrigerator or freezer.

Remove fallen leaves, diseased fruits, and twigs from beneath trees. Don't prune now except to remove dead or broken limbs. Mulch fig trees and blueberry bushes with porous material, but don't mulch other fruits. If mulches are needed around very young trees, use a doughnut, or ring, around them, leaving three or four inches of air space around the trunks.

Wrap the trunks of young fruit trees with burlap strips or commercial tree wrap, or at least paint them with white latex paint, to prevent the winter sun from warming the south and southwest sides and producing sunscald, or the splitting of bark. Diseases enter young trees through split bark; older trees, which have thicker bark, do not need protection as much.

This is a good time to set out fruit trees that have been ordered from mail order firms, since they can root and establish themselves before spring. Fruit trees are not generally available in local nurseries before late December or early January, but you can go ahead now and prepare the soil so that it is mellow and ready regardless of the weather when the trees actually arrive.

Ornamentals   Plant bulbs, tubers, and corms this month. Hardy perennials include daffodils, Dutch iris, allium, garlic, amaryllis (in most areas), hybrid lilies, iris, peony, and muscari, or grape hyacinth. Perennials planted earlier will be fine, although some will have their foliage exposed to extreme weather a little too soon (they will not die but will be unattractive). Fertilize with a well-balanced bulb food rather than with the single-nutrient bone meal.

When you buy bulbs, save a few to set in pots of water and gravel for indoor blooming. Paperwhite and Soleil d'Or are good for the purpose.

Pansies should be in the ground and watered well by now. After a couple of frosts and freezes, any residual heat will be gone from the soil, and the pansies should be mulched to keep weeds under control.

Cut the frosted brown foliage from banana trees and other perennials now. Dig tuberoses, dahlias, and cannas if your area is too cold for them to overwinter. Otherwise, mulch them heavily. Mulch shrubs as well, especially those planted within the past couple of years. Label clumps of flowers now while you know where they are, or at least mark them to avoid accidentally digging into them later.

Water is the critical factor in the survival of many half-hardy, young, or shallow-rooted shrubs, and rainfall is sparse this month.

To keep container plants from having their roots freeze, group them together, and mulch the pots and surrounding area. Alternatively, bury them up to their rims in soil for the winter.

Prune overgrown sprouts and neaten up hedges after a killing

Fall, not spring, is the time in this region to clear away dead leaves and branches, to renovate the borders, to start new gardens . . . to set out new perennials and shrubs . . . And even if something is left undone, everyone must take time to sit still and watch the leaves turn.

Elizabeth Lawrence

frost has sent landscape shrubs into full dormancy. Roses should be topped a little so that tall canes don't sway or break, but save most pruning of roses and other landscape plants until late winter or early spring.

Prepare a rose bed or other other perennial garden now, while the weather is warm by day and the soil is workable, in preparation for winter or spring planting.

Lawn   Drain the gas tank of the mower and string trimmer to prevent evaporation and subsequent gumming of the engine, and change the oil. Loosen the sparkplug wire, and clean the air filter. Change or sharpen the blade, and oil it to prevent rust.

Rake the leaves if they are very thick and likely to mat down and smother the lawn before spring. A few leaves won't hurt and may be mowed so that they serve as a mulch. Just don't let them pack down and become slimy.

Reminder   No other seasonal change is as dramatic as the first frost. Don't despair; take a ride in the country and reflect on the ephemeral clothing of the plants which inhabit our land. Enjoy the bounties of the earth and give thanks.

Put up a thistle feeder to attract finches to the winter landscape, and plant daffodils.

DECEMBER

Things to See Now   Trees are mostly leafless (and some are going up in smoke across the rooftops of town and country), but their buds will be swelling even before the month is out. Variegated trunks of quince trees, bark of hickories and ash, and the stark white upper limbs of sycamore contrast with the dull winter colors of azalea and cedar. Within plain sight of everyone are berries and the streaks of red and blue as cardinals and bluejays battle for crumbs flung from the door. Seasonal winter birds are here, but they are still timid at the bath in the face of opposition from locals. Red-headed woodpeckers are more visible now that their tree canopy is gone. Squirrels are amusingly frenetic in their search for booty.

Galls on oak trees are all-too-obvious (and relatively harmless) along with others on the canes of goldenrod and roses, willows, and the fallen live oaks and hackberry leaves. Galls are to be considered as gross ornaments, rather than as a source of worry; they have been compared to insect larvae "gingerbread houses," survival capsules from harsh winter weather.

Nature's ornaments are in abundance now, from trumpet creeper and milkweed pods to sweetgum balls and long black locust beans (the huge spines of this tree alone make nice ornaments). Lichens, mosses, and mistletoe are the stuff of legends and lore, and are as commonly found now as any flower in June. Spanish moss, a relative of pineapple, is our best-known bromeliad and is widespread across the Deep South, draping cypress and oak in spooky gray.

Evergreen shrubs and groundcovers are the backbone of the southern landscape. Chinafirs, junipers, arborvitae, cedars, pines, and the deodar are particularly interesting as they are the South's rare conifers. Junipers alone have an incredible variety of shape, form, size, color, and hue; many are irreplaceable as accents and sun-loving groundcovers. The bald cypress, though deciduous, and the miraculous dawn redwood (once thought to be extinct, but discovered just before the middle of this century in China), both are wonderful in even clay soils, as long as watered in the late summer and fall.

> Once we become interested in the progress of the plants in our care, their development becomes a part of the rhythm of our own lives and we are refreshed by it.
>
> *Thalassa Cruso*

The two main annuals of the flower bed remain the pansy and ornamental kale (flowering cabbage). Herbaceous flowers are for the most part gone by the end of the calendar year, so those that are peeking about are to be treasured: Christmas rose, paperwhite narcissus, perhaps some dianthus or crocus. Shrubs that make the season include the native witchhazel, laurestinus, and two fragrant, large shrubs, the winter honeysuckle and eleagnus. A few azaleas usually bloom out of season before Christmas.

Poinsettias and cheerful displays of holiday spirit light up stores and outdoor shrubbery as if this is the only time of the year extravagance in the landscape is permitted.

Vegetables　Check stored vegetables such as sweet potatoes and winter squash to make sure that they are still firm and in good conditions. Sweet potatoes need to be kept cool and moist and may turn dark if they are too cold, sprout if they are too warm, shrivel if they are too dry, and rot if they are too moist. Storable squash should be cool and dry; check for signs of decay and use it as soon as possible.

It is almost time to plant again, although some of our worst days lie ahead. Onions and Irish potatoes can withstand the most severe weather, provided that your soil has been prepared ahead of time and they aren't set out during blizzards. Asparagus crowns may be planted any time the soil can be deeply prepared so that the permanent bed will always drain well. For asparagus you will need a lot of organic material plus a little lime.

A coldframe can supply you with fresh greens all winter as well as giving you a place to start transplants of cabbage, broccoli, and, later, tomatoes and peppers. Coldframes should be about knee high on the north side and sloping toward the south to catch as much sun as possible. Open the frame on warm days so that it does not become too hot. Cover it with an old piece of rug on very cold nights for added insulation.

Ordering seeds early ensures that you will have time to plant in a leisurely way—or even to order more seeds. Few experiences are more satisfying to the gardener than receiving seed packets in the mail in January and February!

Fruit Plants   Prune a few grape and muscadine vines for wreaths, and use some apple twigs in the fireplace. If the weather is nice (not above 80 degrees and no one is predicting a freeze within two or three days), spray your trees with a dormant oil to control overwintering scale insects.

If you are trying to grow kiwi, be prepared to cover the vines with plastic and to mulch their bases with straw in the event of an ice storm or freeze that may go below 15 degrees.

Ornamentals   Consider using a locally grown Christmas tree this year. Cutting it can provide a fine outing for the family as well

---

Cut a Magnolia?   Magnolia trees have been around much longer than we have, so you'd expect that we would know how big they can get. Yet people still set out the small trees in tiny front yards, like putting a whale in a bathtub. The landscape my wife and I just bought had a fine specimen right smack in the front, and it was blocking the winter sun as well as the summer breeze. I had to spend $600 getting its roots out of my septic line. It had seven phone, power, and cable lines running through its middle. And, perhaps worst of all, the original owner had pruned the limbs up "to let more light in so grass will grow." Unfortunately, no grass would grow anyway, so I got stuck with a lopsided, overgrown, tree.

The lessons are these. First, decide what mature size or shape you want. Look up for power lines. Avoid large trees in small yards. And don't cut the limbs on Southern magnolias, or you will be doomed forever with leaves to rake!

---

as giving you an inexpensive, very fresh specimen for decoration. Pick-your-own trees, usually Virginia or white pine, are almost always less expensive than precut trees. If you buy a precut tree, check for freshness first. Be sure that the needles are pliant and that an excessive number don't fall when the butt of the tree is tapped on the ground. Recut the stump before putting it in the stand, place it out of a draft, and keep the bowl supplied with water. When the holiday is past, Christmas trees may be set in the yard and decorated with popcorn, peanut butter cups, and seed-cakes for the birds.

Other greenery—holly, magnolia, nandina, mistletoe, aucuba, cleyera, smilax, ivy, and boxwood—can be used for seasonal decoration indoors, but take care not to mutilate the plants from which you take the cuttings.

December is better than any other month (except possibly November) for transplanting trees and shrubs. Dig carefully and take as many roots as possible (shallow roots are more important than deep ones). Dig a trench around the root zone, then undercut the root ball before lifting the plant and setting it into previously prepared soil.

To protect landscape plants from severe damage caused by sudden drops in temperature (especially after prolonged dry weather), mulch, water thoroughly at least once every couple of weeks, and wrap the trunks of young trees. Antiwilt sprays will help protect the leaves of broadleaf evergreens from drying winds.

House Plants   Place new plants out of drafts and away from cold windowpanes but in spots where they can get lots of light. Before watering, lift the pot to see whether it is heavy with moisture or is getting light and in need of a soaking. Fertilizers aren't generally necessary now, since most plants are growing slowly. Group plants together to raise the humidity.

Used to be, when times were simpler, southern homes were filled with the sharp fragrance of cedar. A fellow asked me why it seems that odor is gone now, and I was stumped until a couple of dozen callers let me know that it was a memory from before my time, when women used "smoothing irons" (like I have as a doorstop) to press clothes, which they heated on the fire. Before they were used for pressing, the hot irons were run over boughs of cedar to remove the soot.

(And cedar shavings have long been used to repel fleas from doghouses.)

The Sweet Smell of Cedar

Reminder   'Tis the season to be jolly, but don't forget to put fresh water in the bird bath and a few sunflower seeds and raisins out for our feathered friends! Time to turn the page and gird our gardening selves for the new year. Resolve to read another garden book (check the references in the back of this one for some all-time favorites) and try something new or different next month.

One of the best things about a garden, large or small, is that it is never finished. It is a continual experiment.
Margery Bianco

Additional Resources

Agricultural Extension Horticulture Specialists

Within a state, local extension agents may be located in the telephone directory under "Agricultural Agent" or "Extension Service" in the listings for county government. In addition to their own resources, agents can draw on those of the local agricultural college and the United States Department of Agriculture.

Alabama

Extension Horticulture Department, Auburn University, Auburn, Alabama 36849. Tel. (205) 826-4985

Arkansas

Extension Horticulture, 316 Plant Science Building, University of Arkansas, Fayetteville, Arkansas 72701. Tel. (501) 575-2603

District of Columbia

Chairman, Extension Horticulture, 1725, Lincoln Road, N.E., Washington, D.C. 20002. Tel. (202) 576-6951

Extension Horticulture, Department of Environmental Science, University of the District of Columbia, 4200 Connecticut Avenue, N.W., Washington, D.C. 20008. Tel. (202) 282-7370

Florida

Horticulture Department, University of Florida, Gainesville, Florida 32611. Tel. (904) 392-1834 (Many area offices across the state.)

Georgia

Extension Horticulture, University of Georgia, Athens, Georgia 30602. Tel. (404) 542-2861 (Many area offices across the state.)

Louisiana

Department of Horticulture, 214 Knapp Hall, Louisiana State University, Baton Rouge, Louisiana 70803. Tel. (504) 388-4141

Mississippi

Extension Horticulture, P.O. Box 5426, Mississippi State, Mississippi 39762. Tel. (601) 325-3935 (Additional offices around the state.)

North Carolina

Department of Horticultural Science, North Carolina State University, Raleigh, North Carolina 27695–7609. Tel. (919) 737-3131

South Carolina

Department of Horticulture, 161 Plant and Animal Sciences Building, Clemson University, Clemson, South Carolina 29631–0375. Tel. (803) 656-4694

Tennessee

Extension Horticulture, University of Tennessee, Box 1071, Knoxville, Tennessee 37901–1071. Tel. (615) 974-7324

Texas

Department of Horticulture, 201 Horticulture/Forestry Building, Texas A&M University, College Station, Texas 77843. Tel. (409) 845-5341 (Many area specialists around the state.)

Virginia

Department of Horticulture, Virginia Polytechnic Institute, Blacksburg, Virginia 24061. Tel. (703) 961-5451

Books and Pamphlets

Books in the Ortho and Sunset series, available at many nurseries and hardware stores, are often good sources of information. For a list of government publications, write to Superintendent of Documents, U.S. Government Printing Office, Washington, D.C. 20402. Many publications are available, too, from your state's Cooperative Extension Service.

Austin, Richard L. *Wild Gardening: Strategies and Procedures Using Native Plantings.* New York: Simon and Schuster, 1986.

Batson, Wade T. *Landscape Plants for the Southeast: Botanical Sketch of Each Plant.* Columbia: University of South Carolina Press, 1984.

Bubel, Nancy. *The Seed Starter's Handbook.* Emmaus, Pa.: Rodale, 1978.

Bull, John, and Farrand, John. *The Audubon Society Guide to North American Birds: Eastern Region.* New York: Knopf, 1977.

Bush-Brown, James, and Bush-Brown, Louise. *America's Garden Book.* Rev. ed. New York: Scribner's, 1979.

Color Dictionary of Flowers and Plants for Home and Garden. New York: Crown Publishers, Royal Horticultural Society, 1969.

Creasy, Rosalind. *Complete Book of Edible Landscaping.* San Francisco: Sierra Club, 1982.

Crockett, James U. *Crockett's Victory Garden.* Boston: Little Brown, 1977.

Dennis, John V. *A Complete Guide to Bird Feeding.* New York: Knopf, 1978.

Duncan, Wilbur H., and Foote, Leonard E. *Wildflowers of the Southeastern United States.* Athens: University of Georgia Press, 1975.

Encyclopedia of Organic Gardening. Emmaus, Pa.: Rodale, 1978.

Everett, T. H. *The New York Botanical Garden Illustrated Encyclopedia of Horticulture.* 10 vols. New York: Garland, 1980. (Ask your public library to buy this invaluable reference work if it doesn't already have a copy.)

Galle, Fred C. *Native and Introduced Azaleas.* Pine Mountain, Ga.: Ida Cason Callaway Foundation, 1979.

Garden Flowers You Can Grow. Des Moines, Iowa: Better Homes and Gardens, 1980.

Garden Guide. Birmingham, Ala.: Southern Living, Oxmoor House, 1981.

Gardens of the American South. Barre, Mass.: Westover, 1971.

Gardens of the South/Southern Accents. New York: Simon and Schuster, 1985.

Gordon, Lesley. *A Country Herbal.* New York: W. H. Smith, 1980.

Halfacre, R. Gordon, and Shawcroft, Anne. *Carolina Landscape Plants.* Raleigh, N.C.: Sparks Press, 1975.

Hastings, Louise, and Hastings, Donald. *The Southern Gardening Book.* New York: Doubleday, 1948.

Hortus Third. New York: Macmillan, 1976. (A good reference work for your local public library.)

Hunt, William Lanier. *Southern Gardens, Southern Gardening.* Durham: Duke University Press, 1982.

Lacy, Allen. *Farther Afield: A Gardener's Excursions.* New York: Farrar, Straus and Giroux, 1986.

Lacy, Allen. *Home Ground: A Gardener's Miscellany.* New York: Farrar, Straus and Giroux, 1984.

Lawrence, Elizabeth. *A Southern Garden: A Handbook for the Middle South.* Chapel Hill: University of North Carolina Press, 1984.

McEachern, George Ray. *Growing Fruits, Berries, and Nuts in the South.* Houston: Pacesetter Press, 1978.

Martin, Laura C. *The Wildflower Meadow Book.* Charlotte, N.C.: East Woods Press, 1986.

Mitchell, Henry. *The Essential Earthman: Henry Mitchell on Gardening.* Bloomington: Indiana University Press, 1981.

National Gardening Association. *Gardening: The Complete Guide to Growing America's Favorite Fruits and Vegetables.* Reading, Mass.: Addison Wesley, 1986.

North American Horticulture: A Reference Guide. New York: Scribner's, 1982. (Ask your local public library to buy a copy of this book if it doesn't already have one.)

The Ortho Problem Solver. San Francisco: Chevron Chemical Company, 1984. (Excellent for advice on controlling pests and probably available for your use at your local nursery.)

Perenyi, Eleanor. *Green Thoughts: A Writer in the Garden.* New York: Random House, 1981.

Perry, Frances, ed. *Simon and Schuster's Complete Guide to Plants and Flowers.* New York: Simon and Schuster, 1975.

Peterson, Roger Tory. *A Field Guide to the Birds East of the Rockies.* Boston: Houghton Mifflin, 1980.

Peterson, Roger Tory. *A Field Guide to the Birds of Texas and Adjacent States.* Boston: Houghton Mifflin, 1963.

Proctor, Noble. *Garden Birds: How to Attract Birds to Your Garden.* Emmaus, Pa.: Rodale, 1986.

Raymond, Dick. *Dick Raymond's Gardening Year.* New York: Linden Press, Simon and Schuster, 1985.

Raymond, Dick. *Joy of Gardening.* New York: Garden Way, Harper and Row, 1983.

The Reader's Digest Illustrated Guide to Gardening. Pleasantville, N.Y.: Reader's Digest, 1978.

Reader's Digest. *North American Wildlife.* New York: Random House, 1982.

Simmons, Adelma Grenier. *Herb Gardening in Five Seasons.* New York: Hawthorn, 1964.

Stout, Ruth. *Gardening without Work.* New York: Exposition, 1955.

Swain, Roger. *Earthly Pleasures: Tales from a Biologist's Garden.* New York: Scribner's, 1981.

Swain, Roger. *Field Days: Journal of an Itinerant Biologist.* New York: Scribner's, 1983.

Tekulsky, Mathew. *The Butterfly Garden.* Boston: Harvard Common Press, 1985.

Tenenbaum, Frances. *Gardening with Wildflowers.* New York: Ballantine, 1986.

Trees and Shrubs, Groundcovers and Vines. Birmingham, Ala.: Southern Living, Oxmoor House, 1980.

Wigginton, Brooks E. *Trees and Shrubs for the Southeast.* Athens: University of Georgia Press, 1963.

Witty, Helen, ed. *Billy Joe Tatum's Wild Foods Cookbook and Field Guide.* New York: Workman, 1976.

Wyman, Donald. *Wyman's Gardening Encyclopedia.* Rev. and expanded ed. New York: Macmillan, 1977. (Another book for your public library's reference shelf.)

Magazines

In addition to the periodicals listed below, many of the public gardens and arboretums issue newsletters and other publications with useful information.

American Horticulturist, American Horticultural Society, Box 0105, Mount Vernon, Virginia 22121

Avant Gardener, Box 489E, New York, New York 10028

Flower and Garden, 4251 Pennsylvania, Kansas City, Missouri 64111

Herb Quarterly, Uphills Press, Inc., West Street, Box 275, New Fare, Vermont 05345

Horticulture, 300 Massachusetts Avenue, Boston, Massachusetts 02115

Mother Earth News, 105 Stoney Mountain Road, Hendersonville, North Carolina 28791

National Gardening, 180 Flynn Avenue, Burlington, Vermont 05401

Organic Gardening, 33 East Minor Street, Emmaus, Pennsylvania 18049

Southern Accents, W. R. C. Smith Publishing, 1760 Peachtree Road, Atlanta, Georgia 30357

Southern Living, Box C–119, Birmingham, Alabama 35282–9848

Texas Gardener, Suntex Communications, Inc., 2509 Washington, Box 9005, Waco, Texas 76714

Plant Societies

For a more complete list of plant societies, plus garden centers, community gardens, and other places of interest, see North American Horticulture: A Reference Guide.

American Boxwood Society, Box 85, Boyce, Virginia 22620

American Camellia Society, Box 750, Brookhaven, Mississippi 39601

American Daffodil Society, Tyner, North Carolina 27980

American Dahlia Society, 2044 Great Falls Street, Falls Church, Virginia 22043

American Fern Society, Department of Botany, University of Tennessee, Knoxville, Tennessee 37916

American Hemerocallis Society, Route 2, Box 360, DeQueen, Arkansas 71832

American Horticulture Society, Box 0105, Mount Vernon, Virginia 22121

American Hosta Society, 5605 Eleventh Avenue South, Birmingham, Alabama 35222

American Iris Society, 6518 Beachy Avenue, Wichita, Kansas 67206

American Rock Garden Society, Box 282, Route 1, Mena, Arizona 71953

American Rose Society, Box 30000, Shreveport, Louisiana 71130

Azalea Society of America, Box 6244, Silver Spring, Maryland 20906

Holly Society of America, 407 Fountain Green Road, Bel Air, Maryland 21014

International Camellia Society, Box 1217, Fort Valley, Georgia 31030

National Chrysanthemum Society, 2612 Beverly Boulevard, Roanoke, Virginia 24015

National Gardening Association, 180 Flynn Avenue, Burlington, Vermont 05401

Society for the Louisiana Iris, Box 40175 USL, Lafayette, Louisiana 70504

Mail Order Suppliers

Blue Ridge Seed Savers, Box 106, Batesville, Virginia 29924 (An exchange for Virginia gardeners.)

W. Atlee Burpee Company, 300 Park Avenue, Warminster, Pennsylvania 18974

Comstock, Ferre, and Company, 263 Main Avenue, Wethersfield, Connecticut 06109

Daffodil Haven, P.O. Box 218, Hubbard, Oregon 97032

The Daffodil Mart, Route 3, Box 208R, Gloucester, Virginia 23061

Henry Field Seed and Nursery Company, 407 Sycamore Street, Shenandoah, Iowa 06109

Gurney Seed and Nursery Company, Second and Capitol, Yankdon, South Dakota 57079

Joseph Harris Company, 3670 Buffalo Road, Rochester, New York 14624

H. G. Hastings Company, P.O. Box 4274, Atlanta, Georgia 30302 (Fruit trees for the South.)

Heirloom Gardens, Box 138, Guerneville, California 95446 (Herbs; catalog costs two dollars.)

Holbrook Farm, Route 2, Box 223B, Fletcher, North Carolina 28732 (Perennials for the South; catalog costs one dollar, redeemable with coupon enclosed.)

Ison's Nursery and Vineyard, Brooks, Georgia 30205 (Vines and fruits for the South.)

Jackson and Perkins Company, P.O. Box 1028, Medford, Oregon 97501

Johnny's Selected Seeds, Foss Hill Road, Albion, Maine 04910

J. W. Jung Seed Company, 333 South High Street, Randolph, Wisconsin 53956

A. M. Leonard, Inc., 665 Spiker Road, Piqua, Ohio 45356 (Huge selection of horti-cultural tools and supplies.)

Liberty Seed Company, P.O. Box 806, New Philadelphia, Ohio 44663

Lilypons Water Gardens, 1604 Lilypons Road, Brookshire, Texas 77423 (Garden pools, liners, fish, plants, supplies; catalog costs $2.50.)

Louisiana Nursery, Route 7, Box 43, Opelousas, Louisiana 70570 (Unusual perennials.)

Earl May Seed and Nursery Company, 208 North Elm Street, Shenandoah, Iowa 51603

Meyer Seed Company, 600 South Caroline Street, Baltimore, Maryland 21231

Nichols Garden Nursery, 1190 North Pacific Highway, Albany, Oregon 97321

George Park Seed Company, P.O. Box 31, Greenwood, South Carolina 29647

Plant Finders of America, 532 Beaumont, Fort Wright, Kentucky 41044 (World-wide searches for rare plants.)

Rincon-Vitova Insectaries, Box 95, Oak View, California 93022 (Suppliers of live beneficial insects.)

Seed Saver's Exchange, P.O. Box 70, Decorah, Iowa 52101 (Publishes a seed year-book of available varieties; sells an inventory that includes commercial sources for old varieties.)

Shepard's Garden Seeds, 7389 West Zayante Road, Felton, California 95018 (Un-usual vegetable seeds.)

Slocum Water Gardens, Department H-4, 1101 Cypress Gardens Road, Winter Haven, Florida 33880 (Water lilies, supplies.)

Smith and Hawken, 25 Corte Madera, Mill Valley, California 94941 (Quality gar-den tools.)

Stokes Seeds, Box 548, Buffalo, New York 14240

Thompson and Morgan, P.O. Box 100, Farmingdale, New Jersey 07727 (Superior selection of unusual and exotic plant seeds.)

Twilley Seed Company, P.O. Box 65, Trevose, Pennsylvania 19047

Andre Viette Farm and Nursery, Route 1, Box 16, Fishersville, Virginia 22939 (Outstanding perennials; catalog costs one dollar.)

Wayside Gardens, Hodges, South Carolina 29695–0001 (Southern perennials, unusual flowering shrubs and trees; catalog costs one dollar and has discount coupons inside.)

White Flower Farm, Litchfield, Connecticut 06759–0050 (Perennials; catalog costs five dollars and has discount coupon inside.)

Woodlanders, 1128 Colleton Avenue, Aiken, South Carolina 29801 (Native south-ern perennials, trees, shrubs; catalog costs two dollars.)

Public Gardens and Arboretums

Dates of founding or construction appear in parentheses, together with approximate size, where this information was available. Your state garden club headquarters and Cooperative Extension horticulturists can suggest other gardens that you might visit. In addition, the American Horticulture Society prints a list of hundreds of gardens across the nation; for more details, write the Society at Box 0105, Mount Vernon, Virginia 22121.

Alabama

Auburn University Arboretum, Department of Botany, Auburn, Alabama 36849. Tel. (205) 826-4830 (1963; 14 acres)

Birmingham Botanical Gardens, 2612 Lane Park Road, Birmingham, Alabama 35223. Tel. (205) 879-1227 (1962; 67.5 acres)

University of Alabama Arboretum, Box 1927, University, Alabama 35486. Tel. (205) 348-5960 (1958; 60 acres)

Florida

Alfred B. Maclay State Gardens, 3540 Thomasville Road, Tallahassee, Florida 32308. Tel. (904) 893-4455 (1952; 30 acres)

Bok Tower Gardens, Box 268, Lake Wales, Florida 33853. Tel. (813) 676-1408 (1929; 65 acres)

Fairchild Tropical Garden, 10901 Old Cutler Road, Miami, Florida 33156. Tel. (305) 667-1651 (1938; 83 acres)

Florida Cypress Gardens, Box 1, Cypress Gardens, Florida 33880. Tel. (813) 324-2111 (1935; 86 acres)

Florida's Sunken Gardens, 1825 Fourth Street North, St. Petersburg, Florida 33704. Tel. (813) 896-3186 (1903; 7 acres)

Four Arts Garden, Four Arts Plaza, Royal Palm Way, Palm Beach, Florida 33480 (Mail contact preferred.)

Harry P. Leu Botanical Garden, 1730 North Forest Avenue, Orlando, Florida 32803. Tel. (305) 894-6021 (1961; 55 acres)

Marie Selby Botanical Gardens, 800 South Palm Avenue, Sarasota, Florida 33577. Tel. (813) 366-5730 (1973; 11.5 acres)

Preston B. Bird and Mary Heinlein Fruit and Spice Park, 24801 S.W. 187 Avenue, Homestead, Florida 33031. Tel. (305) 247-5727 (1944; 20 acres)

Sarasota Jungle Gardens, 3701 Bayshore Road, Sarasota, Florida 33580. Tel. (813) 355-3505 (1940; 11 acres)

Simpson Park, 55 S.W. Seventeenth Road, Miami, Florida 33129. Tel. (305) 579-6947 (1931; 8.5 acres)

Suncoast Botanical Garden, Inc., 10410 125th Street North, Largo, Florida 33540. Tel. (813) 321-1726 (1962; 60 acres)

Wilmot Gardens, University of Florida, 1543 HSPP Building, Gainesville, Florida 32611. Tel. (904) 392-1831 (1853; 10 acres)

Georgia

Atlanta Botanical Garden, Piedmont Park at South Prado, Box 77246, Atlanta, Georgia 30357. Tel. (404) 876-5858 (1977; 60 acres)

Callaway Gardens, Pine Mountain, Georgia 31822. Tel. (404) 663-2281, ext. 156 (1953; 2,500 acres)

Camellia Gardens of the American Camellia Society, Box 1217, Fort Valley, Georgia 31030. Tel. (912) 967-2358 (1945; 10 acres)

Fernbank Science Center, 156 Heaton Park Drive, N.E., Atlanta, Georgia 30307. Tel. (404) 378-4311 (1966; 78 acres)

Founders Memorial Garden, University of Georgia, Athens, Georgia 30602. Tel. (404) 542-3631 (1941; 2.5 acres)

University of Georgia Botanical Garden, 2450 South Milledge Avenue, Athens, Georgia 30605. Tel. (404) 542-1244 (1968; 293 acres)

Louisiana

American Rose Society Gardens, Box 30,000, Shreveport, Louisiana 71130. Tel. (318) 938-5402 (1899; 118 acres)

Hodges Gardens, Box 921, Many, Louisiana 71449. Tel. (318) 586-3523 (1956; 4,800 acres)

Jungle Gardens, Avery Island, Louisiana 70513. Tel. (318) 365-8173 (1900; 200 acres)

The Louisiana State Arboretum, Box 494, Route 3, Ville Platte, Louisiana 70586 (1964; 301 acres). Tel. (318) 363-6287

Zemurray Gardens, 8313 O'Hara Court, Baton Rouge, Louisiana 70808. Tel. (504) 927-3500 (1936; 150 acres)

Mississippi

Crosby Arboretum, 3702 Hardy Street, Hattiesburg, Mississippi 39401. Tel. (601) 264-5249 (1980; 58 acres)

Gloster Arboretum, Gloster Arboretum Road, Gloster, Mississippi. Mailing address: John James Audubon Foundation, 227 North Thirteenth Street, Baton Rouge, Louisiana 70802. Tel. (504) 383-4447 (1962; 327 acres)

Mynelle Gardens, 4736 Clinton Boulevard, Jackson, Mississippi 39209. Tel. (601) 960-1894 (7 acres)

Wister Gardens, Highway 49W, Belzoni, Mississippi 39038. Tel. (601) 247-3025 (5 acres)

North Carolina

Coker Arboretum, University of North Carolina, Coker Hall 010-A, Chapel Hill, North Carolina 27514. Tel. (919) 933-3776 (1903; 5 acres)

Daniel Boone Native Gardens, Horn in the West Drive, Boone, North Carolina 28607. Tel. (704) 264-2819 (1961; 8 acres)

The Gardens of the University of North Carolina at Charlotte, Biology Department, UNCC Station, Charlotte, North Carolina 28223. Tel. (704) 597-2315 (1965; 9 acres)

Greenfield Gardens, City of Wilmington, Parks and Recreation, Box 810, Wilmington, North Carolina 28401. Tel. (919) 763-9871 (200-acre park with 180-acre lake)

North Carolina Botanical Gardens, University of North Carolina, Totten Center 457-A, Chapel Hill, North Carolina 27514. Tel. (919) 967-2246 (1952; 307 acres)

North Carolina State University Arboretum, NCSU Unit 4 Farm, Beryl Road, Raleigh, North Carolina 27606. Tel. (919) 737-3133 (1976; 8 acres)

Reynolda Gardens of Wake Forest University, 100 Reynolda Village, Winston-Salem, North Carolina 27106. Tel. (919) 761-5593 (1957; 119 acres)

Sarah P. Duke Gardens, Duke University, Durham, North Carolina 27706. Tel. (919) 684-3698 (1932; 60 acres)

University Botanical Gardens at Asheville, Inc., campus of the University of North Carolina, Weaver Boulevard, Asheville. Mailing address: c/o John A. Broadbooks, President, 6 Northwood Road, Asheville, North Carolina 28804. Tel. (704) 274-1551 (1960; 10 acres)

Wing Haven Foundation, Inc., 248 Ridgewood Avenue, Charlotte, North Carolina 28209. Tel. (704) 332-5770 (1971; 3 acres)

South Carolina

Brookgreen Gardens, Box 3, Route 1, Murrells Inlet, South Carolina 29576. Tel. (803) 237-4218 (1931; 300 acres)

Cypress Gardens, Box 304, Charleston, South Carolina 29402. Tel. (803) 577-6970 (1932; 162 acres)

Edisto Memorial Gardens, Box 863, Highway 301 South, Orangeburg, South Carolina 29115. Tel. (803) 534-6376 (1927; 110 acres)

Horticultural Gardens of Clemson University, Department of Horticulture, College of Agricultural Science, Clemson University, Clemson, South Carolina 29631. Tel. (803) 656-3403 (1963; 70 acres)

Magnolia Plantations and Gardens, Route 4, Charleston, South Carolina 29407. Tel. (803) 571-1266 (1870; 50 acres)

Swan Lake Gardens, City of Sumter Parks and Recreation Department, West Liberty Street Extension, Sumter, South Carolina 29150. Tel. (803) 773-9363 (1930; 150 acres)

Tennessee

Dixon Gallery and Gardens, 4339 Park Avenue, Memphis, Tennessee 38117. Tel. (901) 761-5250 (1976; 17 acres)

Memphis Botanic Garden, 750 Cherry Road, Memphis, Tennessee 38117. Tel. (901) 685-1566 (1964; 88 acres)

Rock City Gardens, 1400 Patten Road, Lookout Mountain, Tennessee 37350. Tel. (404) 820-2531 (1932; 10 acres)

Southwestern at Memphis Arboretum, 200 North Parkway, Memphis, Tennessee 38112. Tel. (901) 458-0964 (1955; 100 acres)

Tennessee Botanical Gardens and Fine Arts Center, Inc., Cheekwood, Nashville, Tennessee 37205. Tel. (615) 356-3306 (1959; 55 acres)

University of Tennessee Arboretum, 901 Kerr Hollow Road, Oak Ridge, Tennessee 37830. Tel. (615) 483-3571 (1964; 250 acres)

Texas

Brazos County Arboretum, Department of Horticulture, College Station, Texas 77843. Tel. (713) 845-2844 (1978; 5 acres)

Dallas Arboretum and Botanical Society, 8617 Garland Road, Dallas, Texas 75218. Tel. (214) 324-4879 (1980; 66 acres)

Fort Worth Botanic Garden, 3220 Botanic Garden Drive, Fort Worth, Texas 76107. Tel. (817) 870-7686 (1933; 115 acres)

Fort Worth Water Gardens, Park and Recreation Department, 1501 Commerce, Fort Worth, Texas 76102. Tel. (817) 870-7016 (1974; 4.5 acres)

Houston Arboretum and Botanical Society, 4501 Woodway Drive, Houston, Texas 77024. Tel. (713) 681-8433 (1967; 165 acres)

Judge Roy Bean Visitor Center, Box 160, Langtry, Texas 78871. Tel. (915) 291-3340 (1968; 6 acres)

Virginia

Maymont Foundation, 1700 Hampton Street, Richmond, Virginia 23220. Tel. (804) 358-7166 (1926; 105 acres)

Norfolk Botanical Gardens, Airport Road, Norfolk, Virginia 23518. Tel. (804) 855-0194 (1937; 175 acres)

Orland E. White Arboretum, Blandy Experimental Farm of the University of Virginia, Box 175, Boyce, Virginia 22620. Tel. (703) 837-1758 (1926; 100+ acres)

River Farm, American Horticultural Society, 7931 East Boulevard Drive, Alexandria, Virginia 22308. Tel. (703) 768-5700 (1973; 25 acres)

University of Virginia campus, Charlottesville, Virginia 22903. Tel. (804) 924-7771 (1819; 800 acres)

Gardens of Historic Houses and Estates

Dates of founding or construction appear in parentheses, together with approximate size, where this information was available.

Alabama

Arlington Historic House and Gardens, 331 Cotton Avenue, S.W., Birmingham, Alabama 35211. Tel. (205) 780-5656 (1952; 6.25 acres)

Bellingrath Gardens and Home, Box 60, Route 1, Theodore, Alabama 36582. Tel. (205) 973-2217 (1932; 65 acres)

Florida

Eden State Gardens, one mile north U.S. 98, Point Washington, Florida. Mailing address: Eden State Gardens, Box 26, Point Washington, Florida 32454. Tel. (904) 231-4214 (1895; 10.5 acres)

Edison Winter Home and Botanical Gardens, 2350 McGregor Boulevard, Fort Myers, Florida 33901. Tel. (813) 334-3614 (1947; 14 acres)

John and Mable Ringling Museum of Art, 5401 Bayshore Road, Sarasota, Florida 33578. Tel. (813) 355-5101, ext. 250 (1924; 70 acres)

Vizcaya, 3251 South Miami Avenue, Miami, Florida 33129. Tel. (305) 579-2708 (1914; 10 acres)

Georgia

Atlanta Historical Society Grounds, Tullie Smith House Restoration and Swan House, The Atlanta Historical Society, Inc., Box 12423, 3101 Andrews Drive, N.W., Atlanta, Georgia 30305. Tel. (404) 261-1837 (1926; 23 acres)

Louisiana

Hermann-Grima Historic House, 818 St. Louis Street, New Orleans, Louisiana 70112. Tel. (504) 525-5661 (1831)

Longue Vue House and Gardens, 7 Bamboo Road, New Orleans, Louisiana 70124. Tel. (504) 488-5488 (1968; 8 acres)

Rosedown Plantation, Route 10 East, St. Francisville, Louisiana 70775. Tel. (504) 524-8407 (1964; 28 acres)

R. S. Barnwell Memorial Garden and Art Center, 501 Clyde Fant Parkway, Shreveport, Louisiana 71101. Tel. (318) 226-6495 (1970; 7 acres)

Shadows-on-the-Teche, Main and Weeks Streets, New Iberia, Louisiana. Mailing
address: Shadows-on-the-Teche, Box 254, New Iberia, Louisiana 70560. Tel.
(318) 369-6446 (1834)

Mississippi

Beauvoir, The Jefferson Davis Shrine, U.S. Highway 90, Biloxi, Mississippi. Mailing
address: Box 200, West Beach Boulevard, Biloxi, Mississippi 39531. Tel.
(601) 388-1313 (1941; 74 acres)

North Carolina

Airlie Gardens, seven miles east of Wilmington, North Carolina, 2 miles southeast
of U.S. Highway 17. Mailing address: Box 210, Wilmington, North Carolina
28402. Tel. (919) 763-9991 (Nineteenth century; 100+ acres)

Biltmore House and Gardens, Asheville, North Carolina 28803. Tel. (704) 274-
1776 (Late nineteenth century; 11,000 acres)

Elizabethan Gardens, Manteo, Roanoke Island, North Carolina 27954. Tel. (919)
473-3234 (1951; 10.5 acres)

Marvin and Mary Gourd Museum and Gardens, Box 666, Fuquay Varina, North
Carolina 27526. Tel. (919) 639-2894 (1963; 2 acres)

Old Salem, Inc., Horticulture Department, Salem Station, Winston-Salem, North
Carolina 27108. Tel. (919) 723-3688 (1766; 40 acres)

Orton Plantation Gardens, 17 miles south of Wilmington, North Carolina, on
North Carolina Route 133. Mailing address: Box 3625, Wilmington, North
Carolina 28406. Tel. (919) 371-6851 (1910; 20 acres)

Tryon Palace, Box 1007, 610 Pollock Street, New Bern, North Carolina 28560.
Tel. (919) 638-5109 (1959; 12 acres)

Tennessee

The Hermitage, The Ladies Hermitage Association, Hermitage, Tennessee 37076.
Tel. (615) 889-2941 (1819)

Magevney House, 198 Adams Avenue, Memphis, Tennessee 38103. Tel. (901)
526-4464 (1837; 144 feet by 144 feet)

Texas

Beaumont Art Museum, 1111 Ninth Street, Beaumont, Texas 77702. Tel. (713)
832-3432 (1950; 5 acres)

Virginia

Agecroft Hall, The Agecroft Association, 4305 Sulgrave Road, Richmond, Virginia
23221. Tel. (804) 353-4241 (1967; 23 acres)

Ash Lawn, Charlottesville, Virginia 22901. Tel. (804) 293-9539 (1975; 0.5 acres)

Belle Grove, Box 137, Middletown, Virginia 22645. Tel. (703) 869-2028 (1787; 4
acres)

Carter's Grove Plantation, Colonial Williamsburg Foundation, Williamsburg, Virginia 23185. Tel. (804) 229-1000 (1751; 400 acres)

Colonial Williamsburg. Mailing address: Drawer C, Williamsburg, Virginia 23187.
Tel. (804) 229-1000, ext. 2256 (Eighteenth-century restoration; 170 acres)

Edgar Allan Poe Museum, The Poe Foundation, Inc., 1914–16 East Main Street,
Richmond, Virginia 23223. Tel. (804) 648-5523 (1922; 50 feet by 200 feet)

Gunston Hall, Lorton, Virginia 22079. Tel. (703) 550-9220 (1932; 556 acres)

Kenmore, Kenmore Association, 1201 Washington Avenue, Fredericksburg, Virginia 22401. Tel. (703) 373-3381 (1922)

Mary Washington House Garden, Mary Washington Branch, Association for the Preservation of Virginia Antiquities, 1200 Charles Street, Fredericksburg, Virginia 22401. Tel. (703) 373-1569 (1890; 118 feet by 110 feet)

Monticello, Thomas Jefferson Memorial Foundation, Box 316, Charlottesville, Virginia 22902. Tel. (804) 295-2657 (Eighteenth century; 50 acres)

Mount Vernon, Mount Vernon Ladies Association of the Union, Mount Vernon, Virginia 22121. Tel. (703) 780-2000 (Eighteenth century; 500 acres)

Oatlands, Route 2, Box 352, Leesburg, Virginia 22075. Tel. (703) 777-3174 (ca. 1800; 261 acres)

Stratford Hall Plantation, Robert E. Lee Memorial Association, Inc., Stratford, Virginia 22558. Tel. (804) 493-8039 (1929; 2 acres)

Woodlawn Plantation, Box 37, 9000 Richmond Highway, Mount Vernon, Virginia 22121. Tel. (703) 557-7880 (1949; 150 acres)

Index

ng brightens winter's day

p.m. Feb. 8-9; 10 a.m.-5 p.m. Feb. 10.

Admission is $5 for adults; children under 12 are admitted free.

The centerpiece gardens are being installed by Outdoor Connection and Pettit's Lawnscape.

Lowe's Home Improvement will sell plants in the east wing of the building.

Roger Swain, host of the PBS *Victory Garden*, will conduct free seminars at noon, 3 p.m. and 6 p.m. Feb. 9; and at 11 a.m., 1 p.m. and 3 p.m. Feb. 10.

The Shelby County Agricultural Extension Service will also have a booth where horticulturists will be answering questions and distributing information from the University of Tennessee.

"This is my biggest show ever," said Bill Harper, organizer of the event.

Lemon tree trials

Virginia Jones wants to know how to coax blooms from a lemon tree she grew from seeds of an ordinary su-

Prune raspberry vines

Margaret Spransy of Caruthersville, Mo., wants to know if now is the time to prune her raspberry vines.

It is indeed, said master gardener and expert fruit and vegetable grower Bill Colvard.

"She can cut them all down to about 3 inches," Colvard said. "That will give her the maximum number of berries next fall."

Guacamole hosta

Guacamole was voted the favorite hosta by members of the Mid-South Hosta Society, who now number 304.

Guacamole has chartreuse leaves edged in dark green. It produces fragrant flowers and can take some sun and lots of heat. It also was voted "Hosta of the Year" for 2002 by the American Hosta Growers.

Local hostaholics also voted for Blue Angel, Sum and Substance and Krossa Regal as favorites.

'To improve the views'

Ronnie McCarty, horticulturist at Memphis Botanic

Are you a compulsive gardener?

Ever find a sprig of rosemary (left over from a nice meal out on the town), soaking in a water glass in the bathroom? I have, despite the fact that my wife thinks anyone who brings food home to root has a problem.

Must be an addiction — I can just hear it now, at a 12-step meeting:

"Hi, my name is Felder, and I am a gardener . . ." (In unison, the others reply "Hi, Felder, we're glad you are here.")

"I gardened just this morning.' (Amen.') Pulled a few weeds on the way down to pick up the morning paper, and before I knew it, started dividing daylilies and repainting a fence post. Coming to this GA meeting, I found a mail-order catalog under my car seat, and people behind me at the stoplight had to honk to get my attention back on the road.

"I need help, can't stop gardening on my own. And I am sorry for my family, even though I don't own a bass.boat or play golf, because I spent my last paycheck on a new greenhouse door, a big bucket

FELDER RUSHING
The Southern Gardener

of Miracle-Gro, and some shrubs I don't even need," 'cause they were on sale. . . ."

Sound close to home? Here's a simple test to see if you, too, need help:

Do you grow 10 or more kinds of the same plant (rose, daylily, daffodil, iris, African violet, camellia, tomato, whatever), and know their names? Extra points if they're labeled. Do you subscribe to three or more garden magazines? Do you think Roger Swain (host of *The Victory Garden* on PBS) is funny? Did you ever call a radio show to ask a garden question?

Do you keep a small shovel in your car trunk? Turn your compost weekly? Blow leaves

on Sunday morning? Buy bird seed by the 50-pound sack? Own a pair of Felco pruning shears (bonus points for a leather scabbard)? Are entire flats of flowers still on the driveway because there's simply no more space to plant?

Have you ever willingly taken a tour of a garden by flashlight? Do we need to search your purse or camera case for purloined seeds, after a visit to a botanical garden?

Extra points if your cuticles are dirty right now. And finally, triple points if you would appreciate a special someone sending you a load of manure for an anniversary. . . .

I'm not suggesting we gardeners should quit — though we all claim we can, any time. Maybe our motto should be "One Flower at A Time." And remember, denial is a symptom!

Horticulturist Felder Rushing, author of several garden books, is an eighth-generation Southern gardener. His column runs the first and third Saturdays of each month. Contact felder@teclink.net.